USING CHRIST CENTERED REALITY THERAPY

Christ Centered

CCRT

REALITY THERAPY

Volume 2

Dr. Alan Kitay and Dr. Carrie Kitay

ENDORSEMENT
DR. CEDRIC E. JOHNSON

In this second volume of the Christ-Centered Reality Therapy series, Drs. Alan and Carrie Kitay have once again demonstrated a rare combination of theological integrity, clinical insight, and pastoral sensitivity. If Volume One laid the foundation by establishing the model—what Christ-Centered Reality Therapy is and why it stands upon the unshakable truth of God's Word—then Volume Two answers the question every counselor and pastor eventually asks: How do I actually use this in real life? And what a remarkable answer it provides.

As a pastor, I have counseled countless individuals who sincerely desire change but lack the tools, structure, and spiritual clarity needed to walk that change out. This volume provides all three. Here, the Kitays move beyond explanation and into implementation. They guide the reader step-by-step through the methodology of CCRT, showing not only what needs to be addressed in the heart of a counselee, but how to walk with them biblically, compassionately, and responsibly toward transformation.

What I appreciate most is that this book does not offer shallow encouragement or superficial techniques. Instead, it takes the counselor into the deeper waters of human belief systems, internal conflicts, and spiritual misalignments—while always drawing the reader back to the sufficiency of Scripture and the redemptive work of Christ. The practical tools, session structures, interventions, and real-world applications offered here are invaluable for anyone committed to Christ-centered counseling. They are usable, teachable, and spiritually grounded.

Drs. Kitay write with the heart of shepherds and the precision of skilled practitioners. They understand people. They understand Scripture. They understand suffering and redemption. And through this volume, they help the rest of us understand how to minister more effectively to those God sends our way.

Using Christ-Centered Reality Therapy is not just a continuation of the first book—it is its necessary counterpart. Read it carefully. Study it deliberately. Apply it faithfully. It will strengthen your counseling, deepen your ministry, and equip you to guide others into the life-changing truth that freedom comes only through alignment with Jesus Christ.

This is a needed book. A timely book. And a gift to the Body of Christ.

Dr. Cedric E. Johnson
Senior Pastor, Destiny Church of Clute, Texas
President, Destiny Bible College
Biblical Counselor & Ministry Trainer

ENDORSEMENT
DR. VIRGINIA BIEBER

I want to commend my dear friends and fellow Christian Counselors Dr. Alan and Dr. Carrie Kitay for their contributions to making known to us the knowledge and understanding ***Christ Centered Reality Therapy.*** I met Alan more than twenty years ago at a Christian Therapist Conference in Texas. He was the Dean of Grace Bible Institute, now Destiny Bible College, and it was then that he entrusted me with his curriculum for college based "Biblical Counseling."

Alan and I always had a heart for God's people suffering with dysfunction, a desire to direct people to God's solution and not man's remedy. Alan also wrote a four-semester class for lay people to counsel under their Pastor. They would, upon completion, receive certification. With his curriculum, I started teaching these college classes on Long Island, New York to teachers, nurses, principals, doctors, and pastors, for over twenty years.

Later, when he and Carrie married, they expanded their school and ministry. I know Carrie to have a strong background in ministry and counseling. I know of her specialization in Domestic Violence and Child Abuse. Both of their knowledge and experience is powerful and practical, and will leave you with great hope and success.

As a Biblical Counselor with particular interest and practice, I am pleased and honored to commend "Using Christ Centered Reality Therapy" as a Masterpiece. As I turn the pages, I find all the tools provided for the Therapist, as well as hope. It is clear to see the profound work of the Holy Spirit of the living God in every chapter as Alan and Carrie have provided a realistic and practical elaboration on the counseling process that goes beyond mere advice-giving and scripture quoting. The book provides biblical grounding, as the principles and the reality keys are intentionally aligned with Scripture's view of creation, sin, and redemption. CCRT treats God's design as the baseline for normality, and it treats departure from that design as abnormality, if not treated and redirected. It gives keys such as "God has a master plan." Biblical, behavioral expectations for the Christian are used to connect practical choices to Biblical truths, while protecting the client from shame, sin, and irresponsible behavior. The behaviors contrary to the scriptures are rejected but the person is not condemned.

I have seen so much grief and misunderstanding in counseling sessions. CCRT is a necessity in every Biblical College, Christian School, Pastor's desk, and for the Christian Counselor. CCRT gives understanding of a Christ-centered model and methodology for competent and effective Christian counseling.

Virginia Bieber, Ph.D. Psychology
Board Certified Christian Therapist
President, Household of Faith
Ridge, New York

ENDORSEMENT
DR. DEL SHON WALLER AND DR. SONJA WALLER

Drs. Alan and Carrie Kitay have given us a gift that the Church desperately needs. In *Using Christ Centered Reality Therapy*, they masterfully bridge the gap between sound psychological practice and deep biblical truth in a way that is both accessible and profound.

As a pastor and counselors, we have long searched for resources that don't simply add a prayer to secular therapy or slap a Bible verse on clinical techniques. Drs. Kitay go much deeper. They dive into the very essence of what it means to address the core of human struggles through the lens of Christ-centered reality. This isn't just therapy with Jesus mentioned… this is therapy that flows from the reality of who Christ is and what He has accomplished for us.

What sets this book apart is the book actually shows that Christ Centered Reality Therapy doesn't merely quote Scripture but actually illuminates it, transforms it, and makes it applicable to counseling as it was intended. They demonstrate with clarity and compassion how God's Word speaks directly to the heart of our problems… not just treating symptoms, but addressing the root issues that keep people stuck in destructive patterns.

Whether you're a professional counselor, a pastor doing care ministry, or a lay leader wanting to help others more effectively, this book will equip you with both the theological foundation and practical tools to bring real, lasting change. Drs. Kitay write with the wisdom of seasoned professors, the skills of experienced counselors, and the heart of servant leaders, and demonstrate the attitude of those who genuinely care about people being able to walk in freedom.

We wholeheartedly recommend *Understanding Christ Centered Reality Therapy* to anyone who wants to see broken lives transformed by the power of God's truth applied with Christ centered clinical approach in excellence. This is the kind of resource that will sit on our desk, not our shelves… dog-eared, highlighted, and regularly referenced as we walk alongside those God has entrusted to our care.

Dr. Del Shon Waller, Sr. & Dr. Sonja Waller
BCC Therapists and Counselors
Pastor, Greater Handy AME Church, Angleton, Texas

DEDICATION

This book, Using Christ Centered Reality Therapy, Volume 2 of the Christ Centered Reality Therapy Training Series, is dedicated to a very special community of people who have quietly, consistently, and faithfully breathed life into this work through their encouragement, their persistence, and their trust.

It is dedicated to the friends who never stopped believing—those who checked in, spoke words of affirmation, prayed in private, and reminded us, often at just the right moment, that this calling matters. Your encouragement has been more than kind words; it has been a sustaining force that kept this work moving forward as we try to fulfill our calling within the body of Christ.

It is dedicated to the ministers and former students who have stayed in contact over the years—those who reached out with stories, questions, testimonies, and reflections from real ministry contexts. Your continued engagement has been a powerful confirmation that Christian counseling is not merely an academic exercise, but a living ministry desperately needed within the Church. Your faithfulness in applying what you learned, and your willingness to share how Christ-centered principles are impacting real lives, have shaped and refined the content of this volume more than you may realize.

It is also dedicated to the students who continue to enroll, continue to listen, continue to ask questions, and continue to express confidence in both the message and the messenger. Each class, each conversation, and each expression of trust has reinforced the conviction that the Church needs thoughtful, biblically grounded, and Christ-centered approaches to counseling now more than ever. Your hunger to learn is evidence that God is stirring something deeper—calling His people to shepherd hearts with wisdom, truth, and compassion.

Together, you have formed a living testimony that this work is not finished, that the calling is still active, and that the teaching of Christian counseling has a vital and necessary place within the Body of Christ. This volume exists because you stayed connected, stayed committed, and stayed believing.

Above all, we give thanks to Jesus Christ—who continues to open doors, confirm calling, and provide strength for every step of the journey. May He be honored through this work, and may these pages serve His Church faithfully for generations to come.

In HIS Service,

Drs. Alan and Carrie Kitay

ACKNOWLEDGMENTS

We wish to gratefully acknowledge the countless individuals whose lives, labor, and faith have contributed to this work, whether directly or indirectly.

We acknowledge every minister with whom we have labored, every pastor we have had the privilege to serve alongside, every teacher under whose instruction we studied, and every author whose written work informed, challenged, and sharpened our understanding. Each conversation, sermon, lesson, and book played a role in shaping both our theology and our approach to Christian counseling.

We are deeply grateful to those who came before us, who laid foundations of faith, doctrine, and practice upon which we now stand. We are thankful for those who walk with us in the present—colleagues, students, and fellow servants—who continue to refine, encourage, and strengthen this calling through shared ministry and mutual faith. And we honor those who will follow after us, trusting that they will carry this work forward with wisdom, humility, and devotion to Christ.

We are grateful to all who continue to proclaim and teach the hope and the answer that lies in the relationship and knowledge of Jesus Christ. Above all, we acknowledge and teach that the hope and the answer is not found in methods alone, but in the living relationship and growing knowledge of Jesus Christ. May this work stand as a testimony to His truth, His grace, and His power to transform lives across generations.

Drs. Alan and Carrie Kitay

Table of Contents

FOREWORD
SHARLENE LYNCH

Drs. Alan and Carrie Kitay have woven together Choice Theory by Dr. William Glasser and Christ Centered Reality Therapy by Dr. Tom Barnette in an extremely thorough and effective way in this book, Understanding Christ Centered Reality Therapy. This masterpiece is the first of two books written to explain the model and methodology of Christian counseling using Christ Centered Reality Therapy as the framework. Understanding Christ Centered Therapy, which is volume One, explains the model, the distinctives, and the tools of CCRT.

In Using CCRT, the Kitays explain the methodology of Christ Centered Reality Therapy. They deconstruct the theories into digestible understanding while also showing how they interact with each other. Dr. Barnette based his theory CCRT on Glasser's by expanding it to include Christ as the root of all choices. By taking the CCRT theory one element at a time the Using CCRT enables the counselor to deeply reflect on the intent of the elements while embracing the holiness of Christ throughout. By elaborating to this level, you are able to see how the root of Christian faith is the true base of CCRT, Choice Theory and overall God's original plan of how to deal with the challenges we face in life. It is a timeless rendition of helps well explained for us all. Truly a priceless gem.

The two books were written to help Christian Counselors and Counselors in general effectively apply both Choice theory and Christ Centered Reality Therapy in counseling settings.

The Kitays have decades of practice in Choice Theory and CCRT methods which give them a deep understanding and perspective that takes them past simply knowing CCRT, but elevates them to the level of understanding it, using it, and teaching it to others. They both use these theories not only in their counseling practice but also in their daily lives. They are truly living the theories out effectively and successfully. The deep layers of application of the theories in their practice comes out in what they share in this two-volume set.

The Kitays have knocked this one out of the park, so to speak. It truly is a fantastic addition to any counselor's resources but also a lay person's library, but don't let this one gather dust. They truly encourage you to apply CCRT to your life, not only your practice.

Well done, good and faithful Servants of Christ!

Keep up the Great Works, Drs. Alan and Carrie. You are planting seeds for generations to come.

Sharlene Lynch, MA
CCRT Therapeutic Mediator
Writer and Publicist

AUTHOR'S PREFACE
DR. ALAN KITAY

Writing this second volume of the Christ-Centered Reality Therapy series has been both a continuation and a deepening of the work begun in Volume One. In the first book, Understanding Christ-Centered Reality Therapy, my goal was to establish the model—the theological, philosophical, and psychological framework upon which all Christ-centered counseling must rest. I wrote that first volume with a profound conviction that Christian counselors, pastors, and leaders needed clarity on what CCRT is, why it matters, and how Scripture defines normality, human need, responsibility, and the structure of the human soul.

This second volume, Using Christ-Centered Reality Therapy, moves from foundation to function. It shifts from what CCRT is to how CCRT works. If Volume One explained the architecture, Volume Two explains the construction. It is my desire that this book serves as a bridge between belief and practice, doctrine and method, understanding and application.

Far too many counseling approaches—even Christian ones—attempt to address problems at the level of emotions, memory, or circumstance without examining the belief systems that shape those realities. But Scripture is clear: people do not simply respond to life; they interpret it. They act out of what they believe to be true. And as Jesus taught repeatedly, a person's thoughts, beliefs, and heart-orientation determine the direction of their entire life. Counseling that ignores belief systems merely rearranges symptoms without confronting causes.

Volume Two addresses that concern directly. Here you will not only learn how to structure sessions, develop therapeutic plans, and guide counselees through the steps of change—you will also learn how to uncover the roots beneath their struggles. You will learn how to discern distorted theology, abnormal wants, unmet needs, and self-centered motives. You will see how Scripture, when properly applied, brings correction, clarity, empowerment, and restoration. You will discover why Biblical confrontation is necessary, how to integrate accountability with compassion, and how to guide people from emotional reaction into responsible, Christ-centered action.

I wrote this volume because I have spent decades watching people long for change without knowing how to achieve it. I have watched believers attempt to meet God-given needs through abnormal means. I have watched sincere Christians exhaust themselves with external doing while neglecting internal obedience. And I have watched many counselors desire to help hurting people, yet lack the structure and tools to guide them toward lasting transformation.

My prayer is that this book equips you—not only with knowledge, but with confidence. Confidence to counsel Biblically. Confidence to diagnose problems accurately. Confidence to ask the right questions. Confidence to lead others through the process of repentance, renewal, responsibility, and restoration. And confidence to trust the Spirit of God, who alone transforms the heart.

May this volume strengthen your calling, sharpen your discernment, deepen your understanding, and enrich your ministry. And may every person you counsel find freedom, hope, and healing through Christ-centered reality—the only reality in which true wholeness can be found.

Dr. Alan Kitay, Ph.D., D.Th., CCCRT

AUTHOR'S PREFACE
DR. CARRIE KITAY

It is with great joy and profound gratitude that I share in writing this introduction to Understanding Christ-Centered Reality Therapy. As a co-author and long-time partner in this journey, I am deeply honored to have contributed to a work that brings together the truths of Scripture and the insights of psychology in a way that has the potential to change lives. Having spent over twenty years in the field of Christian counseling and education, I can say without hesitation that this book represents one of the most meaningful collaborations of my career, offering clarity and guidance for those committed to helping others grow in Christ.

Fresh out of college, I worked as a physical therapist assistant. Then I began working as a case manager at a battered women's shelter. It was during this time that I began studying Christian Counseling. In 2007, I received my Bachelor's degree in Christian counseling and was invited to join Grace Christian Counseling Ministries, which was founded by Dr. Alan Kitay in 1999. I continued my studies and eventually earned my Ph.D. in Psychology and became the Director of the women's shelter. After five years, I left the women's shelter and entered full-time ministry as the Director of Grace Christian Counseling Ministries. Alan turned the position over to me when I started teaching Christian counseling through Grace Bible Institute, which he founded in 2002. GBI later became Houston Bible College, and then, in 2022, was again renamed to Destiny Bible College. In addition to my work with GCCM, I also served as a Senior Instructor teaching Christian Counseling and Women's Studies, focusing on Domestic Violence and Family Abuse. In the course of my studies, I started studying the works of Dr. William Glasser, Reality Therapy and Choice Theory, and Dr. Tom Barnette's Christ Centered Reality Therapy. I went on to become a Certified Christ-Centered Reality Therapist, and that has been my chosen method of counseling for many years. Also, during that time, I married Alan Kitay, and we became husband and wife and partners in life and ministry.

When my husband and I began discussing the vision for this project, our shared goal was clear: to create a resource that would speak to counselors, ministers, and psychologists who desire to see people healed through the power of Biblical truth. We both recognized a gap in the world of counseling - a need for a comprehensive model that does not compromise spiritual integrity in favor of modern trends, yet still acknowledges the value of human understanding and emotional awareness. It is exciting to see that this work not only fills that gap but also provides a strong, Christ-centered foundation upon which future generations of counselors can confidently build.

Throughout my years of counseling, I have encountered so many individuals - both those who sit in the counselor's chair and those who sit across from it - who are searching for something more. They long for wisdom that goes deeper than clinical procedure, for a truth that speaks not only to the mind but to the heart and spirit. Christ-Centered Reality Therapy offers exactly that. It brings us back to the foundation of who we are in Christ, reminding both counselor and client that real transformation does not come from human strength alone but from the renewing work of the Holy Spirit as we align our lives with God's truth.

This book is more than theory - it is a bridge between theology and therapy, between the pulpit and the counseling office. It provides a clear model for understanding human behavior through God's design, while equipping the reader with practical steps to help others experience renewal and reconciliation. I have always believed that the most powerful counseling happens when truth and compassion meet, and this book beautifully demonstrates that balance. It allows counselors to be both gentle and direct, empowering them to guide people toward lasting change without losing sight of grace or accountability.

For those who are pastors and ministers, this book offers a framework for shepherding hearts in ways that are Biblically grounded yet psychologically informed. For professional counselors and therapists, it provides a theological compass to navigate the complexity of human emotion while keeping Christ at the center. And for students preparing for ministry or psychology careers, it serves as a roadmap for integrating faith and practice responsibly and effectively. This combination of knowledge and spiritual insight ensures that every reader - regardless of background - can find tools that strengthen their ability to serve with wisdom and integrity.

Co-authoring this work has also reminded me of the great privilege and responsibility that come with the call to counsel. We are entrusted with people's stories, their pain, their hopes, and their struggles. Every session, every conversation, is sacred space. My prayer is that this book will encourage counselors to see their work as a ministry of healing and discipleship—not merely as a profession, but as a divine partnership with the Great Counselor Himself. When we bring His truth into the lives of others, we participate in the holy work of restoration that only God can complete.

In many ways, this project has been the culmination of two decades of shared labor, prayer, and vision. I have seen firsthand how these principles work - in counseling rooms, classrooms, churches, and homes. I have witnessed men and women rediscover hope, marriages restored, addictions broken, and faith renewed. What we present in these pages is not abstract theology; it is living truth that has been tested and proven through real lives transformed by the Word of God. The same Biblical principles that have shaped my own counseling approach continue to demonstrate their effectiveness in every setting where Christ is invited to bring healing.

It is also my hope that this work will inspire a renewed confidence in the sufficiency of Scripture for addressing the deepest needs of the human heart. The Bible is not silent about mental, emotional, or relational health - it speaks directly to them, offering wisdom, correction, and hope. When counselors approach their work through the lens of Christ-centered reality, they not only help people find healing but also lead them into holiness. The process of change becomes not just therapeutic, but spiritual - a journey of becoming more like Christ in thought, behavior, and character.

As you begin reading this book, I encourage you to approach it prayerfully, with an open heart and a teachable spirit. Allow its truths to challenge and inspire you. Let the principles of Christ-Centered Reality Therapy deepen your understanding of both human nature and divine grace. My prayer is that, through these chapters, you will not only gain knowledge but also catch a vision of the incredible privilege we have as counselors, pastors, and believers - to participate in the redemptive work of God in people's lives.

To every counselor, teacher, pastor, and student who will read this book: know that you're calling matters. What you do changes lives. And when you anchor your work in God's truth, the impact extends far beyond what you can see. This book was written to equip you, encourage you, and remind you that no one is beyond the reach of grace. Healing is possible. Transformation is real. And Christ remains the ultimate source of both.

It has been an honor to be part of this journey, and I am genuinely excited to see the impact these books will have in the years to come. May they serve as tools of wisdom, compassion, and truth for all who seek to bring light into the lives of others. And may every page point us back to the One who makes all healing possible - our Lord Jesus Christ.

In HIS Service,

Dr. Carrie Kitay, Ph.D., BCCT, CCCRT.

INTRODUCTION TO VOLUME TWO

USING CHRIST-CENTERED REALITY THERAPY

BY DR. ALAN KITAY

Christian counseling requires more than compassion, scriptural familiarity, or the desire to help hurting people. It requires a framework—a coherent, biblically grounded understanding of what it means to be human, how people change, and why spiritual and emotional problems emerge in the first place. Volume 1 of this series, Understanding Christ-Centered Reality Therapy, was written to provide this essential foundation. It established the theological model of CCRT by defining the nature of man, the meaning of normality, the structure of the human person, and the relationship between belief, behavior, and spiritual alignment. In that first volume, the reader encountered the philosophical and theological architecture upon which all Christ-centered counseling must rest. Before any counselor can responsibly guide a person toward transformation, he or she must understand how God designed the human soul and what Scripture reveals about the roots of human behavior. Volume 2 builds directly upon that crucial foundation.

Understanding the distinction between model and methodology is vital, for it is this distinction that gives rise to the necessity of a second volume. A model answers questions such as: What is human nature? Why do people think, feel, and behave as they do? What does Scripture define as normal or abnormal? How does sin distort the mind, emotions, and choices? And what is God's design for restoration? These questions form the philosophical and theological lens through which all counseling must be viewed. Without a model, counseling risks becoming subjective, inconsistent, and emotionally driven rather than truth-driven. Model is the compass; it orients both counselor and counselee to the truth of God's Word.

Methodology, however, is the path. Methodology explains how counseling is done—how the truths of the model become the lived experience of the counselee. It is the process by which Biblical truth is applied to real people with real struggles in real situations. A counselor may know the theological foundation, but without methodology, sessions become scattered, repetitive, or emotional rather than transformative. A counselor may be compassionate and knowledgeable, but without structure, people leave encouraged rather than changed. Methodology transforms understanding into practice, belief into action, and Biblical principles into step-by-step direction. It provides clarity, order, and consistency so that the counseling process does not drift from session to session, but moves forward with purpose and precision.

Volume 2, Using Christ-Centered Reality Therapy, therefore exists to translate the model into a reproducible method. It teaches counselors how to move from theological conviction to therapeutic implementation. This volume explains how sessions are structured, how to identify the counselee's belief systems, how to assess unmet needs, how to evaluate distorted thinking, and how to construct a Biblical plan for change. The book explains how to diagnose spiritual and behavioral problems using the Five Needs/Five Conflicts framework, how to integrate Scripture into every step of counseling, and how to ensure that each session leads the counselee closer to responsibility, repentance, and renewal. The focus is not merely on what the Bible says, but on how to help people live what the Bible says.

Volume 1 introduced the reader to the six core needs of humanity—five identified by Dr. William Glasser (survival, love, power, freedom, joy) and a sixth added within CCRT: the need to know God. It explained how God designed these needs, how sin distorts them, and how abnormal wants emerge when needs are met outside God's plan. Volume 2 expands that understanding by showing how the counselor identifies these needs in real time and how distorted wants influence relationships, emotions, and behavior. This volume teaches counselors how to confront the false beliefs that create abnormal wants, how to guide individuals toward Biblical ways of meeting their needs, and how to redirect counselees from self-centered desires to God-centered obedience.

One of the central contributions of this volume is its presentation of the CCRT tools and interventions that make counseling effective and measurable. Readers will learn how to implement tools such as the Therapeutic Plan (Mind–Body–Spirit), the Rule of 52 (Learned vs. Earned), Here-and-Now questioning, the Action Plan worksheet, the Time-Tracker Sociogram, and the Reality Keys. Each of these tools provides structure, accountability, and clarity—ensuring that counseling does not remain vague or conversational, but instead progresses with purpose. These tools help the counselor expose distorted beliefs, analyze behavioral patterns, measure spiritual growth, and establish realistic steps of obedience rooted in Scripture. They move the process beyond emotional processing and into spiritual transformation.

Volume 2 also addresses the essential role of Biblical confrontation and responsible decision-making in CCRT. Human problems cannot be resolved through emotional validation alone. Biblical counseling requires the courage to confront sin, expose self-deception, and redirect the counselee toward obedience to God's Word. This volume explains how to do so with grace, compassion, and clarity—never harshly, but always firmly. It teaches counselors how to help individuals examine their choices, evaluate their motives, and accept responsibility for the consequences of their behavior. It provides practical tools for challenging self-centered thinking, correcting false theology, and guiding individuals toward renewed thinking as described in Romans 12:1–2.

Another unique feature of this volume is its extensive use of Biblical case studies. Scripture provides abundant examples of individuals who struggled with fear, anger, pride, guilt, rebellion, insecurity, doubt, and misplaced desires. Through the stories of David, Elijah, Jonah, Peter, Samson, Hagar, Demas, and others, counselors will see how the human heart responds to unmet needs, distorted beliefs, and spiritual conflict—and how God intervenes to correct, restore, and transform. These case studies demonstrate that people today are not fundamentally different from people in the pages of Scripture. Their struggles are familiar, their temptations recognizable, and the solutions God provides remain unchanged. By studying these examples, counselors gain insight into how the principles of CCRT can be applied with precision and compassion in modern counseling settings.

Volume 2 also explores the Biblical change process in depth. Change is not merely cognitive—it is spiritual. True transformation requires repentance, renewed thinking, responsible behavior, spiritual submission, and disciplined obedience. This book shows how to walk counselees through that process, helping them move beyond superficial modifications and into lasting, Spirit-driven transformation. It explains how to replace distorted thoughts with Scripture, how to redirect self-centered desires, how to guide counselees into daily disciplines that reinforce obedience, and how to help individuals cultivate habits that lead to long-term stability and growth.

Finally, this volume warns counselors about common pitfalls that undermine effective counseling. Many counselors fall into the temptation of offering comfort without correction, encouragement without accountability, or empathy without truth. Others focus too heavily on emotions while neglecting belief systems, or they become so concerned with the past that they fail to address the counselee's present choices. Some counselors unintentionally enable avoidance, self-pity, or passivity. Volume 2 provides clear instruction on how to avoid these errors by grounding every session, every question, and every directive in the authority of Scripture and the structure of CCRT methodology.

Together, the two volumes form a complete and unified Christian counseling system. Volume 1 establishes the model—what is true, what is normal, and how God designed the human soul. Volume 2 applies that model—showing how to guide people toward repentance, responsibility, and renewed alignment with God's will. When used together, they equip counselors, pastors, teachers, and ministry leaders with the knowledge, tools, and structure needed to help others experience genuine transformation through Christ.

It is my prayer that this expanded introduction prepares your mind and heart for the chapters ahead. May this volume deepen your understanding of the counseling process, sharpen your skill in applying Scripture, and equip you to guide others toward the fullness of life that Christ offers. Counseling is not merely a profession—it is a calling. And through Christ-Centered Reality Therapy, that calling becomes a powerful means of bringing truth, healing, and transformation to those God entrusts to your care.

Dr. Alan Kitay

SECTION IV

THE COUNSELING PROCESS

SECTION IV - TABLE OF CONTENTS

INTRODUCTION TO SECTION IV

Section 4 of this volume represents one of the most significant and integrative portions of the CCRT counseling framework. This section serves as the bridge between the counselor's theoretical understanding of human nature and the active process of helping counselees interpret, evaluate, and change their patterns of thinking and behavior. While the earlier sections of this book focus on foundational concepts—defining human needs, exploring distorted belief systems, and identifying the difference between self-centered and Christ-centered living—Section 4 turns toward the deeper analysis of how these realities manifest in everyday life. It equips the counselor to diagnose problems Biblically, confront dysfunctional thinking, and guide counselees toward healthy patterns of responsibility, obedience, and renewed alignment with God's truth.

A central premise of Section 4 is that people do not simply have problems—they interpret life through internal belief systems that shape their emotions and guide their choices. This section emphasizes that the role of the counselor is not merely to listen or provide comfort, but to help the counselee uncover these belief systems and assess whether they are grounded in Biblical reality or shaped by self-centered desires. Through this lens, the section introduces the concept of the Christian Counseling Circle, contrasting the self-centered life, which revolves around personal desires, external approval, and self-preservation, with the Christ-centered life, which is oriented toward obedience, humility, and spiritual maturity. This distinction becomes the foundation upon which the rest of the section develops, as it allows counselors to identify the true roots of the counselee's emotional and relational conflicts.

Another major emphasis in Section 4 is the role of needs and wants in shaping human motivation. The section clarifies that while God created every person with legitimate needs—such as love, belonging, acceptance, purpose, and spiritual connection—individuals often develop abnormal wants that lead them away from God's design. These wants may appear harmless on the surface, but they produce significant internal conflict because they cannot satisfy the deeper needs of the soul. This part of Section 4 guides counselors in identifying the ways counselees pursue fulfillment through performance, control, relationships, pleasure, or material achievement. It further demonstrates how unmet needs and misdirected wants combine to create patterns of frustration, avoidance, dependency, or emotional instability. By understanding these dynamics, counselors become better equipped to redirect counselees away from destructive desires and toward Biblical pathways of fulfillment.

Section 4 also introduces one of the most crucial distinctions in the entire CCRT model: the difference between symptoms and root causes. Many counselees come to counseling describing their circumstances but not the underlying beliefs that shaped those circumstances. They present emotions such as fear, anger, guilt, or discouragement as if these emotional reactions are the central problem. Section 4 teaches counselors that these emotions are spiritual and psychological indicators—not the final destination of counseling but the starting point for deeper exploration. The diagrams and examples provided illustrate how emotional experiences reveal inner conflicts, distorted expectations, and unbiblical perspectives. Through this material, counselors learn to interpret emotional reactions in ways that point to the heart-level beliefs that must be corrected for true transformation to occur.

A significant portion of this section is devoted to exploring the spiritual roots of mental and emotional dysfunction. Section 4 emphasizes that while biology and environment may influence behavior, the foundational cause of most psychological distress is spiritual misalignment. Whether the issue is anxiety, anger, bitterness, addiction, or relational conflict, this section demonstrates how these problems often arise from patterns of self-centered thinking, unconfessed sin, unresolved guilt, or unmet relational and spiritual needs. The section uses Scriptural examples and practical illustrations to show that internal conflict arises when individuals attempt to live independently of God's order. By helping counselees see their struggles through this Biblical lens, counselors can guide them toward repentance, renewed thinking, and restored fellowship with God.

Another key feature of Section 4 is its exploration of human reactions to frustration, disappointment, and unmet expectations. This section explains that people often construct personal narratives about unfairness, entitlement, or victimhood, which fuel emotional instability and relational division. Counselors are taught to identify patterns of manipulation, avoidance, aggression, blame-shifting, and emotional withdrawal. Using relatable illustrations, the section reveals how these reactions flow from deeper belief structures—and how the counselor can redirect counselees toward responsibility and truth. This analysis gives counselors practical tools for dealing with resistance, deflection, or emotional exaggeration during the counseling process.

In the latter part of Section 4, attention shifts toward actionable components of the counseling process. This includes identifying distorted thoughts, evaluating a counselee's motivational patterns, addressing abnormal desires, and constructing a Biblical plan of change. Section 4 highlights the importance of helping counselees move from emotional reaction to deliberate responsibility, using structured questioning and targeted interventions. This part of the section ties together the theological and psychological elements of CCRT, showing how Scripture provides the foundation for correction, instruction, and restoration. The counselor is encouraged to use Biblical truth as both a mirror and a guide—revealing the counselee's current condition while pointing them toward God's intended pathway for transformation.

Ultimately, Section 4 functions as the diagnostic and interpretive core of the CCRT methodology. It equips counselors to go beyond surface-level conversation and into the deeper spiritual and psychological structures that shape human behavior. By understanding the dynamics outlined in this section—self-centeredness versus Christ-centeredness, needs versus wants, symptoms versus causes, and truth versus deception—the counselor becomes capable of addressing problems at their root. Section 4 prepares counselors to guide individuals from confusion to clarity, from emotional instability to spiritual grounding, and from self-directed living to Christ-centered obedience.

This section, therefore, is not merely informational; it is foundational for the practice of Christ-Centered Reality Therapy. It provides the conceptual depth, diagnostic insight, and practical wisdom necessary to understand the true condition of the human heart and to guide counselees toward meaningful, lasting change. Section 4 teaches counselors to interpret human problems through a Biblical lens and equips them with the tools needed to help others embrace the truth that leads to freedom.

CHRISTIAN COUNSELING CIRCLE

A Self-Centered Life focuses on personal desires, ambitions, and comfort, often measuring success by status, possessions, or self-fulfillment. Decisions are made primarily based on what benefits the individual, and relationships may be used as means to personal ends.

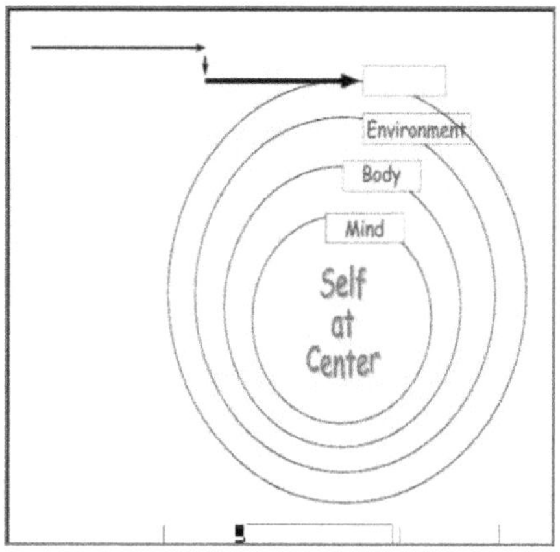

VERSUS

In contrast, A Jesus Centered Life is focused on a life of humility, love, and obedience to God's will. It seeks to follow Christ's example of service, sacrifice, and righteousness. Instead of asking "What's best for me?" a Jesus-centered person asks, "What would glorify God?" and "How can I serve others?" (Philippians 2:3-5; Matthew 6:33).

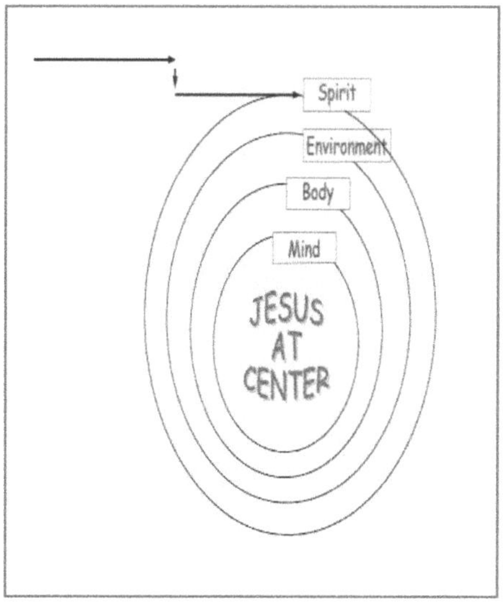

SELF CENTEREDNESS

Christ-Centered Reality Therapy (CCRT) states that a primary source of human suffering stems from a self-centered approach to life, a stark departure from the other-focused ethos found in Biblical teachings. This inward focus, according to CCRT, is not merely a personality quirk but a fundamental violation of God's design, resulting in far-reaching consequences that impact an individual's mental, emotional, and spiritual well-being, as well as their relationships, family, and work life. As CCRT argues throughout Christ Centered Reality Therapy for the 21st Century, a focus on the self is a deviation from the absolute standard of normality set by God.

CCRT emphasizes that God is the ultimate standard of normality, and any deviation from His will constitutes abnormality or sin. The graphic "Self at Center" exemplifies this deviation, placing the "Self" at the heart of existence, encircled by external fulfillments like money, leisure, looks, fame, things, and church. This arrangement, as illustrated, inherently prioritizes personal gratification over service and connection with others. In contrast, Biblical principles underscore the importance of humility, selflessness, and love for neighbor, as evidenced in Matthew 22:39, which stated, "Love your neighbor as yourself". When external validations and temporal accomplishments replace this divine calling to serve, it causes long-term personal harm.

Self at Center

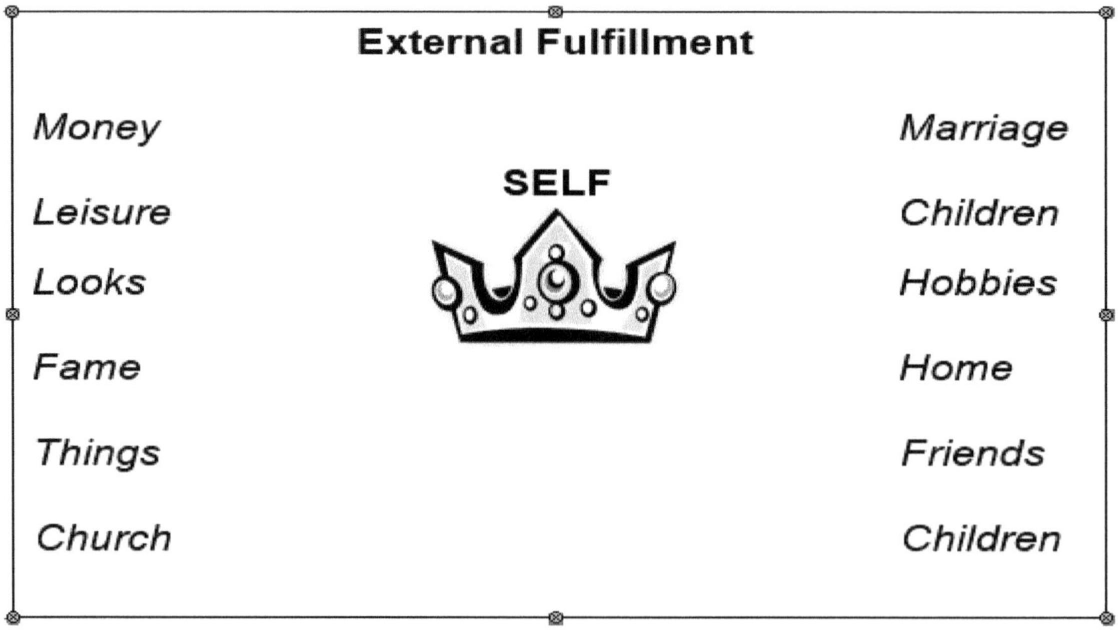

The diagram, "Self at Center" and "The Christian Deception of External Fulfillment," visually depict the problem. The "Self" is positioned as the central focus, surrounded by external measures of success and fleeting pleasures like money, leisure, looks, fame, possessions, and even church activities. The "External Fulfillment" diagrams illustrate that what can be considered inherently good turns sinful when used in an effort to become self-serving. This model, according to CCRT, inherently prioritizes personal gratification over genuine service and authentic connection with others. This mirrors the warnings found throughout Scripture against materialism and the pursuit of worldly possessions (Matthew 6:19-21). The Scriptures state: "Lay not up for yourselves treasures upon earth, where moth and rust doth corrupt, and where thieves break through and steal: But lay up for yourselves treasures in heaven, where neither moth nor rust doth corrupt, and where thieves do not break through nor steal: For where your treasure is, there will your heart be also." A self-serving heart, will also have self-serving behaviors.

A self-centered existence, from a CCRT perspective, breeds a host of negative consequences. Placing one's self-worth and happiness in external achievements and possessions, as depicted in the images, creates a precarious foundation for well-being. Read Ecclesiastes 2:1-11 to see how it illustrates that a life focused solely on pleasure and personal attainment ultimately leads to vanity and vexation of spirit, highlighting the emptiness of pursuing solely external fulfillment.

The very definition of "normality" within CCRT underscores this point. As Page 9 states: "There is no normal outside of the will of God, only degrees of abnormal. Thus, we have all sinned and fallen short of God is normal." This emphasis positions God as the unshakeable benchmark, and self-centeredness as a departure from this baseline inherently leads to dysfunction and imbalance. This concept is further reinforced when one remembers this is God's rule, not my rule

The Christian's Deception of External Fulfillment

However, focusing on the "doing" aspect of external fulfillment, leads to a sense of "earning" favor with God or others. The "Christian Deception of External Fulfillment" diagram demonstrates this, where activities like witnessing, teaching Sunday school, and attending meetings become self-serving efforts to validate one's faith rather than expressions of genuine service and love. Romans 14:17 reminds that "the kingdom of God is not meat and drink; but righteousness, and peace, and joy in the Holy Ghost." It is not about "doing" but about "being".

While people are more and more involved in the Church, and doing things for the Church, and feeling good about the Church, families are falling apart, children are falling behind, divorce is increasing, alcohol, drug use, suicide, pregnancies and abortions, are increasing…and more and more people are turning to mental health professionals, Zen, and New Age therapy than at any other time in history. Why? People are more preoccupied with things and doings for the wrong reasons.

The self-centered violation causes harm on multiple levels. Mentally, it fosters a distorted perception of reality, blinding individuals to their own flaws and faults and inhibiting genuine self-reflection. Emotionally, it leads to a cycle of dissatisfaction, emptiness, and a dependence on external validation. Spiritually, it disconnects individuals from God's purpose for their lives, preventing them from experiencing true joy, peace, and fulfillment. In relationships, it breeds selfishness, control, and a lack of empathy, leading to conflict, alienation, and broken connections. It can damage families, as they often become nothing but objects and tools to get one's selfish needs met. At work, a self-centered attitude fosters a lack of teamwork, ethical compromises, and a focus on personal gain over the well-being of others.

The Christian's Deception of External Fulfillment Chart

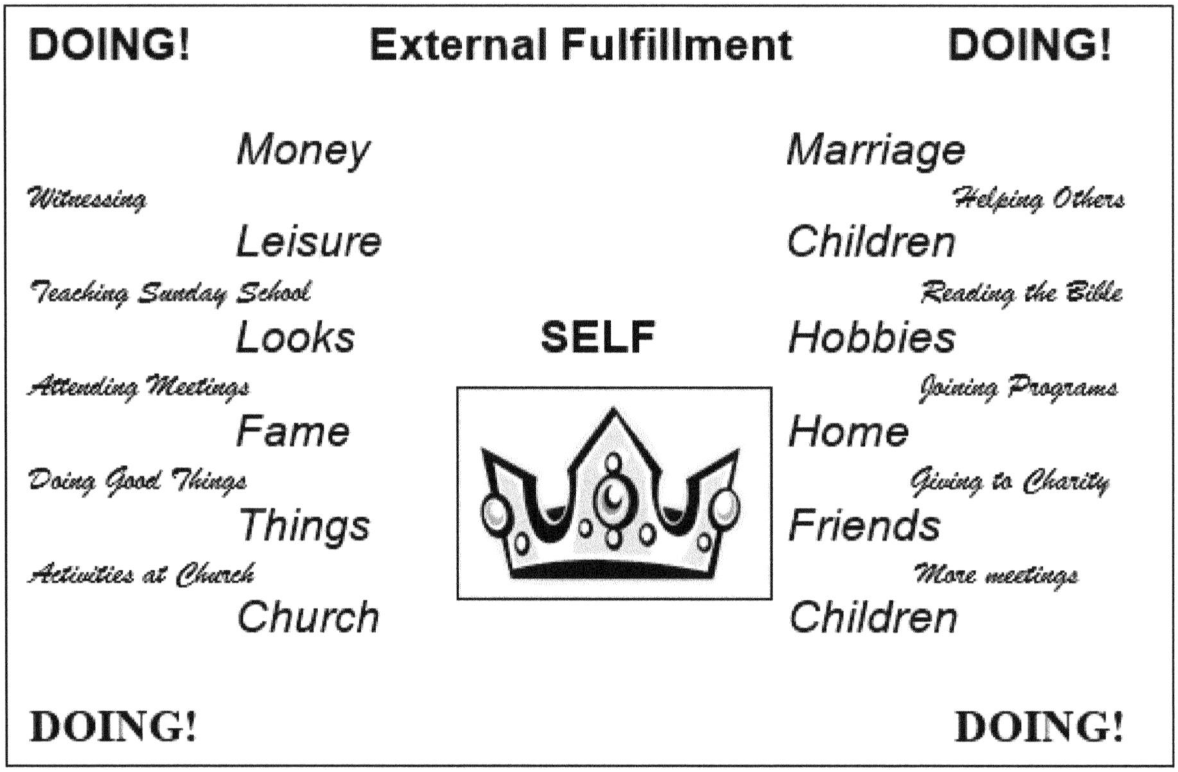

CCRT emphasizes the critical need to shift from a self-centered to a God-centered worldview. It states that true fulfillment lies not in pursuing external validations or pleasures but in aligning one's life with God's purpose and demonstrating love and service to others. This transformation requires acknowledging one's self-centered tendencies, repenting of past actions, and making a conscious decision to prioritize God's will and the needs of others in all aspects of life. Just as stated in Proverbs 14:12 "There is a way which seemeth right unto a man, but the end thereof is the ways of death". A self-centered life, while perhaps at times feels good and right, ultimately leads to death.

While seemingly paradoxical, it is necessary to acknowledge that an adequate amount of self-care is necessary. We must, as the document has pointed out, not "be so heavenly minded that we are no earthly good" and lose ourselves and families on the path of service. To be useful to God and others, we must take care of ourselves. Galatians 6:7 reminds us, "Be not deceived; God is not mocked: for whatsoever a man soweth, that shall he also reap". There is an element of individual need. A healthy harvest is only reaped after we water, fertilize, and protect the land and crops- or family- that we are caring for.

Several Biblical figures provide compelling examples of the pitfalls of self-centeredness. Consider King Saul, whose early reign was marked by humility and obedience to God. However, as he gained power and popularity, his focus shifted to self-preservation and upholding his own image. He disobeyed God's explicit commands, like the instruction to utterly destroy the Amalekites (1 Samuel 15), prioritizing political expediency over divine obedience. This self- centered disobedience led to his downfall and the loss of his kingdom. In fact, 1 Samuel 15:22 - 23 states it clearly: Hath the LORD as great delight in burnt offerings and sacrifices, as in obeying the voice of the LORD? Behold, to obey is better than sacrifice, and to hearken than the fat of rams. For rebellion is as the sin of witchcraft, and stubbornness is as iniquity and idolatry. Because thou hast rejected the word of the LORD, he hath also rejected thee from being king.

Another potent example is Judas Iscariot, whose self-serving desire for money led him to betray Jesus. His focus on personal gain blinded him to the true significance of Jesus' mission and ultimately led to his eternal ruin. Consider too, the account of the rich young ruler (Matthew 19:16-22) who came to Jesus seeking eternal life. He claimed to have followed all the commandments from his youth, but when Jesus challenged him to sell his possessions and follow Him, the young man walked away sorrowful, unable to relinquish his attachment to earthly wealth. His self- centered desire for security and status ultimately prevented him from embracing the true riches of a life dedicated to God.

The consequences of self-centeredness, according to CCRT, permeate all aspects of life. In close relationships, self-centeredness results in selfishness, control, and a lack of empathy, leading to conflicts, alienations, and broken relationships. On pg. 43, it states the toxic person has a distorted self-image. When the only thing of real value is the self, there will be no room for a true and reciprocal bond with others.

CCRT stresses that true healing involves a radical shift from a self-centered to a Christ-centered perspective. This transformation requires acknowledging one's inherent selfishness, repenting of past transgressions, and making a conscious decision to prioritize God's will and the needs of others in all aspects of life. CCRT emphasizes throughout the text that a "plan" that is centered on a self-serving life will inevitably lead to a point of implosion. God did not call us to focus only on our needs.

In contrast to an easy journey, CCRT claims the journey of self-actualization from this life can be met by a personal relationship with Jesus Christ. On page 76, there is a "Reality Key": If you are in the lowest part of life's desert experience, then you are in a good place to be remade into the finished work." In other words, Jesus comes to comfort and deliver all to a place of self-actualization in serving him. It is not possible to be a Christ follower without this core truth. It is only through seeking God, and a personal relationship with Jesus, can an individual see past the noise of the world and truly grasp that a self-centered life is incompatible with Christian doctrine and leads to suffering.

Ultimately, CCRT offers a framework for understanding how a self-centered approach to life is fundamentally incompatible with Biblical principles and detrimental to all aspects of human flourishing. By embracing humility, selflessness, and a commitment to serving others, individuals can break free from the chains of self-centeredness and experience the abundant life that God has designed for them.

UNDERSTANDING YOUR PROBLEM

Understanding your problem from a Christ Centered Reality Therapy (CCRT) standpoint begins with a radical redefinition of what a "problem" actually is. In most secular counseling models, problems are typically viewed as rooted in past trauma, environmental circumstances, or psychiatric dysfunction. While these models may identify real pain and dysfunction, CCRT asserts that problems must be understood in the present, within the context of violated spiritual and moral absolutes, and addressed through Biblically-grounded choices and behavioral transformation.

1. The Problem is in the Present, Not the Past

CCRT strongly asserts: *"Jesus Christ, first and foremost, would always deal with a person (a sinner) in their immediate present condition".* From this CCRT viewpoint, therapy is not about wallowing in the past but facing the current reality of sin, disobedience, or misalignment with God's standards. A person may have experienced past trauma, but unless that issue is brought to Christ for reconciliation, it becomes a present spiritual and behavioral stronghold.

As Paul reminds us in *Colossians 1:21*, *"And you, that were sometime alienated and enemies in your mind by wicked works, yet now hath he reconciled."* The past only ceases to be a problem when it is brought under the blood of Jesus and aligned with God's truth.

Biblical Example: The woman at the well (John 4) was burdened by relational failures and sin, but Jesus addressed her present behavior and pointed her toward spiritual transformation, not past analysis.

2. Your Problem Begins in Your Thoughts

CCRT teaches that all behavior is a product of belief systems, and faulty belief systems result in faulty behavior. This directly supports the Biblical teaching in *Romans 12:2*: *"Be ye transformed by the renewing of your mind."* CCRT insists that a toxic belief system must be confronted and replaced with truth. The person must recognize whether they are operating from a *God-centered belief system* or a *self-centered, world-defined system.*

In CCRT, understanding your problem starts with recognizing that how you perceive your reality (your mind) shapes how you feel (your emotions), which then shapes how you behave (your choices). This aligns with Jesus' teaching in *Matthew 5–7*, where He exposes heart motives behind behaviors.

Biblical Example: King Saul (1 Samuel 15) believed partial obedience was acceptable. His belief system contradicted God's commands, leading to disobedience and eventual destruction.

3. The Root of the Problem: Violation of God's Law

CCRT defines sin not only as rebellion but as *abnormality*—a departure from God's original design. Problems arise when individuals violate God's principles, either knowingly (*James 4:17*), unknowingly (*Luke 12:48*), or through habitual sin (*John 8:34*). CCRT states, *"God is the absolute baseline for what is normal. There is no normal outside the will of God, only degrees of abnormal"*.

Understanding your problem from a CCRT lens requires acknowledging that sin—however subtle—is the source of psychological, emotional, and relational dysfunction. Whether it's anxiety, addiction, or broken relationships, each issue ultimately reflects a misalignment with God's moral and spiritual order.

Biblical Example: David's sin with Bathsheba (2 Samuel 11–12) was a violation of multiple divine principles. His internal conflict and spiritual decay were only resolved when he repented and aligned with God's standard (*Psalm 51*).

4. The False Solution: External Fulfillment and Religious Doing

Many Christians, as the uploaded document warns, fall into the trap of *external doing*—serving in ministry, attending church, helping others—all while ignoring internal spiritual disobedience and unresolved personal sin. This is the illusion of fulfillment without transformation.

CCRT warns that such doing can be self-deceptive: *"People are more preoccupied with things and doings for the wrong reasons"* (Understanding Your Problem, p. 111). CCRT echoes this by highlighting that abnormal belief systems produce false solutions: *"Behavioral failure occurs when a want is abnormal and creates a false belief system replacing normal reality with abnormal and false desires"*.

Scriptural Warning: Matthew 7:22–23: "Many will say to me in that day, Lord, Lord, have we not prophesied in thy name? ... And then will I profess unto them, I never knew you."

Biblical Example: The Pharisees (Matthew 23) were full of religious activity but blind to their spiritual need for repentance and truth.

5. The Only True Solution: Reconciliation, Choice, and Change

A. Reconciliation in Christ

A problem is not resolved until it is brought to Christ. *Colossians 1:21* reminds us that we were once enemies "in our minds by wicked works," but reconciliation changes the entire equation. CCRT teaches that healing cannot occur apart from the spiritual restoration offered through Jesus Christ.

B. A Choice is Required

"I have set before your life and death... choose life" (Deut. 30:19). According to CCRT, human beings possess *free will*, and with that comes the responsibility to choose either obedience or sin. Neutrality is not an option. *"Neutral does not exist in nature. There is always a transformation process for a want to become abnormal.*

Biblical Example: Joshua calls the people to choose whom they will serve (Joshua 24:15), underscoring those spiritual problems always hinge on personal responsibility.

C. A Change is Required

True healing involves transformation, not merely relief. *Romans 12:1–2* demands a change in mind and body. CCRT integrates this truth by emphasizing that individuals must redirect their behavior toward Biblical absolutes, not relative moral standards.

Biblical Example: Zacchaeus (Luke 19:1–10) experienced a total change in direction after his encounter with Christ, marked by restitution and behavioral change.

6. The Six Needs and the Misunderstood Problem

CCRT identifies **five basic human needs**: survival, love, power, freedom, and joy. I have added a sixth need, the need to know God. Problems arise when these needs are met through *abnormal wants* instead of God's design.

Need	Biblical Example	Abnormal Attempt to Meet It
Survival	Joseph (Genesis 37– 50) trusted God's plan	Hoarding, greed, control
Love	Ruth and Naomi (Ruth 1–4)	Co-dependency, promiscuity
Power	Paul (Philippians 3:4–14) through Christ	Pride, manipulation, dominance
Freedom	Daniel (Daniel 6) remained obedient	Rebellion, lawlessness
Joy	David dancing before the Lord (2 Sam. 6:14)	Substance abuse, escapism, distraction
Need to Know God	Jesus said," John 17:3 (KJV) [3] And this is life eternal, that they might know thee the only true God, and Jesus Christ, whom thou hast sent." John 17:3	Worship God in their own way. Cain. Genesis 4:5

When these needs are unmet, or met through worldly systems, the result is spiritual dysfunction and eventual collapse. CCRT helps clients identify which need is unfulfilled and what abnormal want is being used to fill the gap.

Conclusion: Understanding Your Problem Through CCRT

Understanding your problem requires more than identifying symptoms—it requires spiritual discernment, Biblical alignment, and therapeutic redirection rooted in the absolute truth of God's Word. CCRT provides a uniquely powerful and Biblically faithful model for seeing our problems clearly: not as random or medically detached, but as spiritual misalignments that can be corrected through the power of Christ, the guidance of Scripture, and the wise integration of behavior, belief, and responsibility.

In Christ, your problem has a solution. But it will require honesty, choice, and change.

"If the Son therefore shall make you free, ye shall be free indeed." – John 8:36

"I can do all things through Christ which strengtheneth me." – Philippians 4:13

MEETING YOUR NEEDS BIBLICALLY

In Christ Centered Reality Therapy (CCRT), the core premise is that human beings were designed by God with intrinsic, legitimate needs. These needs—*survival, love, power, freedom,* and *joy*—are part of God's original and perfect design. In CCRT, the foundation for meeting human needs is rooted not in self-help or worldly philosophies, but in the divine revelation of Scripture and the absolute truth of God's design. As CCRT writes, "God created all of man's original needs… God met each of humans' needs through intelligent design. God's normal master plan and original design was perfection. Outside of the master design is imperfection". The problem arises not from the needs themselves, but from how individuals, often influenced by culture or wounded belief systems, attempt to fulfill those needs through abnormal or sinful means.

From a CCRT viewpoint, meeting your needs Biblically begins with acknowledging that God alone defines what is *normal*. "There is no normal outside the will of God, only degrees of abnormal," This theological absolute sets CCRT apart from secular psychology, which often encourages individuals to define truth based on emotion, past trauma, or relative standards. Instead, CCRT asserts that the believer must submit every desire, motive, and behavior to the unchanging standard of Scripture (2 Timothy 3:16–17). God's Word is not just suggestive—it is definitive for what is necessary to live a godly and fulfilled life (2 Peter 1:3).

1. The Bible Is the Source for Meeting All Needs

God has not left us without guidance. Scripture declares that all we need for life and godliness has already been provided:

"According as his divine power hath given unto us all things that pertain unto life and godliness, through the knowledge of him that hath called us to glory and virtue" (2 Peter 1:3).

As CCRT notes, the Word of God is the absolute standard for what is normal; any solution that departs from this foundation results in increasing abnormality. The Apostle Paul confirms this when he writes that *"all Scripture is given by inspiration of God... that the man of God may be perfect, thoroughly furnished unto all good works"* (2 Tim. 3:16–17).

Biblical Example: Jesus in the wilderness (Matthew 4:1–11) resisted Satan's temptation to meet legitimate needs (hunger, identity, power) through illegitimate means. Instead, He relied solely on Scripture to meet His needs within God's will.

2. The Problem with the World's Way of Meeting Needs

CCRT teaches that all people share the same five core needs: survival, love, power, freedom, and joy. However, problems arise when individuals attempt to meet these needs through the world system, which is not of God. 1 John 2:15-17, "15 Love not the world, neither the things that are in the world. If any man loves the world, the love of the Father is not in him. 16 For all that is in the world, the lust of the flesh, and the lust of the eyes, and the pride of life, is not of the Father, but is of the world. 17 And the world passeth away, and the lust thereof: but he that doeth the will of God abideth forever. that replaces normal with abnormal. Proverbs 14:12 warns us: "There is a way which seemeth right unto a man, but the end thereof are the ways of death." Colossians 2:8- 10 further cautions us against "philosophy and vain deceit… and not after Christ."

The world's methods—self-indulgence, addiction, escapism, or control—promise fulfillment but lead to destruction. Only Christ offers a complete and righteous way to meet our needs: *"Ye are complete in Him, which is the head of all principality and power"* (Col. 2:10).

Biblical Example: King Solomon (Ecclesiastes) pursued every worldly avenue—pleasure, wealth, wisdom—yet concluded it was all vanity. True fulfillment could only come through reverence and obedience to God.

3. The Tools for Biblical Recovery

CCRT integrates Scripture, the Holy Spirit, prayer, and the Church as essential tools for addressing problems and restoring normality. These tools are not optional; they are God's divinely ordained means of recovery.

1. The Word of God – Provides correction, instruction, and truth (2 Tim. 3:16).
2. The Holy Spirit – Indwells and empowers the believer to choose rightly (John 14:26; Rom. 8:14).
3. Prayer – Opens communion with God and invites divine help (Phil. 4:6; James 1:5).
4. The Church – A body of believers that exhorts, edifies, and bears burdens (Heb. 10:24-25; Gal. 6:1-2).

"We must face reality, acknowledge the truth, assume personal responsibility, and recover ourselves" (Meeting Your Needs Biblically, p. 1; CCRT, p. 7). This mirrors Paul's command in Romans 12:1–2 that we must be "transformed by the renewing of our minds."

Biblical Example: The prodigal son (Luke 15:11–32) used worldly means to meet his need for freedom and joy, but ultimately repented, returned to his father, and was restored. His recovery required truth, humility, and re-alignment with the father's design.

4. Meeting Each of the Six Needs God's Way

1. Survival – God provides for our material needs as we trust Him (Matthew 6:25–33).

Biblical Example: Elijah was fed by ravens and a widow during famine (1 Kings 17), showing God's provision in desperate times.

2. Love – True love is found in God and expressed in sacrificial relationship.

"We love him, because he first loved us" (1 John 4:19).

Biblical Example: Jonathan and David's friendship illustrates mutual, godly love (1 Samuel 18).

3. Power (Self-Worth) – Real power comes from identity in Christ, not performance.

"I can do all things through Christ" (Phil. 4:13).

Biblical Example: Gideon saw himself as weak, but God called him a mighty man of valor (Judges 6).

4. Freedom – God-given free will is fulfilled through obedience, not rebellion.

"If the Son therefore shall make you free, ye shall be free indeed" (John 8:36).

Biblical Example: Daniel maintained spiritual freedom even under Babylonian captivity by remaining faithful to God (Daniel 6).

5. Joy – Joy is not found in pleasure or circumstance but in relationship with God.

"In thy presence is fullness of joy" (Psalm 16:11).

Biblical Example: Paul and Silas sang praises in prison, showing joy in trial (Acts 16:25).

6. The Need to Know God – God has given us everything we need through the knowledge of Him. "According as his divine power hath given unto us all things that pertain unto life and godliness, through the knowledge of him that hath called us to glory and virtue:" (2 Peter 1:3)

Each of the six basic needs can be met in either a *normal (Biblical)* or *abnormal (sinful)* way. According to CCRT, "A want is abnormal when it is a replacement for a basic need".). When individuals seek to satisfy their God-given needs through worldly substitutes—such as substances for joy, manipulation for power, or promiscuity for love—they deviate from God's intended path and produce dysfunction and spiritual dissonance.

Proverbs 14:12 warns, "There is a way which seemeth right unto a man, but the end thereof are the ways of death." This includes seemingly innocent choices that attempt to meet real needs in ungodly ways.

For example, the need for **love** is often distorted into unhealthy attachments or self-centered dependency. CCRT explains that "Love is God-created and God-centered. If a person's understanding of love is perverted or distorted, then all other needs will suffer malfunction", The Biblical remedy is not just to "feel loved," but to understand love through Christ's sacrificial example (John 15:13). Consider the Apostle John, who referred to himself as "the disciple whom Jesus loved" (John 13:23). His security in Christ's love anchored his identity and enabled him to meet other needs, such as joy and freedom, with stability and truth.

The **need for power** often becomes confused with control, dominance, or self-assertion. He writes, "When the basic need for power is unmet, people will seek to fill it with substitutes—revenge, intimidation, or self-pity". Biblically, power is not about asserting one's will, but surrendering to God's authority and receiving strength through Him. *"I can do all things through Christ which strengtheneth me"* (Philippians 4:13). Gideon, for instance, initially viewed himself as weak, yet God called him a "mighty man of valor" (Judges 6:12). His power was not found in self-belief, but in God's calling.

Freedom is another core need that is frequently misunderstood in modern contexts. Rather than defining freedom as autonomy or self-governance, Scripture defines true freedom as the ability to walk in righteousness and obedience to God. Jesus said, "If the Son therefore shall make you free, ye shall be free indeed" (John 8:36). CCRT warns, "Freedom without moral accountability is merely licensed rebellion". Daniel is a Biblical example of one who preserved true freedom—even while politically enslaved—by refusing to compromise his worship and values (Daniel 6).

Joy is perhaps the most easily counterfeited. Many chase fleeting pleasures under the illusion that they will produce lasting joy. But CCRT teaches that "joy is the byproduct of correctly fulfilling all the other needs" CCRT, p. 17). This aligns with Psalm 16:11: *"In thy presence is fullness of joy."* Paul and Silas, singing in prison (Acts 16:25), demonstrated that joy is not tied to circumstances but flows from a Spirit-filled life.

To meet your needs Biblically, you must first examine your belief system. As CCRT emphasizes, "All behavior stems from belief. Wrong behavior is the result of wrong belief". If someone believes that survival depends on deceit, or that love must be earned, or that power means domination, they will behave abnormally and produce spiritual consequences. Romans 12:2 commands believers to "be transformed by the renewing of your mind," which CCRT interprets as the replacement of toxic, self-centered beliefs with Biblical truth.

5. Responding to Temptation and Emotional Distress

CCRT teaches that it is not merely the events in life that defeat us, but how we respond to them. *"It is how we respond to them that gets us down"* (Meeting Your Needs Biblically, p. 2). Paul writes in 1 Corinthians 10:13 that God always provides "a way of escape" from temptation. Through Biblical tools, we are equipped not just to cope but to overcome.

Biblical Example: Joseph, though betrayed and enslaved, responded with faith and integrity. He refused to sin with Potiphar's wife and later forgave his brothers, understanding that *"God meant it for good"* (Genesis 50:20).

6. The Hope of Transformation

Transformation is not only possible; it is required. CCRT contends that *knowledge and action are not the same thing.* 10). God expects obedience, not just awareness. Romans 12:2 calls us to be "transformed by the renewing of your mind," which is the process of exchanging faulty beliefs with Biblical truth.

This transformation takes place not through effort alone but by the empowering presence of the Holy Spirit, the authority of God's Word, and support of the church. CCRT is clear: *"Each person has five basic core needs... A want is different from a need. A want is always driven by culture and society. A need is an individual, naturally occurring process".*

Conclusion

From a CCRT perspective, Biblical counseling is not about self-improvement, but about submission to God's design. Meeting your needs Biblically involves understanding what those needs truly are, rejecting worldly strategies, embracing divine tools, and living in obedience to God's Word. As you realign your beliefs, behavior, and desires with the will of God, you will find that your needs are not only met but redeemed, restored, and reoriented for His glory. *"And ye are complete in Him, which is the head of all principality and power."* – Colossians 2:10 Recovery is therefore not just emotional or cognitive—it is *spiritual.* Recovery begins at the point of repentance and transformation begins when a new belief system is chosen over the old. This process involves the Holy Spirit (John 14:26), the Word of God (Psalm 119:105), prayer (James 1:5), and the support of the Church (Hebrews 10:24–25). These tools function as the *means of grace* through which God realigns the heart and mind, enabling believers to meet their needs in harmony with His will.

Ultimately, meeting your needs Biblically is not about suppression, but submission. It is about trusting that God's design for survival, love, power, freedom, and joy is not only sufficient but superior. When our needs are aligned with His provision, we are not enslaved by our desires, but fulfilled by His Spirit. *"Delight thyself also in the LORD; and he shall give thee the desires of thine heart."* – Psalm 37:4

SYMPTOMS OR ROOT CAUSES

Understanding the distinction between a *symptom* and a *root cause* is fundamental in Christian counseling, particularly within the framework of Christ Centered Reality Therapy (CCRT). Without this discernment, a counselor may spend valuable time treating behavioral manifestations (symptoms) rather than helping the counselee confront and correct the underlying belief systems or heart conditions that drive the behavior. As CCRT articulates, "All behavior stems from belief. Wrong behavior is the result of wrong belief". This critical concept highlights those behaviors we often label as the problem are, in reality, only *surface-level indicators* of deeper spiritual or psychological roots.

CCRT emphasizes the critical distinction between surface-level symptoms and the underlying root causes that fuel human suffering. Many therapies, according to CCRT, focus solely on alleviating symptoms, offering temporary relief but failing to address the foundational issues that perpetuate dysfunction. However, many counselors respond to what the client describes as the problem. However, experience has taught "the problem is rarely the problem". The symptoms that a client describes need to be traced to the actual root causes." Drawing from Biblical principles, CCRT aims to identify and address these root causes, paving the way for genuine healing and lasting transformation.

The provided image categorizes the root causes of many problems into "Pride of Life," "Lust of the Eyes," and "Lust of the Flesh." It links these root causes to specific surface causes (e.g., inferiority, frustration, anger; envy, insecurity, ungratefulness; guilt, lust, pride) and ultimately to surface problems (e.g., wrong appearance, wrong motives, wrong language; lying, stealing, destruction; avoidance, addictions, adultery). These "surface-level" symptoms are often what individuals present in therapy or in their own lives, leading to a cycle of repeated and often ineffective attempts at fixing the problem.

1 John 2:15-17 illustrates the root causes: "Love not the world, neither the things that are in the world. If any man loves the world, the love of the Father is not in him. For all that is in the world, the lust of the flesh, and the lust of the eyes, and the pride of life, is not of the Father, but is of the world. And the world passeth away, and the lust thereof: but he that doeth the will of God abideth forever." This passage forms the backbone of this therapy.

Many Biblical Figures exhibit a focus on "surface" or visible indicators. Consider the Pharisees, who sought to show good and just behavior through public displays, as well as rigid rules for public order, but did not live right behind closed doors. A prime example is in Luke 18:9-14, where a self-righteous pharisee thanked God he was not evil like a tax collector, but a tax collector beat his breast in repentance and went home justified because he humbled himself before God.

Root Causes	Root Problem	Surface Causes	Surface Symptom
	Bitterness		Wrong Appearance Wrong Motives Wrong Language Wrath Hatred Heresies Variance Seditions Gossip Arguments
Pride of Life		Inferiority Frustration Anger	
Lust of the Eyes	Covetousness	Envy Insecurity Ungratefulness	Lying Stealing Destruction Adultery Covetousness Materialism Envying
Lust of the Flesh	Moral Impurity	Guilt/Lust Pride	Avoidance Addictions Adultery Drunkenness Emulations Idolatry Lasciviousness Murders Reveling Sexual Immorality Smoking Strife Uncleanness

King David, who committed adultery with Bathsheba and then orchestrated the murder of her husband, Uriah, provides another example (2 Samuel 11). David's actions stemmed from a "lust of the flesh", or acting on one of the flesh's needs. While David's action had the effect of destroying a marriage, what he reported at the surface to others (and perhaps himself) was that he was a man after God's own heart. The reality, was at the surface, he was a liar, an adulterer, and a murderer.

The consequences of focusing solely on symptoms, according to CCRT, are far-reaching. While temporarily alleviates their issue, they tend to have long-term personal and generational consequences. Moreover, focusing only on surface level interactions blinds one to seeing the truth about a situation, which inhibits their power to act within it, and to ask God for a relationship with Jesus to become freed.

The Surface Causes often include emotional responses such as anger, envy, insecurity, guilt, and ungratefulness. These emotional responses are tied to incorrect thought patterns or distorted perceptions but are still not the root. Dealing with only these emotional layers may bring temporary relief but rarely leads to lasting transformation.

Beneath these layers, the chart identifies Root Problems like bitterness, covetousness, moral impurity, inferiority, and pride. These deeper conditions of the heart reflect moral and spiritual disconnections from God's truth and righteousness. Yet, even these are linked to Root Causes, which, according to both the chart and 1 John 2:15–17, are the *lust of the flesh, lust of the eyes, and the pride of life*. These three spiritual categories describe the fundamental orientations of sin that govern worldly behavior and separate us from godly living: As CCRT articulates, "All behavior stems from belief. Wrong behavior is the result of wrong belief". This critical concept highlights that behaviors we often label as the problem are, in reality, only *surface-level indicators* of deeper spiritual or psychological roots.

This verse serves as a theological key to understanding the human condition. In CCRT, these root causes align with what CCRT identifies as *toxic beliefs*—false worldviews that shape one's identity, purpose, and choices. If a counselor does not help the client identify and confront these toxic roots, then any behavioral change will be short-lived. CCRT insists, "Unless you have a success plan to maintain the new ideas, there will be no change". The success plan must begin with replacing wrong beliefs at the root level with Biblical truth.

In therapeutic practice, a CCRT-informed counselor would use the chart as a diagnostic and conversational tool. For example, a counselee may present with alcoholism (a surface problem). Through dialogue, the counselor uncovers deep feelings of inferiority and frustration (surface causes), which stem from unresolved bitterness and rejection (root problems). But ultimately, the counselee's worldview is shaped by a prideful refusal to accept God's love and grace— a manifestation of the *pride of life* (root cause). By exposing this root, the counselor can then lead the counselee to repentance, confession, and transformation through God's Word.

Scriptural examples further reinforce this process. Consider Cain in Genesis 4. His outward act—murder—was preceded by surface emotions: envy and anger. But God diagnosed the root: an unsubmitted heart unwilling to accept God's authority. God said, *"If thou doest well, shalt thou not be accepted?"* (Genesis 4:7). The failure to do right was not due to emotion alone but belief in self-righteousness and pride.

Jesus also modeled this approach. In Mark 7:21–23, He declares that evil actions proceed from the heart: "For from within, out of the heart of men, proceed evil thoughts... thefts, covetousness, wickedness... pride, foolishness: All these evil things come from within, and defile the man." He did not treat behaviors as isolated or accidental but as fruit produced by corrupt roots.

Therefore, in a CCRT therapeutic session, the chart becomes more than a visual—it is a Biblical map. The counselor guides the counselee downward through the layers of behavior, emotion, belief, and spiritual condition. Once the root is revealed, the healing process begins with targeted Scriptures, Holy Spirit conviction, confession, and renewal of the mind (Romans 12:2). The counselor helps the counselee understand that they are not merely to stop sinning but to start believing rightly.

In conclusion, the difference between symptoms and root causes is not merely semantic—it determines the *depth and durability of healing*. Christian counselors who fail to recognize this distinction risk applying superficial solutions to deeply rooted spiritual dysfunction. But those who, through prayer and Scripture, help their counselees identify and uproot false beliefs aligned with the world can witness true transformation. This is the goal of Biblical counseling: not behavioral compliance, but rooted spiritual maturity.

THE ROOT OF MENTAL ILLNESS

Christ-Centered Reality Therapy (CCRT) offers a unique perspective on the etiology of mental illness, asserting that the core of many psychological struggles stems from a fundamental triad: a lack of satisfying significant relationships, unmet emotional needs, and unbiblical beliefs that promote unbiblical behavior. This framework posits that these three elements are inextricably intertwined, and their combined presence creates fertile ground for the development of mental and emotional distress. Moreover, CCRT contends that the root is rebellion from God, and all "needs" and "wants" are simply byproducts of not following God's will.

Within the CCRT framework, a counseling client's arrival at the therapist's door is a tacit acknowledgement of these three interconnected factors. On the point of mental health needing a Christian component on pg 12., it states Reality Therapy exclusively focuses on the mind and body, and it never addresses the spiritual nature of man. Most counseling modalities focus on the mind and body. Whereas Christian counseling typically focuses exclusively on the client's spiritual needs. Let me remind you what is known about your client before he/she arrives:

1. **There is a Lack of a Satisfying Significant Relationships:** Humans are inherently relational beings, designed to connect with others in meaningful ways. CCRT recognizes the importance of belonging, love, and positive relationships as fundamental needs, as highlighted on pg 13. When these needs are unmet, individuals may experience feelings of isolation, loneliness, and a lack of worth, creating a void that can be filled by unhealthy coping mechanisms. Without a Godly relationship with peers, or family, there is no way to experience true satisfaction- there is always a level of want.
2. **Basic Emotional Needs are not being met:** CCRT acknowledges a spectrum of emotional needs for humans including: Mental, emotional, physical, and spiritual needs. There are some that believe humans need "happiness" "purpose" and even "satisfaction". To that end, the second PDF emphasizes the same point. However, from pg. 16 it states "You are either going to be growing, or dying." and this applies to one's inner and outer self. It is possible, in a nonbiblical relationship, to receive false affirmation to be on track- but if it is a distorted view of reality, there is in reality no growth occurring at all- regardless of the actions. These needs, as presented include love, power, freedom, and fun/joy, and the need to know God.All have to be met to have good mcntal and cmotional wcllbcing.
3. **Unbiblical Beliefs Promoting Unbiblical Behavior:** At the heart of CCRT lies the conviction that adherence to Biblical principles is essential for well-being. When you look at both sides, as a test to determine Godly morality is often used, to determine there is both good, and bad. Without God's input and guidance, humans don't know the difference- and as highlighted on pg. 33, what will always begin as a simple matter, will become so twisted that only failure can result. It is a slow boil, of all wrong ingredients- that always comes back to a relationship with Christ as the only safe and secure path.

In the meeting the needs with what is right comes from the fact our soul will be satisfied by it- with what is of God will bring the inner peace needed to carry on, not the instant relief at the moment, but the long haul.

Biblical figures often struggled with the consequences of broken or strained relationships. David's complicated and destructive family dynamics, which is what happens with any relationship as they get away from what is right.

Ultimately, CCRT proposes that we can see the patterns and the solutions are presented. We all had at least a 20% good in life - but with some self-reflection and by following the way laid out by Christ, in our relationship with Christ, can change it to 100% for all our interactions and to solve our problem with what would have otherwise become an ever downward spiral. It is never a point where some cannot be won over if they try. We are to follow the teachings and guidelines in that to help us come to the solution. It is essential to be a constant reminder to follow with the teachings. As stated by Charles Spurgeon "I never can comprehend how the snails managed to get into the ark, yet they did; they must have started very early."

Throughout the annals of psychological thought, many theories have emerged, each seeking to unravel the complexities of the human experience, particularly in the realm of mental health. CCRT suggests that individuals are driven by basic emotional needs and that all behavior is a purposeful attempt to satisfy these needs. When these needs are not adequately met, distress and what are often labeled as "mental illnesses" can arise. Complementing this perspective, the timeless wisdom of the King James Version (KJV) of the Bible offers a moral and relational compass, emphasizing the importance of covenant, love, and obedience to divine principles for holistic well-being. Integrating these two seemingly disparate domains offers profound insights into the nature of mental health and potential pathways toward healing and restoration. CCRT shows that almost all emotional problems stem from unsatisfying relationships. When people are asked why they are unhappy, almost all of them blame someone else for their misery—lovers, wives, husbands, exes, children, parents, teachers, students, or people they work with. There is hardly a person alive who hasn't been heard saying, "You're driving me crazy.... That really upsets me. Don't you have any consideration for how I feel? You make me so mad, I can't see straight." It never crosses their minds that they are choosing the misery they are complaining about.

CCRT, at its core, asserts that human beings are primarily motivated by five basic needs: survival, love and belonging, power, freedom, and fun, and I add a sixth one, the need to know God, among these, the need for love and belonging is paramount, as it forms the bedrock of our relationships and social connections. Again, all long-lasting psychological problems are relationship problems. When individuals experience a lack of meaningful and satisfying relationships, their emotional needs go unmet, leading to distress, anxiety, depression, and other manifestations of psychological unease. The absence of this bedrock foundation will most certainly give rise to mental illness.

Correspondingly, the Bible places immense emphasis on the significance of relationships, particularly within the context of covenant. From the creation narrative in Genesis, where God establishes a covenant with humanity, to the teachings of Jesus Christ in the New Testament, the importance of love, fidelity, and reciprocal commitment resonates throughout Scripture. The Bible posits that the most essential commandment is to love God with all one's heart, soul, and mind, and to love one's neighbor as oneself (Matthew 22:37-39). Disobedience to these commandments, particularly in the form of broken relationships and disregard for the well-being of others, is portrayed as a departure from divine order, resulting in disharmony and suffering.

One might consider the character of King David, a figure revered in the Old Testament yet plagued by relational turmoil. Despite his initial devotion to God and his divinely ordained role as king, David's life was marred by instances of adultery, deceit, and violence, most notably in his affair with Bathsheba and the subsequent murder of her husband, Uriah (2 Samuel 11). These actions not only violated the commandments of God but also shattered the bonds of trust and fidelity within David's family and kingdom, leading to strife, rebellion, and personal anguish.

CCRT offers a lens through which to understand David's actions, suggesting that his choices, though morally reprehensible, were driven by his attempt to satisfy his needs, albeit in destructive ways. His pursuit of power and sexual gratification ultimately came at the expense of his relationships, leaving him isolated and remorseful. Even though David repented, the sins of his relational choices gave rise to an ever-increasing cycle of pain and suffering.

Again, in the realm of counseling, the integration of CCRT and Biblical principles offers a potent framework for addressing the root causes of mental illness and facilitating healing. When an individual seeks counseling, three fundamental premises often hold true:

1. There is a lack of a satisfying significant relationship: Individuals grappling with psychological distress often find themselves isolated, disconnected, or embroiled in dysfunctional relational patterns.
2. Emotional needs are not being met: The unmet needs for love and belonging, power, freedom, and fun manifest as a sense of emptiness, frustration, and overall dissatisfaction with life.
3. There is an unbiblical belief that promotes unbiblical behavior: Cognitive distortions, flawed belief systems, and moral deviations often contribute to maladaptive behaviors and relational conflicts, furthering psychological distress.

Conclusion

CCRT accepts the Biblical truth that teaches that the **root cause of mental illness** is found in humanity's **original sin**, which corrupted mankind's entire nature—mind, body, and spirit—thus creating an abnormal condition that pervades all aspects of human existence (pp. 6–7). CCRT explains that God's original design for man was perfect, with all needs—mental, emotional, physical, and spiritual—met in harmony with His will. When Adam and Eve sinned, this divine order was disrupted, and humanity became w the "Natural Toxic Man," choosing to meet needs through abnormal, man-made sources instead of God's perfect provision (p. 7). This break from God's absolute standard for normalcy introduced toxic belief systems and destructive behavioral patterns into the human condition, which became universally embedded in every generation after the Fall.

In CCRT, mental illness is therefore not viewed solely as a biological or psychological malfunction, but as the *symptom* of a deeper spiritual disorder—separation from God's normal reality. This separation leads to a distorted view of self, others, and the world, resulting in destructive choices and false belief systems (p. 7). These abnormal beliefs and behaviors integrate into all three dimensions of man—mental, physical, and spiritual—creating patterns of thought and action that damage relationships, erode self-worth, and perpetuate dysfunction. CCRT emphasizes that original sin "gave birth to all abnormal bad behavior and toxic abnormal belief systems" (p. 7), and that these systems are at the foundation of much of what is diagnosed today as mental illness.

From a CCRT perspective, the cure is not found in merely treating symptoms or altering behavior in isolation, but in restoring man to God's design through Christ. This involves confronting false, sin-based belief systems with the absolutes of God's Word and replacing abnormal wants with Biblically normal needs (pp. 6–7). Thus, while chemical imbalances, trauma, or environmental factors may contribute to the manifestation of mental illness, CCRT holds that the ultimate root cause is the spiritual corruption of mankind's nature through original sin—a condition that only reconciliation with God through Jesus Christ can fully heal.

UNDERSTANDING THE WORLD'S SYSTEM OF MENTAL DISORDERS.

The human experience is inherently fraught with challenges and adversity. From the minor inconveniences of daily life to the profound crises that test our resilience, problems are an inevitable part of the human condition. However, the impact of these challenges on our mental, emotional, and spiritual well-being is not solely determined by the nature of the problem itself but rather by our attitude and response to it. As explored in the text, Christ Centered Reality Therapy for the 21st Century (CCRT), attitudes towards a problem are a core component.

Drawing from this understanding, alongside the teachings of the Bible, particularly the wisdom of the Apostle Paul in Philippians 4:4-9, a powerful synergy emerges, offering guidance on cultivating a resilient and transformative approach to life's inevitable adversities.

CCRT emphasizes the importance of aligning one's thoughts, behaviors, and beliefs with Biblical principles for holistic well-being. He writes, "Every time someone sins someone else pays the price. Socially accepted abnormality reality costs everyone. It causes chaos in the lives of everyone" (Chapter 3). This aligns with the Biblical understanding of sin and its far-reaching consequences, emphasizing the interconnectedness of individuals within a community of faith.

Furthermore, CCRT underscores the power of choice in shaping our responses to life's circumstances. This aligns with the Bible's emphasis on free will and personal responsibility. While external factors may influence our experiences, the Bible posits that we retain the agency to choose our attitudes, behaviors, and beliefs in the face of adversity.

Paul, in his letter to the Philippians, exemplifies this principle of choice in the face of challenging circumstances. From a CCRT therapist's lens, Philippians 4:4–12 sketches a remarkably complete "mental hygiene" plan that aligns point-for-point with how Christ Centered Reality Therapy defines **normal** thinking and living. CCRT begins by anchoring "normal" in God Himself: "GOD is the absolute baseline for what is normal. There is no normal outside of the will of God, only degrees of abnormal" (p. 10). Because humans are created as a unity of "Mind, Body and Spirit" (p. 11) and God "created the human mind, body, and spirit…[and] humans are only a total person when the three- dimensional person is intact" (p. 15), mental health in CCRT is never merely managing feelings; it's aligning thought, desire, and behavior to God's design so needs are met in **normal** (not toxic) ways.

Imprisoned and facing potential persecution, Paul exudes an attitude of unwavering joy and contentment, urging his readers to "Rejoice in the Lord always: and again I say, Rejoice" (Philippians 4:4). This call to rejoice is not a naive dismissal of suffering but rather a deliberate choice to focus on the transcendent presence of God amidst trials, tapping into a source of strength and hope that transcends earthly circumstances. "Rejoice in the Lord always" (v. 4) is not denial; it's a disciplined return to the original design where **joy** is a core, God-given human need. CCRT explicitly reframes "fun" as "JOY" and asserts, "The Master Designer created man's existence to be in a perpetual state of joy. JOY is the real normal for humanity" (p. 25). That means rejoicing is both **possible** and

therapeutic, even before circumstances change—because "It is never about how you feel. How you feel is a result of being either sick or healthy" across mind, body, and spirit (p. 19). And Jesus sets a "behavioral expectation" for believers (p. 10): rejoicing is an act of obedience that re-centers the person on God's normal rather than on fluctuating emotions.

Paul goes on to outline a set of positive thought processes that can cultivate this resilient attitude. He says in Philippians 4:4-9, " *Rejoice in the Lord always: and again I say, Rejoice. Let your moderation be known unto all men. The Lord is at hand. Be careful for nothing; but in everything by prayer and supplication with thanksgiving let your requests be made known unto God. And the peace of God, which passeth all understanding, shall keep your hearts and minds through Christ Jesus. Finally, brethren, whatsoever things are true, whatsoever things are honest, whatsoever things are just, whatsoever things are pure, whatsoever things are lovely, whatsoever things are of good report; if there be any virtue, and if there be any praise, think on these things. Those things, which ye have both learned, and received, and heard, and seen in me, do: and the God of peace shall be with you."* Let's consider this from a psychological perspective."

From a CCRT) therapist's perspective, Philippians 4:4–9 provides what is essentially a sequenced, present-focused therapeutic protocol that walks a person from emotional instability toward stability, hope, and peace—using God's absolutes as the standard for "normal" behavior and thinking. In CCRT terms, *"GOD is the absolute baseline for what is normal. There is no normal outside of the will of God, only degrees of abnormal"* (Ch. 1, p. 2). This verse not only aligns with CCRT's definition of normalcy but also matches its insistence on actionable, measurable behavioral change: *"There is a behavioral expectation for Christians... regardless of the individual's mental condition"* (Ch. 1, p. 2).

The command, *"Rejoice in the Lord always: and again I say, Rejoice"* (v. 4), directly relates to CCRT's fifth universal human need—Fun or Joy—which CCRT reframes as the *"real normal for humanity"*. CCRT states, *"The Master Designer created man's existence to be in a perpetual state of joy... All of mankind is still trying to get back to the garden"* (Ch. 2, p. 16). Choosing rejoicing in all circumstances is not psychological denial—it is a conscious re- alignment with God's original design, which in CCRT restores a person's normalcy and protects against abnormal coping mechanisms: *"Love meets all three [emotional, spiritual, and physical needs] simultaneously... Finally, love can only be generated and flourish in normalcy"* (Ch. 2, p. 14).

The next statement, *"Let your moderation be known unto all men. The Lord is at hand"* (v. 5), reinforces what CCRT identifies as Spirit-produced self-control and gentleness—virtues that are outwardly visible and relationally restorative. Emotion is the byproduct of the need… Abnormality is always destructive and corrosive to all love. (Ch. 2, p. 14). Moderation also protects the God-given gift of Freedom (Need #4): "Free will is a gift from God… Normalcy is mankind making choices good or bad but free. Abnormal is man's removal of freedom" (Ch. 2, p. 15).

Moderation isn't passivity; it's governed responsiveness. CCRT is blunt: "emotion is neutral; it is the choices made which become abnormal or normal" (p. 34). Gentleness, then, is the chosen, practiced behavior of a Spirit-led mind— visible, reliable, and healing to relationships.

Verse 6, "Be careful for nothing; but in everything by prayer and supplication with thanksgiving let your requests be made known unto God", maps precisely onto CCRT's rejection of passivity and overthinking. Knowledge and action are never the same thing. This is an absolute. Real change comes through active, repeated spiritual practices. He even prescribes forgiveness through intercessory blessing: "If you cannot forgive someone... pray for God to bless them. This is not optional—it is the command of God" (Ch. 12, p. 192). Thanksgiving, likewise, shifts mental focus: "Behavioral failure occurs when a want is abnormal and creates a false belief system replacing normal reality with abnormal... You must add all the reality and meaning into the statement to be honest and factual" (Ch. 2, p. 18).

"Be careful [anxious] for nothing, but...by prayer...with thanksgiving" (v. 6) is CCRT's move from treating symptoms to treating causes. CCRT warns that focusing on feelings misses the cure: "How you feel is dealing with your emotions, not the individual core conflict. Feelings are a byproduct of a conflict, not the conflict itself" (p. 32). Prayer with thanksgiving re-aligns the person to God's normal (baseline), restores the spirit's primacy within the mind–body–spirit whole (p. 15), and specifically counteracts stress—CCRT notes plainly that everyday stress "steals Joy" (p. 28). The promised result, "the peace of God...shall keep your hearts and minds" (v. 7), is exactly the protective integration CCRT seeks: spiritual peace stabilizing cognition ("minds") and emotion ("hearts") through Christ.

Verse 7 promises, *"And the peace of God, which passeth all understanding, shall keep your hearts and minds through Christ Jesus"*. CCRT recognizes peace as a measurable therapeutic outcome when mind, body, and spirit are addressed together: *"God created all of man's original needs... God's normal master plan and original design was perfection. Outside of the master design is imperfection"* (Ch. 1, p. 7). That perfection includes inner stability; Restored spiritual alignment allows a person's "heart and mind" to be "kept" from relapse into abnormality.

Paul's thought-discipline in verse 8 ("whatsoever things are...") functions like CCRT's cognitive gatekeeping— choosing inputs that support normal need-meeting rather than toxic want-chasing. True: CCRT teaches that abnormal systems thrive when "abnormal wants are relabeled as needs" (p. 27); dwelling on truth dismantles that self- deception and restores clean motives. Honest/honorable: CCRT pushes clients to stop psychobabble and face reality; "words...are not powerful until a person emboldens the words to action," so honesty must shape choices, not just talk (cf. p. 26). **Just**: justice expresses the **Power** need (healthy self-worth) without exploiting others; CCRT emphasizes that **real** power is internal, not borrowed from applause or control (p. 23). **Pure**: purity guards the **Love** need (healthy attachment) from toxic substitutes; CCRT shows how seemingly attractive shortcuts (e.g., sexualized coping) are abnormal wants that "appear to be the solution, but...create...problems" (pp. 18–20). **Lovely**: focusing on what is relationally beautiful strengthens pro-social, constructive bonds—exactly how CCRT defines healthy love as "positive, constructive relationships" (p. 22). **Of good report**: nourishing testimonies and trustworthy reports counter the world-system's cynicism and normalize gratitude-shaped thinking; CCRT's point about words gaining power as they move into action (p. 26) applies here—repeat the good on purpose. **If there be any virtue**: cultivate excellence rooted in the **Power** need rightly met—again, "Real power is generated from within...Man has the power to transcend any situation drawing upon the reservoir of internal power" (p. 23). **If there be any praise**: thanksgiving is not cosmetic; it is a chosen stance that re-primes the joy-system (p. 25) and re-anchors the will to God's baseline (p. 10).

Verse 9 ("do...practice these things") lands squarely on CCRT's change model. Dr. Glasser's maxim—quoted approvingly in CCRT—fits Paul perfectly: "If you want to change attitudes, start with a change in behavior" (p. 21). And CCRT cautions that the "revolving door" remains when clients "never complete the treatment" or "never start the treatment.... Knowledge and action are never the same thing" (p. 19). Paul says: take what you've *learned* and *do* it; CCRT says: finish the plan and make it behavioral. Verse 9 (“do…practice these things”) lands squarely on CCRT’s change model

Finally, verses 10–12 center the learned skill of **contentment**. Paul says, “I have learned…to be content” and “I know how to be abased, and…to abound.” It is important to reflect on those words. Paul learned…that means that it did not come naturally, somebody taught him, and he listened and made a choice to obey and change. That is textbook CCRT: contentment is not innate temperament; it’s a trained discipline of need-meeting in God’s way regardless of circumstance. Two CCRT pillars explain how Paul got there: (1) **Internal power**— “Real power is generated from within” rather than from external circumstances (p. 23); (2) **Free will**—“Freedom—Free will” means the person can choose God-aligned responses even under constraint (p. 23). Add CCRT’s joy baseline (p. 25) and symptom/cause clarity (p. 32), and contentment emerges as a practiced, spirit-led mental habit—exactly what Paul claims to have **learned**.

In short, Philippians 4:4–12 lays out the mental requirements CCRT would call **normal**: rejoice (activate the joy system, p. 25), embody gentleness (govern emotion by choice, p. 34; Gal. 5:22–23, p. 11), replace anxiety with prayerful thanksgiving (treat causes, not just feelings, p. 32; protect joy from stress, p. 28), curate your thought life (resist relabeled wants, p. 27; feed truth, justice, purity, love, and excellence, pp. 22–23), practice consistently (behavior change leads attitude change, p. 21; finish the treatment, p. 19), and **learn** contentment (internal power and free will under God’s absolute baseline for normal, pp. 10, 23). Do these, Paul says, “and the God of peace shall be with you”—exactly the outcome CCRT is built to cultivate.

The World's System of Mental Disorders

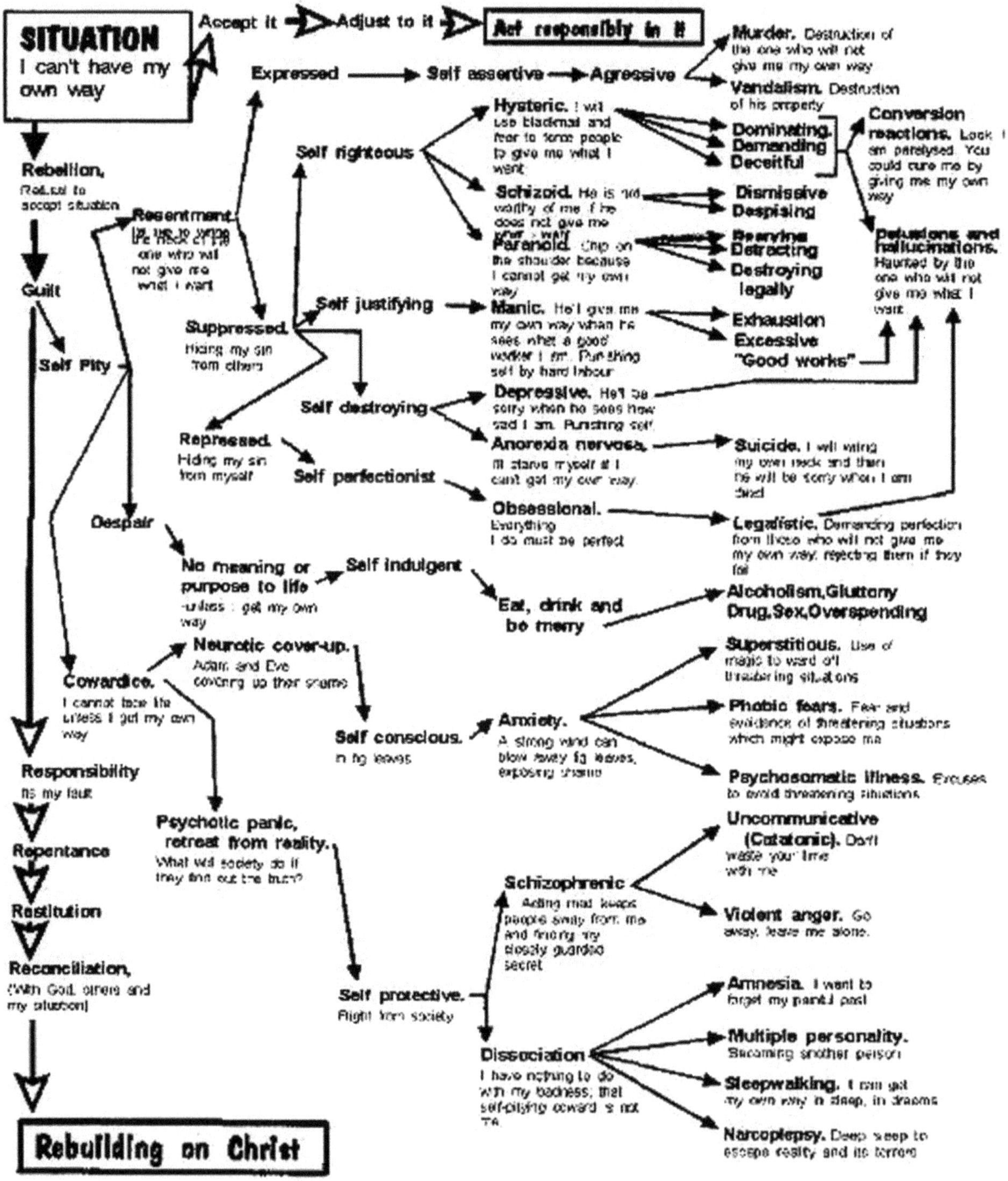

Understanding the Mental Disorders Chart

Although the chart looks rather complicated with all the different types of mental disorders, it is really very simple to understand.

Let me provide a very simple context to set the framework for understanding. A young boy, a senior in high school asks his dad, "May I use the car tonight? I want to go to the school football game."

The boy's father replies, "I'm sorry son, I need to work tonight and I need the car. I wished you had asked me sooner."

Now, look at the top left corner of the chart. There is a situation where the young man does not get his way – does not get what he wants. So, look at how he responds to his father's authority. Look to the right – he accepts the answer, adjusts to it, and acts responsibly. He asks his father, "Do you mind if I call my friend and ask if he can pick me up to go to the game?"

The father says, "No, I don't mind. I don't mind you going to the game, I just need the car to go to work.:

The situation is resolved. The son responded Biblically, He honored and obeyed his father and no conflict occurred.

Now, let's look at the same scenario with a different outcome. The boy asks his dad, "May I use the car tonight? I want to go to the school football game."

The boy's father gives the same reply, "I'm sorry son, I need to work tonight and I need the car. I wished you had asked me sooner."

Now look down the left side. The boy responds with rebellion, a bad attitude, and anger. He refuses to quietly accept the decision, and storms off. After a little time, he starts to feel guilt for his response. Now the boy is at a junction and has to make a decision about how he will act. Will he act responsibly or react feeling sorry for himself? He decides to act responsibly. Continue down the page; He goes to his father, apologizes, repents, and with his words, his promise not to act that way again, makes restitution. The boy and his father are reconciled, and once again the father says, "Son, I don't mind you going to the game, I just need the car to go to work. Why don't you call one of your friends?"

By both rebuilding of Christ, the boy apologizes, the father forgives, and offers a solution, the conflict is over without escalation.

Now let's look at a third scenario. The boy is at the junction and has a decision to make. Will he act responsibly or react feeling sorry for himself? This time he gives into anger, pride, and self-pity. Now his abnormal, unbiblical thoughts lead him to abnormal, unbiblical behavior. He is where the so-called "mental disorders start. Zhe can react with depression. He can react with aggression. He starts his angry self-talk, and starts lying to himself. (Incidentally, this is what Elijah did in 1 Kings 19:) Once you start responding contrary to God's will, there is no telling with the distortions of you mind will carry you. But, notice, the root of all th possible "mental disorders are very simple – anger and pride. Anger says, "I didn't get my way." Pride says, "I have a right to get my way." Now depending how long the boy remains angry and entertains the Unbiblical thoughts determines how long he will choose to give into abnormal, unbiblical behavior. That is why the Bible gives a very succinct way of dealing with anger. **Ephesians 4:26-27 (KJV)**

[26] Be ye angry, and sin not: let not the sun go down upon your wrath: [27] Neither give place to the devil. Some people say this is the cure for mental disorders, but actually it is the prevention of mental disorders.

How a CCRT Therapist Might Counsel the Young Boy

Philippians 4:4-9 (KJV) [4] Rejoice in the Lord always: *and* again I say, Rejoice. [5] Let your moderation be known unto all men. The Lord *is* at hand. [6] Be careful for nothing; but in everything by prayer and supplication with thanksgiving let your requests be made known unto God. And the peace of God, which passeth all understanding, shall keep your hearts and minds through Christ Jesus. [8] Finally, brethren, whatsoever things are true, whatsoever things *are* honest, whatsoever things *are* just, whatsoever things *are* pure, whatsoever things *are* lovely, whatsoever things *are* of good report; if *there be* any virtue, and if *there be* any praise, think on these things. [9] Those things, which ye have both learned, and received, and heard, and seen in me, do: and the God of peace shall be with you.

A CCRT therapist might open by framing Philippians 4:4–9 as the session's working map and then:

1. Assess which of the Five Needs are currently deprived, with special attention to Belonging (love) and freedom
2. Build a one-week plan with three daily micro-behaviors: *Moderation* (one tangible gentleness act toward a named relationship to strengthen Love; Need #2), and *Prayer-with-Thanksgiving* (two minutes naming requests plus two gratitude's, ending with a blessing prayer for any offender—an intervention that directly targets forgiveness and restores Freedom; Need #4). (Ch. 2, p. 16; Ch. 10/12, p. 192).
3. Institute a Philippians 4:8 Thought Audit (three entries/day where each primary thought is labeled *true/just/pure/lovely/good report* or discarded) to retrain attention per CCRT's choice-driven emotional model.
4. Add note taking homework where the boy writes down the triggers that he responds unbiblical to.
5. Close with a measurable next step that embodies "*do*": one concrete repair or service act (Love), one boundary that protects moderation (Freedom), and one replacement behavior for an unmet want— remembering CCRT's rule that, for change to hold, the want to stop must outweigh the perceived need to continue, and vice-versa.

Across the week, the expected payoffs in CCRT terms are
(a) restored JOY and lowered stress load (v. 4),
(b) visible gentleness/regulation in relationships (v. 5),
(c) anxiety displacement by prayerful dependency and gratitude (v. 6),
(d) a *felt* peace that stabilizes affect and cognition (v. 7),
(e) disciplined attention that starves abnormal wants and feeds truth (v. 8), and
(f) practiced, modeled obedience that moves change from insight to habit (v. 9).

That is precisely the arc CCRT predicts when God's absolutes set the target and the client is held lovingly but firmly to actionable steps in the present. (Ch. 12, pp. 189–190, 184).

Paul provides hope that those well versed in Scripture had had an encounter with its living author Jesus Christ. "Remember, all toxic relationships begin with a purely selfish act. (Chapter 3). The words on this list which can provide support and hope for all whom were created. Paul's words were not passive, but those of action; thus enabling the modern Christian to experience the freedom promised in Scripture and in Reality.

CCRT provides a comprehensive and transformative approach to addressing the challenges of life and cultivating mental well-being. By embracing personal responsibility, aligning our thoughts and behaviors with Biblical truth, and actively nurturing meaningful relationships, we can navigate the inevitable adversities of life with resilience, grace, and unwavering hope, as intended by a creator which gives all things richly to enjoy (1 Timothy 6:17).

Application in a Therapy Session:

Here's a possible Therapy Session Outline for Philippians 4:4–9 written from a CCRT perspective, structured so a counselor could follow it step-by-step in-session. Every phase is rooted in both the Scripture and CCRT principles.

Session Theme: Rejoicing, Moderation, Prayer, Peace, and Thought Discipline

Session Goal: Guide the client to address unmet needs and abnormal wants by implementing the six sequential principles in Philippians 4:4–9, aligning them with CCRT's Five Basic Needs and the Biblical standard for normal.

1. **Session Opening —stablishing the Baseline (10 min) Scripture Focus: Phil. 4:4**
    - Read aloud: "Rejoice in the Lord always: and again I say, Rejoice."

CCRT Principle: "The Master Designer created man's existence to be in a perpetual state of joy… All of mankind is still trying to get back to the garden" (Ch. 2, p. 16).

Therapeutic Action:

- Ask: "On a scale of 1–10, how present is joy in your life right now?"
- Identify which of the Five Needs (Survival, Love, Power, Freedom, Joy) is least fulfilled—focusing on Joy first.
- Assign micro-step: Begin each morning with 60 seconds of verbal praise to God, regardless offeelings.

2. **Moderation and Relational Regulation (10 min) Scripture Focus: Philippians 4:5**
    - Read aloud: "Let your moderation be known unto all men. The Lord is at hand."

CCRT Principle: "Free will is a gift from God… Normalcy is mankind making choices good or bad but free. Abnormal is man's removal of freedom" (Ch. 2, p. 15).

Therapeutic Action:

- Explore where the client's reactions have been extreme or emotionally driven.

- Ask: "What one relational interaction this week can you intentionally approach with gentleness and self- control?"
- Assign: Choose one specific person to practice moderation with; note the result for discussion in the next session.

3. **Replacing Anxiety with Prayer and Thanksgiving (15 min) Scripture Focus: Philippians 4:6**
   - Read aloud: "Be careful for nothing; but in everything by prayer and supplication with thanksgiving let your requests be made known unto God."

CCRT Principle: "Knowledge and action are never the same thing. This is an absolute" (Ch. 2, p. 10).

Therapeutic Action:

- Instruct client to write down current top three worries.
- Teach the "Prayer Swap": For each worry, pray a specific request to God, then name two related things to thank Him for.
- Incorporate the forgiveness assignment: *"If you cannot forgive someone... pray for God to bless them"* (Ch. 12, p. 192).
- Assign: Daily 5-minute "Prayer with Gratitude" block; track prayers answered or perspectives changed.

4. Cultivating the Peace of God (5 min) Scripture Focus: Philippians 4:7
   - Read aloud: "And the peace of God, which passeth all understanding, shall keep your hearts and minds through Christ Jesus."

CCRT Principle: "God's normal master plan and original design was perfection. Outside of the master design is imperfection" (Ch. 1, p. 7).

Therapeutic Action:

- Have client describe what "peace" would look and feel like in their daily life.
- Link peace to need fulfillment: Peace comes when needs are met God's way, not through abnormal wants.

5. **Thought Audit and Cognitive Replacement (15 min) Scripture Focus: Phil. 4:8**
   - Read aloud: "Whatsoever things are true... honest... just... pure... lovely... of good report; if there be any virtue, and if there be any praise, think on these things."

CCRT Principle: "Words in and of themselves are not powerful until a person emboldens the words to a concept; then the words give rise to action... Abnormality will not exist until the individual integrates the abnormal into their belief system" (Ch. 3, p. 25).

Therapeutic Action:

- Teach client to "filter" thoughts through the Philippians 4:8 list.
- Practice in-session with one troubling thought: Does it meet the list? If not, discard and replace with a God- aligned truth.

- Assign: Three times daily, audit a primary thought and replace it if it fails the Philippians 4:8 test.

6. Action and Accountability (5 min) Scripture Focus: Phil. 4:9

- Read aloud: "Those things, which ye have both learned, and received, and heard, and seen in me, do." **CCRT Principle:** "There is a clear wrong direction and a clear right direction in all plans… It is always necessary to have the right direction mapped out" (Ch. 3, p. 33).

Therapeutic Action:

- Identify one practical, measurable behavior changes to implement before the next session.
- Set up an accountability system: daily journal entries or a text check-in with the therapist or a trusted person.

7. Session Closing — Prayer and Recommitment (5 min)

- Pray over the client, committing each assignment to the Lord.
- Remind: "Your choice, you can plan for success or plan for failure, but you cannot do both" (Ch. 3, p.33).

Summary of Assignments for the Week:

1. **Joy Practice:** 60 seconds of morning praise daily.
2. **Moderation Practice:** One intentional act of gentleness toward a specific person.
3. **Prayer Swap:** Replace top three worries with specific prayer + thanksgiving; pray blessing over offenders.
4. **Thought Audit:** Three Philippians 4:8 thought checks per day.
5. **Action Step:** One measurable behavior change linked to unmet need.

MISDIRECTED ANGER

Anger is a fundamental human emotion, a natural response to perceived threats, injustice, or frustration. A simple definition of anger is simply the thoughts a person has when he does not get what he wants. I put a dollar in the candy machine, make my selection, push the button, and nothing happens. I think, "Oh, no, the candy didn't come out. Drat!' See, there! I just got angry, so I push the button again. Same result, no candy. I say, "Stupid machine!" and I walk away. There, I got angry, but I behaved responsibly. When dealing with Anger, it is not the thought that is sinful (I didn't get what I want), it is how I choose to respond (behave) based upon that thought that leads to problems. The way we choose to express our anger can have profound consequences, shaping our relationships, our mental well- being, and our connection to God.

From a CCR and Biblical perspective, misdirected anger—whether aimed upward at God, outward at others, or inward at oneself—is ultimately destructive and stands in stark contrast to the path of healing and wholeness offered through Christ.

I. Misdirected Anger

1. Anger Directed Upward: Blaming God

When faced with suffering, loss, or injustice, it's not uncommon for individuals to direct their anger at God. Questions like, "Why did God let this happen?" or "How could a loving God allow such evil?" reflect a deep sense of frustration and disillusionment. While acknowledging the pain and confusion inherent in these questions, CCRT and the Bible offer a different perspective.

Why It's Unbiblical: Blaming God for our circumstances often stems from a misunderstanding of His nature and sovereignty. While God is all-powerful, He does not always intervene to prevent suffering. As Romans 8:28 reminds us, "And we know that all things work together for good to them that love God, to them who are the called according to his purpose." This verse does not promise a life free of hardship but assures us that God can use even painful experiences for our ultimate good.

Why It's Self-Harming: Holding onto anger toward God creates a barrier in our relationship with Him, hindering our ability to receive His comfort, guidance, and healing. It fosters a spirit of bitterness and resentment, preventing us from experiencing the peace that surpasses all understanding (Philippians 4:7).

Examples from CCRT and Scripture:

CCRT emphasizes the importance of recognizing God as the source of all good. Directing anger toward God ultimately distances us from the source of true comfort and healing. (p.12). The center point for man is God, and He expresses this in His Word, the 66 books of the Bible. This provides the absolute unlimited baseline for normal. It can be inferred then that the opposite is true, directing your anger toward God is abnormal.

The story of Job: Though Job experienced profound suffering, he never cursed God. As Job 2:10 states, "But he said unto her, Thou speakest as one of the foolish women speaketh. What? shall we receive good at the hand of God, and shall we not receive evil?" Job's unwavering faith in God, even in the face of immense pain, serves as a powerful example of how to navigate suffering without succumbing to anger and resentment.

2. Anger Directed Outward: Blaming Others

Another common response to anger is to direct it outward, blaming others for our pain and frustration. This can manifest as verbal abuse, physical violence, resentment, and a desire for revenge. While it's natural to feel hurt and angered by the actions of others, directing our anger outward is ultimately destructive.

Why It's Unbiblical: Jesus calls us to love our enemies and to forgive those who have wronged us. Matthew 5:44 states, "But I say unto you, love your enemies, bless them that curse you, do good to them that hate you, and pray for them which despitefully use you, and persecute you." Holding onto anger and seeking revenge perpetuate a cycle of violence and division, hindering reconciliation and healing.

Why It's Self-Harming: Directing anger outward often leads to broken relationships, isolation, and a deep sense of bitterness. It consumes our thoughts and emotions, preventing us from moving forward and experiencing joy and peace.

Examples from CCRT and Scripture:

CCRT warns of the dangers of toxic relationships, where anger and abuse are used to control and manipulate others. In toxic relationships, redirection happens and you are next justifying bad behavior. The inability to forgive creates an "I have to use porn to get my fix," mentality (p.37). "You won't have sex with me, so I have to use porn to get my fix."

Cain's anger towards Abel: Driven by envy and anger, Cain murdered his brother Abel (Genesis 4:3-8). This act of violence not only destroyed Cain's relationship with Abel but also alienated him from God, leading to a life of wandering and isolation.

3. Anger Directed Inward: Blaming Yourself

Some individuals respond to anger by directing it inward, blaming themselves for their problems and harboring feelings of guilt, shame, and self-hatred. While acknowledging our own shortcomings is essential for growth, excessive self-blame can be equally destructive.

Why It's Unbiblical: The Bible teaches that we are all sinners in need of God's grace and forgiveness. Holding onto excessive guilt and self-condemnation prevents us from receiving the freedom and healing offered through Christ's sacrifice.

Why It's Self-Harming: Inwardly directed anger can lead to depression, anxiety, low self-esteem, and self-destructive behaviors. It creates a cycle of negativity, preventing us from recognizing our worth and potential.

Examples from CCRT and Scripture:

CCRT emphasizes the importance of self-compassion and recognizing our inherent worth as children of God, even in the face of our failures. This compassion helps us break free from the cycle of self-blame and cultivate a more loving and accepting relationship with ourselves.

Judas's remorse: After betraying Jesus, Judas experienced intense remorse and self-condemnation (Matthew 27:3-5). Rather than seeking forgiveness and redemption, he succumbed to despair and took his own life.

A Path to Healing and Wholeness

Instead of misdirecting our anger, CCRT and the Bible offer a pathway to healing and wholeness through Christ- centered thinking:

- Acknowledge and Validate Your Feelings: Don't suppress or deny your anger. Acknowledge that it is a valid emotion, but choose how you will express it.
- Seek God's Guidance: Turn to God in prayer, asking for wisdom and guidance in dealing with your anger.
- Practice Forgiveness: Forgive those who have wronged you, releasing the bitterness and resentment that consume your heart.
- Extend Grace to Yourself: Recognize that you are not perfect and that you will make mistakes. Extend compassion and forgiveness to yourself, just as God has forgiven you.
- Focus on What You Can Control: Take responsibility for your own actions and attitudes.
- Refocus on God: The very first step is to "center all" to God, the way you are supposed to. It's a plan. It's His master design. (p. 27)

By embracing these principles, we can transform our anger from a destructive force into a catalyst for growth, healing, and a deeper relationship with God.

More Biblical Examples:

Biblical Characters Demonstrating Misdirected Anger

The Bible offers numerous accounts of individuals who struggled with anger, providing valuable lessons on the dangers of misdirected emotions and the importance of seeking God's guidance in managing our feelings. Here are some key examples:

1. Cain (Genesis 4:3-8): Anger Outward - Leading to Murder

Context: Cain's anger stemmed from God's acceptance of Abel's offering over his own. Driven by envy and resentment, Cain allowed his anger to fester, ultimately leading him to murder his brother.

Incorrect Display: Cain's outward anger manifested as violence and a complete disregard for the sanctity of human life. He failed to address the root of his anger, instead choosing to lash out in a destructive way.

Lessons: Cain's story serves as a stark warning about the dangers of unchecked anger and the destructive consequences of allowing envy and resentment to control our actions.

2. Moses (Numbers 20:10-12): Anger Outward - Disobeying God and Losing a Blessing

Context: After leading the Israelites through the wilderness for decades, Moses was tasked by God to provide water from a rock. Frustrated with the Israelites' constant complaining and lack of faith, Moses struck the rock twice instead of speaking to it as God commanded.

Incorrect Display: Moses's anger led him to disobey God's instructions and to take credit for God's power. He was angry at the Israelites and took the direction of "hitting".

Lessons: While Moses's anger may have been understandable given the circumstances, his response demonstrated a lack of self-control and a failure to fully trust in God. As a result, he was denied entry into the Promised Land.

3. Jonah (Jonah 4:1-11): Anger Towards God - Lacking Compassion and Questioning Divine Justice

Context: Jonah was sent by God to preach repentance to the people of Nineveh, a wicked and violent city. When the Ninevites repented, God spared them, causing Jonah to become exceedingly angry.

Incorrect Display: Jonah's anger was directed towards God for showing mercy to his enemies. He lacked compassion for the Ninevites and questioned God's justice, prioritizing his own personal preferences over God's will.

Lessons: Jonah's story highlights the dangers of self-righteousness and the importance of aligning our hearts with God's boundless love and compassion.

4. Saul (1 Samuel 18:6-9): Envious Anger

Context: Saul, the first king of Israel, started out right, leading the army, but soon became jealous of the fame that David was receiving.

Incorrect Display: Saul let jealously and then anger control him and began trying to kill David.

Lessons: King Saul provides that there are times when fame is not a good thing, that jealously and anger are not to be held on to.

5. The Disciples (Luke 9:51-56): Anger leading to a vengeful spirit:

Context: Samaria was not a friend of the Israelites, and the Samaritans were not going to let Jesus and the disciples pass through their area. James and John wanted to call down fire from heaven and destroy them for their actions,

Incorrect Display: James and John wanted to lash out in anger at those who were being disrespectful to them.

Lessons: Jesus rebuked them for not understanding what spirit they were of. You must not take personal insults and turn them into personal vendettas, or use the excuse to take violence for personal feelings.

6. The Older Brother (Luke 15:11-32): The Parable of the Prodigal Son

Context: The younger son asked for, and received his inheritance early, then went off and squandered it. He returned home, and the father celebrated his return.

Incorrect Display: The older brother was mad. After following all the rules, working hard, he saw the father rejoicing about the returned son, and was filled with anger.

Lessons: He represents self-righteousness and the inability to celebrate the joy of others. As CCRT states, some will maintain the sin. He is unable to accept and be thankful.

7. Naaman (2 Kings 5:1-14): Anger at Simplicity

Context: Naaman was the commander of the army, but he had leprosy. God had used Naaman to give victory to Syria, and the king held him in high esteem.

Incorrect Display: Elisha gave the leper to go wash 7 times in the river. The Leper got mad and asked, aren't our rivers better?

Lessons: There are times, when you must put your pride away and follow directions, even if they are humble.

These stories demonstrate that anger, when misdirected, can lead to destructive consequences, both for ourselves and for those around us. The scriptures also present a powerful contrast to such negative examples. Jesus in Mark 3:5 shows an example of righteous anger, that is appropriate anger that leads to appropriate action: "He looked around at them in anger and, deeply distressed at their stubborn hearts, said to the man, "Stretch out your hand." He stretched it out, and his hand was completely restored." Jesus displayed many times the wisdom and control over his emotions.

To help deal with anger, The Bible, in contrast, shows people how to be good, rather than how not to be good. In Ephesians 4:26-27 the direction states "Be ye angry, and sin not: let not the sun go down upon your wrath: Neither give place to the devil."

II. COUNSELING INTERVENTION

While it is necessary to identify anger and deal with it, there are appropriate and inappropriate reasons to be angry. There are also appropriate and inappropriate responses to anger. And since all "feelings" are the result of how one perceives an event (thinks), it is necessary to fully evaluate the reality and the legitimacy of our perceptions.

Is Anger always a Sin?

The Bible teaches that there is an anger based in righteousness and an anger based in unrighteousness (sin).

Righteous anger is not quick, reactive, or self-serving. It is the lawful administration of judgment or consequence. Unrighteous anger is self-serving and punitive.

- Matthew 5:22 But I say unto you, that whosoever is angry with his brother *without a cause* shall be in danger of the judgment:
- Ephes. 4:26 Be ye angry, and sin not: let not the sun go down upon your wrath: This verse teaches that you may be angry, but not sin.

These verses teach that there may be a reason (a cause) to be angry:

Appropriate: Proverbs 17:27-28 He that hath knowledge spareth his words: and a man of understanding is of an excellent spirit. [28] Even a fool, when he holdeth his peace, is counted wise: and he that shutteth his lips are esteemed a man of understanding.

Inappropriate: - Proverbs 29:22 An angry man stirreth up strife, and a furious man aboundeth in transgression.

Guidelines for Anger (For the Immature Christian – Legality)

Eph. 4:26-32 Be ye angry, and sin not: let not the sun go down upon your wrath: [27]

Neither give place to the devil. [28] Let him that stole steal no more: but rather let him labor, working with his hands the thing which is good, that he may have to give to him that needeth. [29] Let no corrupt communication proceed out of your mouth, but that for children which is good to the use of edifying, that it may minister grace unto the hearers.

Guidelines for Anger (For the Mature Christian – Grace)

[30] And grieve not the holy Spirit of God, whereby ye are sealed unto the day of redemption. [31] Let all bitterness, and wrath, and anger, and clamor, and evil speaking, be put away from you, with all malice: [32] And be ye kind one to another, tenderhearted, forgiving one another, even as God for Christ's sake hath forgiven you.

Summary:

- Anger is acknowledged (not condoned) v. 26
- You can control yourself when angry v. 26
- Anger should have a duration v. 26
- Anger can give opportunity to the Devil v. 27
- Anger should be put away v. 31
- Bitterness, wrath, anger, etc. all related. v. 31
- Anger is a choice v. 32
- Anger can be conquered through forgiveness v. 32

1. Why Do People Get Angry and Respond unbiblical?

1. All anger is chosen.
2. Anger reveals the true nature of a person (Luke 6:45)
3. Unrighteous anger is an emotion of selfishness and self-centeredness
4. Unrighteous anger focuses on the faults of others and ignores the faults of self
5. Unrighteous anger focuses on the damage to self
6. Unrighteous anger wants to control and coerce
7. Unrighteous anger is influenced by many aspects of our life
8. Unrighteous anger is a (lazy) shortcut to a (false) solution
9. Unrighteous anger is reactive instead of planned and thoughtful
10. Unrighteous anger is the influence of our sinful nature

Unrighteous Anger Causes

1. Pride. Proverbs 21:24
2. Cruelty. Genesis 49:7; Proverbs 27:3-4
3. Clamor and evil-speaking. Ephes. 4:31
4. Malice and blasphemy. Col. 3:8
5. Strife and contention. Proverbs 21:19; Proverbs 29:22;
6. Jealousy 1 Sam. 18:
7. Frustration

Questions to Ask Your Client to Identify Cause of Anger

1. What are your thoughts about this situation?
2. Why are you choosing to be angry?
3. Are you responding or reacting?
4. Is there an injustice that warrants action?
5. Are you reacting out of pride or unmet expectation?
6. How does the other person view this situation?
7. What part do you have in contributing to this situation?
8. What are you really angry about?
9. Are you angry because of the situation or because of my current mood?
10. Are you dealing with the issue or with the self?

Emphasize:

1. Anger can be positive or negative - it is your motivation and your response that decides.
2. Anger can reveal your true nature.
3. Anger can reveal past hurts that are still within you.
4. Anger can reveal your inappropriate ways of meeting your needs.
5. Anger can demonstrate your standing with God.
6. Anger can help you realize areas of your life that need changing.
7. Anger appropriately displayed is used by God to convict others.
8. Anger handled correctly is a powerful witness and testimony.

If Your Client is Dealing with Anger in Self

1. Realize that anger is a choice you make - No one makes you angry
2. Pause before speaking
3. Decide what the real issue is before responding
4. Evaluate their Feelings
5. Determine what is the motivation for your anger
6. Determine if there is a need for anger
7. Address the real issue\object of your anger
8. Acquire information before reacting
8. Be conscious of the presence of God as you respond to an issue
9. Talk to God about your feelings

If Your Client is Dealing with Anger in Others, tell them

1. Remain calm - Proverbs 15:1 A soft answer turneth away wrath: but grievous words stir up anger.
2. Control Your Response - Proverbs 16:32 He that is slow to anger is better than the mighty; and he that ruleth his spirit than he that taketh a city.
3. Avoid sarcasm - Proverbs 29:8 Scornful men bring a city into a snare: but wise men turn away wrath.
4. Choose the right time to respond - Eccles. 3:7 A time to rend, and a time to sew; a time to keep silence, and a time to speak;
5. Be constructive when speaking - Col. 4:6 Let your speech be always with grace, seasoned with salt, that ye may know how ye ought to answer every man.
6. Be patient and understanding - Proverbs 25:15 By long forbearing is a prince persuaded, and a soft tongue breaketh the bone.
7. Be willing to forgive the offender - Ephes. 4:32 And be ye kind one to another, tenderhearted, forgiving one another, even as God for Christ's sake hath forgiven you.
8. Pay attention to what you say - Psalm 39:1 I said, I will take heed to my ways, that I sin not.

Injunctions against *un-righteous* anger

- Psalm 37:8 Cease from anger, and forsake wrath: fret not thyself in any wise to do evil.
- Eccles. 7:9 Be not hasty in thy spirit to be angry: for anger resteth in the bosom of fools.
- Job 5:2 For wrath killeth the foolish man, and envy slayeth the silly one.
- Proverbs 15:18 A wrathful man stirreth up strife: but he that is slow to anger appeaseth strife.
- Proverbs 16:32 He that is slow to anger is better than the mighty; and he that ruleth his spirit than he that taketh a city.
- Proverbs 19:19 A man of great wrath shall suffer punishment: for if thou deliver him, yet thou must do it again.

- Proverbs 21:19 It is better to dwell in the wilderness, than with a contentious and an angry woman.
- Proverbs 22:24-25 Make no friendship with an angry man; and with a furious man thou shalt not go: [25] Lest thou learn his ways, and get a snare to thy soul.
- Proverbs 27:3-4 A stone is heavy, and the sand weighty; but a fool's wrath is heavier than them both. [4] Wrath is cruel, and anger is outrageous; but who is able to stand before envy?
- Col. 3:8 But now ye also put off all these; anger, wrath, malice, blasphemy, filthy communication out of your mouth.
- James 1:19-20 Wherefore, my beloved brethren, let every man be swift to hear, slow to speak, slow to wrath: [20] For the wrath of man worketh not the righteousness of God.
- Proverbs 27:3-4 A stone is heavy, and the sand weighty; but a fool's wrath is heavier than them both. [4] Wrath is cruel, and anger is outrageous; but who is able to stand before envy?
- Col. 3:8 But now ye also put off all these; anger, wrath, malice, blasphemy, filthy communication out of your mouth.
- James 1:19-20 Wherefore, my beloved brethren, let every man be swift to hear, slow to speak, slow to wrath: [20] For the wrath of man worketh not the righteousness of God.

Conclusion

Key Takeaways from CCRT and the Bible

- Anger is a Choice: While anger is a natural emotion, our response to it is a choice.
- God's Presence is Key: As referenced throughout the book, God is in the center to be effective (p.25).
- Forgiveness and Self-Compassion Are Essential: These components are also essential for a positive emotional well-being.
- Positive Emotions Are Essential: We see this throughout Philippians 4, joy and hope is a great recipe to get to where you want to go.
- Action and Implementation: CCRT is focused on getting the help, and implementing a plan.

By understanding the dangers of misdirected anger and embracing the principles outlined in CCRT and the Bible, we can learn to navigate our emotions in a healthy and constructive way, fostering healing relationships and a deeper connection with God.

Christ Centered
CCRT
Reality Therapy

COMPONENTS OF THE CHANGE PROCESS

In this CHART, each row represents a variation of the change process with one essential component missing. The absence of any component in the first six squares disrupts the effectiveness and integrity of the change effort, resulting in a specific negative outcome shown in the seventh square of each row.

Aim & Purpose	Knowledge & Skill	Motivation & Buy-In	Resources	Action Plan/ Blueprint	Feedback & Assessment	Quality/Change Positive Env.
	Knowledge/ Skill	Motivation/ Buy-In	Resources	Action Plan/ Blueprint	Feedback & Assessment	Confusion & Conflict
Aim & Purpose		Motivation/ Buy-In	Resources	Action Plan/ Blueprint	Feedback & Assessment	Fear of Failure Anxiety
Aim & Purpose	Knowledge/ Skill		Resources	Action Plan/ Blueprint	Feedback & Assessment	Passivity & Compliant
Aim & Purpose	Knowledge/ Skill	Motivation/ Buy-In		Action Plan/ Blueprint	Feedback & Assessment	Frustration & Overload
Aim & Purpose	Knowledge/ Skill	Motivation/ Buy-In	Resources		Feedback & Assessment	Fragmentation & Resentment
Aim & Purpose	Knowledge/ Skill	Motivation/ Buy-In	Resources	Action Plan/ Blueprint		Illusion of Change Uncertainty

By understanding the fundamental steps in the change process. The counselor has a greater chance of identifying the problem, where the main hindrance or contribution to the problem lies, and where he needs to start to provide a workable, manageable solution. Below is a detailed, paragraph-level explanation of each row, outlining what happens when each specific component is missing and why that component is vital to successful, lasting change:

Each of these components is interdependent, and the absence of even one weakens the entire change process. Together, they form a comprehensive system designed to lead individuals or organizations from intention to transformation. Recognizing and addressing each area is crucial for achieving quality change in a positive environment.

Column 1–6 list the components of change; if a component is missing, column 7 shows the unfavorable result. I'll use these six components throughout: **(1) Aim & Purpose, (2) Knowledge & Skill, (3) Incentives, (4) Resources, (5) Action Plan, (6) Accountability/Timeline**; column 7 is the **Result**. I'll weave in CCRT logic (absolutes, plan + resolve + accountability, meeting needs God's way) and Biblical principles.

1. All components present --- Sustained, visible change (favorable).

When aim & purpose are clear, skills are taught and practiced, incentives are meaningful, resources are in place, the action plan is concrete, and there's real accountability with dates and reviews, change sticks. In CCRT terms, this aligns the person's wants with God's way of meeting needs, then reinforces that alignment through a disciplined plan and ongoing accountability. Biblically, this looks like wise planning plus diligent follow-through: "For which of you, intending to build a tower, sitteth not down first, and counteth the cost…?" (Luke 14:28–29, KJV). Everything pulls in one direction, so efforts translate into stable behavior and growing peace.

2. Missing Aim & Purpose --- Confusion and Conflict.

If the "why" is fuzzy, people work hard but scatter energy. In CCRT, God's absolutes define normal; without a clear aim anchored in those absolutes, counseling degrades into chasing symptoms. Practically, sessions feel busy yet aimless; clients ask, "What are we even trying to accomplish?" Biblically: "Where there is no vision, the people perish…" (Proverbs 29:18, KJV). Remedy: establish a shared, written aim tied to God's purposes (e.g., reconciliation, sobriety, truth-in-love), then trace every step back to that aim.

3. Missing Knowledge & Skill --- Anxiety.

People can know the goal and even want it, but if they've never learned *how* to do it—how to have a hard conversation, how to interrupt a craving loop, how to pray and reframe thoughts (Philippians 4:6–8, KJV)— they feel exposed and afraid. CCRT insists on equipping: teach, model, rehearse, and assign practice so the counselee can meet needs in God's way, not by defaulting to old, abnormal wants. Biblically, God supplies wisdom for skill-gaps: "If any of you lack wisdom, let him ask of God…" (James 1:5, KJV).

4. Missing Motivation and Buy- (Incentives0 --- Passivity and Compliant.

When people don't *see* why the change is worth the cost, they push back. In CCRT, motivation is strengthened by installing hope, clarifying payoffs that honor God (peace, restored trust, health), and making wins tangible. Biblically, Jesus "for the joy that was set before him endured the cross" (Hebrews 12:2, KJV). We surface God-honoring incentives (joy, freedom from shame, repaired relationships) and link them to daily steps. No incentives = "Why bother?"; good incentives = "This is hard, but it matters."

5. Missing Resources --- Frustration and Overload.

You can have aim, skills, and motivation, but if you lack resources such as time, tools, support people, transportation, or practical helps (e.g., a budget worksheet, meeting list, childcare), change stalls, producing frustration and overload. In CCRT, we do not prescribe what the environment makes impossible; we right-size goals and supply the supports so the plan is executable. Biblically, asking people to "make bricks without straw" breeds despair (cf. Exodus 5). God's promise steadies us: "According as his divine power hath given unto us all things that pertain unto life and godliness" (2 Peter 1:3, KJV). We locate and install those "things."

6. Missing Action Plan --- Fragmentation and Resentment.

Vision, skills, motivation, and resources still won't move the needle unless they're converted into *who does what, by when, and how we'll know.* CCRT emphasizes concrete next steps, sequencing, and measurable targets (mind, body, spirit). Biblically, builders who count the cost then *build* (Luke 14:28–30) show the pattern: specify steps, start, review, adjust. Without a plan, people "try harder" in vague ways, relapse into old ruts, and conclude change "doesn't work."

7. Missing Feedback and Assessment --- Illusion of Change and Uncertainty

Without dates, check-ins, and a named person to ask, "Did you do what you said?", even good plans fade and people are unsure of the progress, can only speculate as to outcome, delivery, and quality. CCRT treats accountability as a stabilizer: regular reviews, time-tracking, celebrating small wins, and tightening weak links. Biblically, we're commanded to *mutually* spur one another on: "And let us consider one another to provoke unto love and to good works… exhorting one another" (Hebrews 10:24–25, KJV); "Iron sharpeneth iron" (Proverbs 27:17, KJV). No accountability = short bursts, long plateaus, and quiet backsliding.

Biblical Understanding

Below is a theological integration of the change process chart with Scripture from the King James Version (KJV) of the Bible. Each paragraph correlates to one row in the chart, elaborating on the problem caused by the missing component of change and demonstrating how Scripture affirms the necessity of that component through direct passages and Biblical narratives.

1. Missing "Aim & Purpose" --- Result: Confusion & Conflict

Without a clear aim and purpose, people are left in disarray, unable to unite around a shared mission. Scripture affirms that divine purpose is foundational to all fruitful endeavor: *"Where there is no vision, the people perish: but he that keepeth the law, happy is he"* (Proverbs 29:18). When Israel wandered in the wilderness, much of their conflict and rebellion arose from their disconnection from

God's purpose and promises. They grumbled and rebelled against Moses because they lacked faith in the purpose behind their deliverance (Numbers 14:1-4). The Apostle Paul, in contrast, speaks of pressing "toward the mark for the prize of the high calling of God in Christ Jesus" (Philippians 3:14). This illustrates how a divinely revealed aim focuses the believer, reduces division, and channels effort toward God-honoring ends.

2. Missing "Vision & Direction" --- Result: Fear of Failure / Anxiety

Lacking vision and direction causes fear and paralysis. The Israelites experienced this at the edge of the Promised Land, when the spies returned with a discouraging report. Although they had God's aim (to inherit Canaan), they lost sight of His direction and became fearful: *"And all the congregation lifted up their voice, and cried; and the people wept that night"* (Numbers 14:1). In contrast, Joshua and Caleb, who held fast to God's vision, were fearless: *"If the LORD delight in us, then he will bring us into this land, and give it us"* (Numbers 14:8). The New Testament reinforces this principle. Jesus tells His disciples, *"Let not your heart be troubled: ye believe in God, believe also in me"* (John 14:1), anchoring their emotional peace in the clarity of His redemptive mission. Vision dispels fear by reminding believers of God's sovereignty and the path forward.

3. Missing "Knowledge & Skill" --- Result: Passivity & Compliance

When knowledge and skill are absent, even willing participants become disengaged. Hosea writes, *"My people are destroyed for lack of knowledge: because thou hast rejected knowledge, I will also reject thee"* (Hosea 4:6). The importance of equipping people with understanding is evident throughout Scripture. For instance, when Ezra returned from exile to restore the law among the Jews, he read and explained it to the people so they could act on it: *"So they read in the book in the law of God distinctly, and gave the sense, and caused them to understand the reading"* (Nehemiah 8:8). Without such knowledge, the people would have fallen into legalistic compliance rather than heartfelt obedience. Likewise, Jesus trained His disciples for ministry so they could become effective ambassadors rather than passive observers (Luke 24:45, "Then opened he their understanding, that they might understand the scriptures").

4. Missing "Motivation & Buy-In" --- Result: Frustration & Overload

Motivation is the inner conviction that propels change forward. Scripture illustrates that even strong leaders falter without heart-level buy-in. When Moses attempted to deliver Israel by his own timing and strength, he was met with rejection and frustration: *"Who made thee a prince and a judge over us?"* (Exodus 2:14). Later, even when the people were willing, they were prone to grumbling under the weight of their burdens, revealing that willingness must be sustained by spiritual motivation (Numbers 11:10-15). In the New Testament, Paul instructs believers to serve *"not with eye service, as men pleasers; but as the servants of Christ, doing the will of God from the heart"* (Ephesians 6:6). Genuine transformation occurs when individuals are internally persuaded and energized by divine purpose, not simply complying out of obligation.

5. Missing "Resources" --- Result: Fragmentation & Resentment

A lack of resources often causes division and bitterness, even among those who are committed. When Nehemiah led the rebuilding of Jerusalem's walls, he not only cast vision but ensured that the workers were armed and supplied (Nehemiah 4:16-18). He understood that spiritual fervor alone could not overcome physical exhaustion or vulnerability. Similarly, when the early church failed to distribute food equitably, it led to complaints: *"And there arose a murmuring of the Grecians against the Hebrews, because their widows were neglected"* (Acts 6:1). The apostles quickly addressed the issue by appointing deacons, ensuring resources were properly managed. This prevented resentment and preserved unity. Paul reinforces this principle, admonishing believers to share in one another's needs: *"But to do good and to communicate forget not: for with such sacrifices God is well pleased"* (Hebrews 13:16).

6. Missing "Action Plan / Blueprint" --- Result: Illusion of Change

An action plan converts intention into obedience. James warns against deceiving oneself by only hearing the Word but not acting on it: *"But be ye doers of the word, and not hearers only, deceiving your own selves"* (James 1:22). Jesus also emphasized the danger of religious performance without real transformation, rebuking the Pharisees: *"This people draweth nigh unto me with their mouth... but their heart is far from me"* (Matthew 15:8). The Tower of Babel offers a negative example of misapplied planning—human effort without divine alignment (Genesis 11:1–9)—but in godly settings, strategic planning empowers fulfillment. Noah followed God's blueprint for the ark precisely, and it saved his family (Genesis 6:14-22). Planning alone is not sufficient, but in cooperation with divine instruction, it enables visible, lasting change.

7. Missing "Feedback & Assessment" --- Result: Uncertainty

Feedback is essential for guidance, correction, and affirmation. The book of Proverbs stresses this repeatedly: *"Reprove not a scorner, lest he hate thee: rebuke a wise man, and he will love thee"* (Proverbs 9:8); *"The ear that heareth the reproof of life abideth among the wise"* (Proverbs 15:31). Biblical leaders regularly sought feedback from God. David often inquired of the Lord before making decisions (1 Samuel 23:2-4), and when he failed to assess his behavior—such as with Bathsheba—he suffered greatly until confronted by Nathan (2 Samuel 12:1-13). In the New Testament, Paul exhorts the Corinthians to *"Examine yourselves, whether ye be in the faith"* (2 Corinthians 13:5). Without regular reflection and evaluation, believers are prone to drift, confusion, or self-deception. Assessment fosters clarity and course correction, safeguarding the process of sanctification.

Together, these Scriptures affirm that each component of the change process—purpose, vision, knowledge, motivation, resources, planning, and feedback—has a theological foundation. When any one of them is absent, the results are predictable and spiritually consistent with the Biblical record. The Bible offers not only a spiritual roadmap for personal and communal transformation but also practical wisdom that affirms the psychological and organizational truths reflected in this change process model.

CCRT, guised by Biblical principles helps clients understand the process of change, the practical steps to achieve change, and the Biblical principles defining proper change.

FIVE STEP COUNSELING MODEL

A Practical Application of Biblical Counsel: A Five-Step Model Combining 2 Timothy 3:16-17 & CCRT

Step 1 Listen	Step 2 Determine Problem	Step 3 Compare with Scripture	Step 4 Gain Commitment	Step 5 Implement Change

UNBELIEVER
• Denies God
• Denies Word
	LOOK FOR:
	• Symptoms
	• Problems
	• Root Causes
		EVANGELIZE UNBELIEVER
		• God (Plan of God)
		• Word (Perfect)
		• Jesus (Redemption)
		• Spirit (Sanctifier)
			UNBELIEVER
			• Repentance
			  • Confession of faith
			  • Baptism
			  • Read the Bible
				GIVE HOPE TO ALL
				
				GO OVER STEPS TO ACCOMPLISH CHANGE.
				• Look at short and long term goals
				• Decide on intervention techniques
				• Discuss Spiritual aspects of change
				• Discuss physical aspects of change

BELIEVER (Sin) • Focus on self • Rejection of God's viewpoint • Patterns of self sufficiency • Rebellion • Blames others • Denial of Reality	**DECISIONS TO BE MADE:** • Prioritize Problems • Decide greatest need • Determine wrong beliefs • Determine wrong thoughts • Determine wrong motives • Determine wrong behaviors • Determine wrong feelings • Determine Treatment Plan	**NOUTHETIC APPROACH FOR BELIEVER IN SIN** • Warn - feelings • Admonish - thoughts • Correct - behavior	**BELIEVER (Sin)** • Repentance • Confession of sin • Agreement to change life	
BELIEVER (Over-whelmed) • Lack of understanding • Grief • Depression • Victimization • Events & Circumstance		**PARAKLECTIC APPROACH FOR OVERWHELMED BELIEVER** • edify - thoughts • exhort - behaviors • comfort - feelings Show the advantages of God's way and the disadvantages and consequences of man's way.	**BELIEVER (Overwhelmed)** • show God's purpose • show God's love • show how event can be used for good	

The Five-Step Counseling Model and 2 Timothy 3:16-17

From a CCRT perspective, the fourfold process of doctrine, reproof, correction, and instruction in righteousness described in 2 Timothy 3:16 (KJV)— "All scripture is given by inspiration of God, and is profitable for doctrine, for reproof, for correction, for instruction in righteousness"—provides a complete Biblical blueprint for counseling. It is clear that CCRT is anchored in the conviction that "The center point for man is God, and He expresses this in His Word, the 66 books of the Bible. This provides the absolute unlimited baseline for normal" This process is not theoretical; it is both theological and therapeutic, offering a structured progression that moves the counselee from understanding God's standard, to confronting what is wrong, to redirecting toward what is right, and finally to training in how to live it out daily.

The process begins with **doctrine**—establishing "what is right." In CCRT, this is identifying God's design for human behavior, relationships, and thought life, rooted in Christ as the model for normalcy (p. 35). Here, the counselor helps the counselee understand God's truth about their situation, much like how Paul instructed Timothy to use Scripture to define correct belief and conduct.

The next step reproof, "what is being done wrong," mirrors CCRT's diagnostic phase, where the therapist confronts faulty belief systems and sinful behaviors that stem from unmet needs or unbiblical thinking. CCRT emphasizes that identifying wrong actions or beliefs is not condemnation but a loving exposure of what hinders mental, emotional, and spiritual health. This is akin to Nathan confronting David over his sin with Bathsheba (2 Samuel 12:1-9), where truth was spoken to reveal the wrong.

- The next step, correction, "what should be done," aligns with CCRT's intervention stage, where the counselor guides the counselee toward replacing faulty thinking and sinful actions with Biblically correct alternatives. This involves "helping the counselee see the Biblical way of meeting their needs". For example, Jesus' restoration of Peter in John 21:15-19 both acknowledged past failure and redirected him toward faithful service.

The final step, Instruction in righteousness, "how to do it," corresponds to CCRT's skill-building and discipleship phase. This is where the counselor equips the counselee with the practical steps and spiritual disciplines needed to walk in obedience and maintain change. Lasting transformation occurs when the counselee not only knows what is right but practices it daily, empowered by the Holy Spirit. The mentoring relationship between Paul and Timothy itself is a Biblical model—Paul not only taught Timothy doctrine but also modeled righteous living (Philippians 4:9).

Throughout, both 2 Timothy 3:16 and CCRT view counseling as a cycle rooted in Scripture: define truth, expose error, redirect toward right action, and equip for ongoing righteousness. Biblical examples—David's repentance (Psalm 51), Josiah's reforms after hearing the Book of the Law (2 Kings 22–23), and the transformation of the Corinthian church after Paul's corrective letters—show this fourfold pattern in action. In each case, God's Word provided the doctrinal foundation, the reproof of sin, the correction toward God's will, and the instruction for continued

A detailed therapeutic example: Imagine a woman named Sarah who is in counseling due to chronic resentment toward her sister over a business betrayal.

- In the doctrine stage, the CCRT therapist shows Sarah passages like Colossians 3:13, defining God's standard of forgiveness. Sarah begins to see that withholding forgiveness is not aligned with Christ's model.
- In reproof, the counselor gently confronts Sarah's belief that "forgiving means I'm letting her win," exposing this as a worldly, self-protective mindset that contradicts God's truth (Romans 12:17–21).
- In correction, the counselor guides Sarah to replace her resentment with intentional acts of kindness, as commanded in Luke 6:27–28, explaining how obedience can break the cycle of bitterness.
- In instruction in righteousness, the counselor equips Sarah with a weekly accountability plan, daily Scripture meditation on forgiveness, and prayer assignments, ensuring she knows how to live out this change going forward.

In this way, 2 Timothy 3:16 becomes not just a theological statement but a **practical clinical flow** in CCRT: God's Word defines reality, exposes distortion, offers the right path, and trains the believer to walk in it. Biblical history is filled with examples—David's repentance, Josiah's national reforms, Peter's restoration—all demonstrating that real change begins when God's truth is taught, sin is exposed, correction is embraced, and righteous living is learned and practiced.

Explaining the Five Step Chart

The Five Step Chart was, of course, modeled to reflect 2nd Timothy 3:186-17, and to provide the counselor with a little more insight into the counseling process.

Step 1: Listen (Foundation of Understanding)

Before any meaningful intervention can occur, the counselor must cultivate a space of genuine listening and empathy. This involves creating a safe and non-judgmental environment where the client feels heard, understood, and validated. As Proverbs 18:13 states, "He that answereth a matter before he heareth it, it is folly and shame unto him." Effective listening provides valuable insights into the client's state.

View of God/Reality (Unbeliever/Believer): Is the client's starting point one of truth or denial? The counselor's first step is to know this before providing direction. Is the client an unbeliever or a believer. If the client is an unbeliever, the counselor must first establish a common framework for counseling. If the client does not accept the truth of the existence and presence of God and Divine authorship of the Bible, will the client concede that the principles taught in the Bible provide a framework for healing and good mental health, and the pursuit of a normal, fulfilling life. If the client will accept this as a starting point, counseling can be profitable, and future evangelism possible.

If the counselor determines, the client is a believer, the next step is to identify the type of problem the client is facing. Is the issue of blatant sin, or is the client being overwhelmed by issues that the client doesn't know how to respond to correctly? Is the person a victim of events outside of of the ability to control them? Being positively aware of the new client's spiritual state is imperative in forming a treatment plan.

CCRT Connection: At this stage the counselor assess the client's level of spiritual understanding, identifies their core beliefs, and seeks to understand their overall worldview. "The hearing ear and the seeing eye, the Lord hath made even both of them." (Proverbs 20:12 KJV).: The deeper the counselor listens and truly understands the client's life, then better are the chances for successful intervention to happen. There is power in truly understanding!

Step 2: Determine the Problem (Discerning Truth from Error -Doctrine)

Having listened intently, the next step is to help the client identify the core problems and challenges they are facing. This involves moving beyond surface-level symptoms to uncover the underlying issues (root causes) that are driving their thoughts, emotions, and behaviors. This requires:

- Prioritizing Problems: Addressing the most pressing and impactful issues first.
- Identifying Unmet Needs: This is necessary to determine the best place to start and what is the best area that can make an immediate change, for good? "If you want to change attitudes, start with a change in behavior." You can start the process by suggesting a conscious change in behavior even if the attitude, value, or belief is not yet changed. For example, a person can quit vocalizing complaints about things at work even if he believes his complaints are valid. Explain thaqt y changing what you do first, then attitudes, belief, and then faith comes. The only behavior one can change his own. But, by changing his

behavior, he can influence change in others. In the case of the complainer who quits vocalizing the complaints, others may become more probe to listening to his opinion when he is asked.

- Challenging Wrong Beliefs and Thoughts: The counselor, having knowledge from the Word, what would be considered not healthy, must show and then offer. "What will people in the church say if I got a divorce?", or, "it is so great to do drugs and party, it's the only way I have friends."

CCRT Connection: When implementing Biblical truth, the client must understand that there are three dimensions: thoughts, actions, and beliefs contribute to the chosen behavior. CCRT warns of the dangers of "learned abnormality" and the "world system" which can distort our perceptions and lead us astray. (pp. 12, 25) Identifying and challenging these distorted beliefs is a critical part of the therapeutic process.

Step 3: Compare with Scripture (Reproof)

This is where Christian counseling truly distinguishes itself. By grounding the therapeutic process in the timeless truths of Scripture, the counselor helps the client evaluate their thoughts, feelings, and behaviors in light of God's Word. This involves:

- Evangelizing the Unbeliever: Sharing the message of God's love, forgiveness, and salvation through Jesus Christ. What are the tools you use? You need to remember that you must get to know the bible.

CCRT Connection: As the "CCRT" key points for the individual state, the first point is to believe, not just that you know.

- Offering a Nouthetic Approach for the Believer in Sin: What steps can change you? The point is there! (You must take these steps!)

CCRT Connection: Showing the Advantages of God's Way and the Disadvantages of Man's Way: If not, why do anything? To compare the value, and the results is key in giving any hope. God has a "design", but to the world, it is to force. The world has the power of sin, but you have the "authority and the power" of Jesus!

Step 4: Gain Commitment (Motivating Change - CORRECTION)

Understanding the truth is not enough; the client must also be motivated to embrace it and take action. This involves:

- Unbeliever: Repentance, Confession of faith, Baptism, and read the Bible. You can't use the truth, if you do not have any!

CCRT's first two steps are to focus in on the client's "I am" in order to bring about the good, for that can also bring in a "I have" to the good as well.

- Overwhelmed: Show the God's purpose and God's love.

CCRT Connection: This step aligns with the "CCRT" emphasis on integrating Christian absolutes into the therapeutic process. By emphasizing love, the client has more hope of freedom, not just to be helped. They are now helping in order to grow

Biblical Example: Confession and Repentance. 2 Timothy 2:25 (KJV) 25 In meekness instructing those that oppose themselves; if God peradventure will give them repentance to the acknowledging of the truth;

Step 5: Implement Change (Transformative Action - INSTRUCTION)

The final step involves putting the plan into action and implementing concrete changes in the client's life. This requires: Show those where to put the effort. "It requires an assessment of what to do. (p.28).

CCRT Connection: This step aligns with the principle of "the power of now in that the decisions we make will shape a future. There needs to be a commitment to the future.

CCRT Connection: "CCRT provides a systematic format of absolutes and normality and abnormality" (p. 6), giving structure where once had none.

Discuss Spiritual and Physical Aspects of Change: Make time for work but also time for the spirit.

Biblical Examples: Galatians 6:10 goes, "As we have therefore opportunity, let us do good unto all men, especially unto them who are of the household of faith." In showing good, you help give the steps to that action.

Conclusion: A Holistic Path to Transformation

The five-step counseling model, when integrated with the principles of 2 Timothy 3:16-17 and "CCRT", provides a comprehensive and Biblically sound approach to guide individuals toward lasting transformation. It moves beyond symptom management to address the root causes of problems, equipping clients with the truth, love, and grace needed to live a life aligned with God's will.

COUNSELING PITFALLS TO AVOID

While Christ Centered Reality Therapy (CCRT) provides a powerful framework for guiding individuals toward wholeness and a restored relationship with God, it's essential for practitioners to be aware of potential pitfalls that can hinder the therapeutic process. Drawing upon the principles of CCRT, scripture, we can identify and address these challenges to ensure our counseling efforts remain grounded in Biblical truth and produce lasting, transformative change.

The Imperative of Avoiding Temptation: A Foundation for Christian Service

Galatians 6:1-10 (KJV), "[1] *Brethren, if a man be overtaken in a fault, ye which are spiritual,*
restore such an one in the spirit of meekness; considering thyself, lest thou also be tempted. Bear
ye one another's burdens, and so fulfil the law of Christ. [3] *For if a man think himself to be something,*
when he is nothing, he deceiveth himself. [4] *But let every man prove his own work, and then shall he*
have rejoicing in himself alone, and not in another. [5] *For every man shall bear his own burden.* [6] *Let*
him that is taught in the word communicate unto him that teacheth in all good things. [7] *Be not*
deceived; God is not mocked: for whatsoever a man soweth, that shall he also reap. [8] *For he that*
soweth to his flesh shall of the flesh reap corruption; but he that soweth to the Spirit shall of the
Spirit reap life everlasting. [9] *And let us not be weary in well doing: for in due season we shall reap,*
if we faint not. [10] *As we have therefore opportunity, let us do good unto all men, especially unto them*
who are of the household of faith. world is crucified unto me, and I unto the world.

The text from Galatians 6:1-10, provides a foundation for the warnings about a person who has lost his way. As it states: "Brethren, if a man be overtaken in a fault, ye which are spiritual, restore such a one in the spirit of meekness; considering thyself, lest thou also be tempted.") This verse provides the tone of what is to come, it warns to avoid temptation, and we should not think highly of ourselves. This lays the foundation for our need to be guarded, and ready for anything. There key area where counselors experience difficulties are:

1. Pride: The Illusion of Superiority ("We are needed, therefore we are right")

One of the most insidious dangers for any counselor, but particularly those working within a Christian framework, is the temptation toward pride. This can manifest as:

- An Attitude of Superiority: Viewing oneself as possessing unique insight or a higher level of spiritual understanding, leading to a judgmental or condescending approach toward clients. CCRT warns that Jesus deals with the person at the present condition. Instead of assuming your ability to save, or acting as the chosen one, you must let Jesus take the lead.
- Over-Spiritualizing/Under-Spiritualizing Problems: Imposing spiritual interpretations on issues that may require practical, psychological, or even medical intervention, or the opposite, avoiding legitimate spiritual intervention due to not wanting to seem

"religious". Recognizing the balance that CCRT notes can be tough, requiring the strength from the Spirit to make an appropriate determination. (p. 3)

- Curiosity and Sexual Attraction: While compassion and concern are essential, it's critical to maintain professional boundaries and avoid inappropriate curiosity or attraction towards clients. Proverbs 4:23 reminds us, "Keep thy heart with all diligence; for out of it spring the issues of life." Guarding our hearts and minds is crucial for maintaining ethical integrity and preventing harm to both ourselves and our clients.
- Opposites Attract: The scriptures ask, "How can two walk together except they be agreed?" This should have weight, for if two sides of the opposite attract, why has the problem even occurred.

Solution: Humility is key. Galatians 6:3, continuing the thought from the beginning of the chapter warns, "For if a man think himself to be something, when he is nothing, he deceiveth himself." (KJV). We must recognize that we are merely vessels through which God's healing power flows, and that true transformation comes from Him, not from our own expertise or efforts. As the bible teaches, "Pride goes before destruction, and a haughty spirit before a fall." (Proverbs 16:18 KJV)

2. Rescuing: Harming with Good Intentions ("We feed instead of teaching others to fish")

The desire to help others is a noble one, but it can easily become distorted if we fall into the trap of rescuing clients rather than empowering them. This may manifest as:

- Fostering Over-Dependency: Solving clients' problems for them, rather than equipping them with the tools and skills they need to address their own challenges.
- Unrealistic Expectations for Self: Creating a standard that isn't Biblical.
- Inability to set Limits for Others: This may manifest as letting friends always overstay their visit, or take advantage of you.
- Motivated by wrong desires This is a self-seeking reason, and it has nothing to do with God's desire for your life.

CCRT: The ultimate goal isn't about fixing anyone but instead letting God provide guidance and wisdom in people's design. The goal is for one to become "self-reliant independence and the ability to individually operate with self- control and independence." (p. 34)

Solution: Empowerment is key. 2 Timothy 1:7 says, "For God hath not given us the spirit of fear; but of power, and of love, and of a sound mind." We must empower individuals to be accountable. Rather than rescuing, we should focus on helping them develop their gifts, skills, and strengths.

3. Avoidance: Neglecting the Call to Serve ("How we avoid helping people")

Sometimes, for a variety of reasons, we may find ourselves avoiding or neglecting the needs of those who seek our help. This can manifest as:

- Favoritism: Showing preferential treatment to certain clients based on personal preferences or biases.
- Uncomfortable: Not being able to connect personally.

- Afraid: Not knowing how to work.
- Don't Know How to Respond
- Don't like the person
- Afraid Our Image will be Ruined
- No Financial Recompense: The calling is for our needs for God.

1 Peter 3:15 urges us to, "be ready always to give an answer to every man that asketh you a reason of the hope that is in you with meekness and fear. Even though we may feel inadequete, to be ready is our calling.

As a "CCRT" counselor you must learn that love does not include society. (p. 22) That is, the needs of the person outweigh any feelings of dislike.

Solution: Obedience is key. As christians we are called to service. Jesus says in John 13:14: "If I then, your Lord and Master, have washed your feet; ye also ought to wash one another's feet." To not respond means you think you are better than the least of His brothers.

Conclusion: Walking the Path of Authentic Service

As Christian counselors practicing CCRT, we are called to a high standard of service. By remaining vigilant, rejecting pride and control, and embrace the path of empowerment and service, we can effectively guide others towards healing, wholeness, and a deeper relationship with God. May our lives be a testament to the transformative power of Christ-centered living, reflecting His love, grace, and unwavering commitment to the lost and hurting.

BIBLICAL CHANGE

How One Changes Biblically – A Christ Centered Reality Therapy Perspective

Biblical change is not merely the improvement of habits or the adjustment of outward conduct; it is a total transformation of the inner man—mind, body, and spirit—through the power of God's Word and the work of the Holy Spirit. As Romans 12:1–2 commands, believers are to "present [their] bodies a living sacrifice, holy, acceptable unto God… and be not conformed to this world: but be ye transformed by the renewing of your mind. This transformation is the return to God's "absolute baseline for what is normal," where normalcy is defined only in relation to God's will and nature (p. 2).

Anything outside of God's will, regardless of how socially acceptable it may appear, is abnormal. Thus, true change begins when a person abandons the world's definitions of good and acceptable and embraces God's absolutes as the sole measure of thought, behavior, and identity.

From a CCRT standpoint, change must begin in the spirit before it can be lasting in the mind and body. As Ephesians 4:22–24 instructs, the believer is to "put off… the old man, which is corrupt according to the deceitful lusts… be renewed in the spirit of your mind… [and] put on the new man, which after God is created in righteousness and true holiness." This is not cosmetic or behavioral reform—it is a supernatural exchange of identity, where the "old man" with his abnormal wants, toxic belief systems, and sinful patterns is replaced with the "new man" aligned with God's character. CCRT stresses that without spiritual regeneration, any behavioral modification will remain superficial and temporary: "Unless there is a change of heart, the change will not be permanent" (p. 34).

The steps of Biblical change, as reflected in Ephesians 5:13–21, mirror CCRT's counseling model: (1) *Awake*— recognizing the reality of one's sinful state; (2) *Arise*—turning decisively toward Christ; (3) *Walk circumspectly*— living intentionally according to God's Word; (4) *Redeem the time*—prioritizing God's purposes; (5) *Be wise*— applying Scripture to decisions; (6) *Be filled with the Spirit*—living under His guidance and power; (7) *Speak correctly*—using speech to edify, not destroy; (8) *Give thanks*—developing a grateful heart; and (9) *Submit*—yielding to God and serving others. These steps reflect what CCRT calls "redirecting reality" toward God's normal (p. 29), replacing abnormal thought patterns with Biblical truth.

Mental and Physical

Romans 12:1-2 I beseech you therefore, brethren, by the mercies of God, that ye **present your bodies a living sacrifice**, holy, acceptable unto God, which is your reasonable service. [2] And be not conformed to this world: but be ye transformed by the **renewing of your mind**, that ye may prove what is that good, and acceptable, and perfect, will of God.

Change is both Physical and Spiritual

Ephes. 4:22-24 That ye put off concerning the former conversation the old man, which is corrupt according to the deceitful lusts; [23] And be renewed in the spirit of your mind; [24] And that ye put on the new man, which after God is created in righteousness and true holiness.

Steps in the Change Process

Ephes. 5:13-21 But all things that are reproved are made manifest by the light: for whatsoever doth make manifest is light. [14] Wherefore he saith, awake thou that sleepest, and arise from the dead, and Christ shall give thee light. [15] See then that ye walk circumspectly, not as fools, but as wise, [16] Redeeming the time, because the days are evil. [17] Wherefore be ye not unwise, but understanding what the will of the Lord is. [18] And be not drunk with wine, wherein is excess; but be filled with the Spirit;

Speaking to yourselves in psalms and hymns and spiritual songs, singing and making melody in your heart to the Lord; [20] Giving thanks always for all things unto God and the Father in the name of our Lord Jesus Christ; [21] Submitting yourselves one to another in the fear of God.

1. Awake
2. Arise
3. Walk circumspectly
4. Redeem the time
5. Be wise
6. 6. Be filled with the Spirit
7. Speak Correctly
8. Give thanks
9. 9. Submit

How change Occurs

1. Change occurs when a counselee desires to change, but unless there is a change of heart, the change will not be permanent.
2. There is no set number of days it takes for change to occur
3. Spiritual change must first occur before a physical change can occur permanently

How Changes Progresses

When a person sincerely desires to change, and offers and yields to the Holy Spirit:

1. Changes come from the regeneration of power of the Holy Spirit
2. The word of God produces change
3. Examples of Godly lives produces changes
4. Principle of Prayer
    - Asking
    - Believing
    - Receiving

Changes occur when the counselee decides to change. But unless change results from guidance from the Holy Spirit, only one's behavior is changed – not their life.

Most counselors seek only to change behaviors. They need to help the counselee change their attitude and change their life.

Ways of implanting change in a counselee

1. People cannot change themselves…they need the Holy Spirit (Rom. 8:13)
2. People must be able to accept that there are Spiritual principles involved
3. Keep in mind that the Bible talks about renewing the mind (Romans 12:1)
4. Keep in mind that the Bible talks about bringing the body under subjection (1 Cor. 9:27)
5. True repentance requires knowledge, understanding, and an acceptance of what the scriptures teach

In order to implement change, the counselee must realize it is a spiritual battle. Make sure the following guidelines have been established:

1. Are the issues clearly defined?
2. Has a Biblical goal for the purpose of counseling been established?
3. Does the counselee believe God can help him?
4. Has the counselee accepted responsibility?
5. Has prayer, repentance, and confession been offered?
6. Are the solutions you are recommending Biblical?

Change is accomplished through the willingness to submit to God and allow God to work in you. One does not make lasting changes through self-effort. (See Romans 8:13)

Too many people think that they need to get "cleaned up" or "straightened out" before they turn their life over to God. However, if they were able to do that, they would not need God. Romans 8:12-14 "Therefore, brethren, we are debtors, not to the flesh, to live after the flesh. [13] For if ye live after the flesh, ye shall die: but if ye through the Spirit do mortify the deeds of the body, ye shall live. [14] For as many as are led by the Spirit of God, they are the sons of God."

Growth and Change

2 Peter 1:5-10 And beside this, giving all diligence, add to your faith virtue; and to virtue knowledge; [6] And to knowledge temperance; and to temperance patience; and to patience godliness; [7] And to godliness brotherly kindness; and to brotherly kindness charity. [8] For if these things be in you, and abound, they make you that ye shall neither be barren nor unfruitful in the knowledge of our Lord Jesus Christ. [9] But he that lacketh these things are blind, and cannot see afar off, and hath forgotten that he was purged from his old sins. [10] Wherefore the rather, brethren, give diligence to make your calling and election sure: for if ye do these things, ye shall never fall:

Focus and be conscious of changing Add to your Faith:

+ Virtue
+ Knowledge
+ Temperance
+ Patience
+ Godliness
+ Kindness
+ Charity

= Fruitful

The Bible s is filled with vivid examples of such change after meeting Jesus.

Saul of Tarsus (Acts 9) was a zealous persecutor of Christians—his worldview rooted in legalism and hostility toward the gospel. His encounter with the risen Christ on the road to Damascus shattered his toxic belief system and redefined his identity. Jesus confronted Saul's sin ("Why persecutest thou me?"), revealed Himself as the truth, and commissioned him for a new purpose. In CCRT terms, Saul's "abnormal wants" of religious dominance and self-righteousness were replaced with God's normal—humble service, love for the church, and a mission to spread the gospel. His life thereafter reflected the spiritual principle that *identity change precedes behavior change*.

Zacchaeus (Luke 19:1–10), a chief tax collector, exemplifies the principle that true repentance leads to immediate, tangible change. Before meeting Jesus, Zacchaeus's life was driven by greed and dishonest gain—abnormal behaviors springing from an abnormal want for wealth at others' expense. After Jesus called him by name and dined at his house, Zacchaeus publicly committed to giving half his goods to the poor and restoring fourfold what he had taken unjustly. This aligns with CCRT's teaching that "each idea, action, or desire starts as a need… how those needs are met will become either normal or abnormal" (p. 17). Zacchaeus's need for security and acceptance was once met through corruption; after encountering Christ, it was met through obedience, generosity, and restored relationships.

The Samaritan woman at the well (John 4) reveals the power of Jesus to address both the presenting symptom and the root cause. Her serial relationships were attempts to fulfill the God- given need for love (CCRT Need #2, p. 14) in abnormal ways. Jesus bypassed superficial conversation, exposed the truth of her life, and offered "living water"—a spiritual solution to her deepest need. After receiving this truth, she left her water pot (symbolizing her old patterns) and became a witness to her community. CCRT emphasizes this principle: *Identify the real need, reject abnormal means of fulfilling it, and replace it with God's provision.*

These transformations share common spiritual principles: recognition of sin (Awake), turning toward Christ in faith (Arise), renewal of the mind through truth (Walk circumspectly), and submission to God's will (Submit). As Romans 8:13 declares, "if ye through the Spirit do mortify the deeds of the body, ye shall live." Mortification—putting to death sinful desires— cannot be achieved through self-effort but only "through the Spirit," in alignment with CCRT's insistence that "people cannot change themselves… they need the Holy Spirit" (p. 129).

In summary, to change Biblically is to experience a Spirit-empowered, Scripture-directed reorientation of one's entire life toward God's standard of normalcy. It is to have the heart transformed, the mind renewed, and the body disciplined under God's authority. The process is the same for all who come to Christ—whether Pharisee, tax collector, or outcast woman: (1) identify and acknowledge the abnormal, (2) encounter and submit to the absolute truth in Jesus Christ, (3) replace toxic belief systems with God's Word, and (4) live out the new identity through Spirit-led obedience. This is the pathway where Biblical truth and CCRT principles meet, producing change that is both eternal and practical, both spiritual and behavioral, both immediate and lifelong.

Biblical Change Process – Integrated with CCRT Principles

The Biblical process of change aligns seamlessly with the counseling framework of Christ Centered Reality Therapy (CCRT), which addresses transformation in the mind, body, and spirit by identifying abnormal patterns and replacing them with God's absolute standard for normalcy.

Ephesians 5:13-21 (KJV)

13 But all things that are reproved are made manifest by the light: for whatsoever doth make manifest is light.
14 Wherefore he saith,awake thou that sleepest, and arise from the dead, and Christ shall give thee light.
15 See then that ye walk circumspectly, not as fools, but as wise,
16 16 Redeeming the time, because the days are evil.
17 Wherefore be ye not unwise, but understanding what the will of the Lord is.
18 And be not drunk with wine, wherein is excess; but be filled with the Spirit;
19 Speaking to yourselves in psalms and hymns and spiritual songs, singing and making melody in your heart to the Lord;
20 Giving thanks always for all things unto God and the Father in the name of our Lord Jesus Christ;
21 Submitting yourselves one to another in the fear of God.

The first step, ***Awake,*** involves recognizing one's sin and spiritual need. Ephesians 5:14 commands, "Awake thou that sleepest, and arise from the dead, and Christ shall give thee light." In CCRT terms, this corresponds to the stage of *Problem Identification*, where the counselee acknowledges the abnormal beliefs or behaviors in their life and admits the need for change. This moment of awakening meets the *Survival* need (Need #1), as the person becomes aware of their spiritual death and their need for eternal life in Christ.

This meets the *Survival* need (Need #1) because the person realizes their spiritual death and need for new life in Christ. An example of this is found in **the Prodigal Son** (Luke 15:11–32), who "came to himself" while starving among the swine. His awakening was the recognition that his abnormal lifestyle had led him to ruin, and that survival could only be found by returning to his father.

The second step, ***Arise,*** calls for a decisive turning to Christ, as demonstrated by Saul's question in Acts 9:6: "Lord, what wilt thou have me to do?" Within the CCRT framework, this is the stage of *Commitment*, where the individual chooses to reject abnormal patterns and embrace God's normal. This step satisfies the *Love* need (Need #2), because true belonging and unconditional acceptance are now rooted in a relationship with Jesus Christ rather than in unhealthy or worldly sources. **Saul of Tarsus** (later Paul) is the prime example—once committed to persecuting Christians, his encounter with Jesus redirected his life's mission from destroying the church to building it, showing that love from God transforms enemies into ambassadors.

Third, ***walk circumspectly*** means living intentionally by God's Word, following the exhortation of Ephesians 5:15: "See then that ye walk circumspectly, not as fools, but as wise." CCRT identifies this as *Behavior Redirection*, the stage where toxic habits are replaced with Biblically aligned actions. This aligns with the *Power* need (Need #3), as obedience to God fosters genuine self-worth and the ability to create lasting, positive change rooted in His authority. **Zacchaeus** (Luke 19:1–10) illustrates this change—once a corrupt tax collector, his encounter with Jesus redirected his behavior immediately. He restored fourfold what he had taken and gave half his goods to the poor, showing that genuine power comes from righteous living, not exploitation.

Fourth, the believer must ***Redeem the time,*** prioritizing God's purposes over personal convenience or worldly pursuits. Ephesians 5:16 warns, "Redeeming the time, because the days are evil." In CCRT, this corresponds to ***Goal Setting,*** where the counselor and counselee establish God-centered objectives for life and relationships. This fulfills the *Freedom* need (Need #4), exercising the God-given gift of free will to choose His will rather than being enslaved by sin or societal pressures. **The Samaritan woman** (John 4) embodies this—once consumed with abnormal relationships to meet her need for love, she redirected her life after meeting Jesus. She left her water pot and spent her energy testifying to her town, using her time for kingdom purposes rather than self-gratification.

Finally, ***be filled with the Spirit*** is the essential element that sustains change. Ephesians 5:18 instructs, "Be filled with the Spirit," indicating continual dependence on God for strength and direction. This is the *Spiritual Empowerment* stage in CCRT, where the counselee relies on the Holy Spirit's power to live out the new life in Christ. It satisfies the *Fun/Joy* need (Need #5), as Spirit-led living produces joy, peace, fulfillment, and the deep contentment of being aligned with God's purpose. **Peter** offers a striking example—once impulsive and fearful, even denying Christ, he was transformed after being filled with the Holy Spirit at Pentecost (Acts 2). The same man who hid in fear boldly preached to thousands, rejoicing even when persecuted for Christ's sake.

When these steps are understood and applied together, they form a cohesive pathway for transformation. The Biblical sequence provides the divine order, while CCRT offers the practical tools for diagnosis, redirection, and growth. Together, they address the deepest needs of the human heart while ensuring that change is not superficial, but rather a Spirit-led reorientation toward God's unchanging standard of normalcy.

When these steps are understood and practiced together, they form a cohesive pathway for transformation. The Biblical sequence provides the divine order, while CCRT offers the practical counseling framework to diagnose, redirect, and guide growth. Through this integration, the believer's deepest needs are met in God's way, ensuring that change is not superficial or temporary, but a Spirit-led reorientation toward God's eternal standard of normalcy—one that is as visible in behavior as it is rooted in the heart.

TEACHER'S OUTLINE

Topic: How One Changes Biblically – A Christ Centered Reality Therapy Perspective

Lesson Goal:

To guide students/counselees in understanding the Biblical steps of lasting change, integrating CCRT principles with Scripture, and applying them to their own lives.

1. Introduction: The Nature of Biblical Change
    - **Key Scripture:** Romans 12:1–2 – Present bodies as living sacrifices, renew the mind, prove God's will.
    - **CCRT Concept:** God is the absolute baseline for normalcy.
    - **Teaching Point:** Lasting change is spiritual first, then mental and physical.

2. Step One – Awake
    - **Scripture:** Ephesians 5:14
    - **CCRT Stage:** Problem Identification – Recognizing abnormal beliefs/behaviors.
    - **Human Need:** Survival (Need #1) – awareness of spiritual death.
    - **Example:** The Prodigal Son (Luke 15:11–32).
    - **Discussion:** What does "coming to yourself" mean spiritually?
3. Step Two – Arise
    - Scripture: Acts 9:6
    - **CCRT Stage:** Commitment – Decision to reject abnormal and embrace God's normal.
    - **Human Need:** Love (Need #2) – receiving belonging in Christ.
    - **Example:** Saul's conversion to Paul.
    - **Discussion:** How does real love change destructive goals?

4. Step Three – Walk Circumspectly
    - **Scripture:** Ephesians 5:15
    - **CCRT Stage:** Behavior Redirection – Replacing toxic patterns with God's ways.
    - **Human Need:** Power (Need #3) – self-worth through obedience.
    - **Example:** Zacchaeus.
    - **Discussion:** Why does obedience create genuine self-worth?

5. Step Four – Redeem the Time
    - **Scripture:** Ephesians 5:16
    - **CCRT Stage:** Goal Setting – God-centered objectives.
    - **Human Need:** Freedom (Need #4) – using will to fulfill God's will.
    - **Example:** Samaritan woman at the well.
    - **Discussion:** How does redirecting time change life purpose?

6. Step Five – Be Filled with the Spirit
    - **Scripture:** Ephesians 5:18
    - **CCRT Stage:** Spiritual Empowerment – Dependence on the Spirit.
    - **Human Need:** Fun/Joy (Need #5) – peace and fulfillment.
    - **Example:** Peter's boldness after Pentecost.
    - **Discussion:** How does the Spirit sustain long-term change?

7. Application and Reflection
    - Identify one "abnormal want" in your life.
    - Replace it with God's normal based on Scripture.
    - Set a concrete, Spirit-led goal for the week.

For the Counselor - Here's a step-by-step, therapist-facing guide to implementing the Biblical change process in a CCRT counseling session.

Step 1 — Establish the frame (Christ as the absolute baseline for "normal").

Open by clarifying the counseling worldview: in Christ Centered Reality Therapy (CCRT), "normal" is defined by God's character and will, not by culture, feelings, or consensus. Briefly explain that the goal is alignment with God's design for the whole person—mind, body, and spirit—rather than symptom management alone. Read Romans 12:1–2 (KJV) aloud and invite consent to this frame: "I beseech you therefore, brethren, by the mercies of God, that ye present your bodies a living sacrifice… And be not conformed to this world: but be ye transformed by the renewing of your mind…" You're setting the expectation that lasting change is spiritual first (repentance and faith), then mental (renewed thinking), and then behavioral (obedience).

Step 2 — Illuminate with Scripture to surface the problem behind the problems.

Use Scripture as light (Eph. 5:13–14) to reveal—not to shame. Ask the counselee to describe the presenting concerns (anger, anxiety, porn use, relational chaos, etc.). Then gently distinguish symptoms from root causes: "What do you want when you feel this? Where do you run to meet that want?" Explain that God-given needs (survival, love/belonging, power/self-worth, freedom/agency, joy) are good, but we often meet them in abnormal ways (sinful "wants" disguised as "needs"). Invite the counselee to consider how their current strategies have replaced God's provision (e.g., intimacy with porn, peace with substances, worth with achievement), and note how these strategies have multiplied consequences.

Step 3 — Map the case using CCRT's Five Needs and Five Conflicts.

Formulate a simple written map together. In one column, list where each of the Five Human Needs is currently unmet or met in unbiblical ways. In a second column, list the Five Common Conflict Arenas that are inflamed (children, money, extended family, sex, religion/faith). In a third column, write "abnormal substitutes" (what the counselee uses to cope or control). This compact conceptualization lets you show how unmet needs drive abnormal substitutes, which then spill into predictable conflicts. Close by normalizing: "The problem isn't that you have needs; it's how you've been trying to meet them."

Step 4 — Invite an "Awake / Arise" decision (conviction --- repentance --- faith).

Read Ephesians 5:14 (KJV): "Awake thou that sleepest, and arise from the dead, and Christ shall give thee light." Ask, "Where do you sense the Lord calling you to wake up?" Then move to Acts 9:6—Saul's surrender: "Lord, what wilt thou have me to do?" Lead a brief prayer of confession and trust in Christ, emphasizing that forgiveness is real and that new obedience flows from grace, not grit. You are helping the counselee cross the line from insight to surrender— turning from abnormal substitutes to the living Christ.

Step 5 — Install the "put off / be renewed / put on" change engine.

Read Ephesians 4:22–24 (KJV) in full: "That ye put off... the old man... And be renewed in the spirit of your mind... And... put on the new man..." Collaboratively identify one or two high-leverage patterns to target. For each, write a three-part replacement plan: (1) *Put off* (what to refuse: situations, scripts, props), (2) *Be renewed* (truth to rehearse: a short KJV verse and a "truth sentence" to speak aloud), and (3) *Put on* (a concrete, godly replacement behavior).

Example: "When lonely at night (trigger), I will *put off* scrolling; I will *renew* with Psalm 16:11 and say, 'Lord, you are my portion'; I will *put on* texting my accountability partner and reading one Psalm before bed."

Step 6 — Anchor the thought-life: Scripture-based cognitive renewal.

Open Philippians 4:6–9 (KJV) and work it into a daily mental routine: "Be careful for nothing... but in everything by prayer and supplication with thanksgiving let your requests be made known unto God... whatsoever things are true... think on these things." Build a two-column thought record the counselee will use all week: (A) anxious/tempted thought + bodily sensations + urge;

(B) prayer + promise (KJV verse) + planned action. Emphasize gratitude as an active ingredient ("with thanksgiving") and assign memorization of one verse that directly counters the dominant lie.

Step 7 — Fill with the Spirit (practice dependence, not mere determination).

Explain Ephesians 5:18 (KJV): "Be filled with the Spirit"—an ongoing posture, not a one-time event. Coach a simple, repeatable practice: morning consecration (Romans 12:1 language, offered aloud), moment-by-moment breath prayers ("Lord, I receive Your help now"), and evening examen (two questions: "Where did I walk with You?" "Where did I walk away?" followed by confession and thanks). Make clear: self-effort can white-knuckle behaviors, but only the Spirit changes desires (Rom. 8:12–14).

Step 8 — Set godly goals and redeem the time.

Move from vague aspirations to time-bound, visible, and relationally meaningful goals that directly oppose the old pattern. Tie each goal to calling and love of neighbor (Eph. 5:16; Luke 10:27). For example: "By Friday, I will confess to my wife where I've hidden spending and show her our budget; we will pray together and choose one cut to make." Schedule rhythms that make obedience easier (church attendance, one-another relationship, service). The aim is not busyness, but redemption—reclaiming hours, energy, and attention for what pleases God.

Step 9 — Require reparative action where sin harmed others.

Use Zacchaeus (Luke 19) as your template: genuine repentance makes concrete amends. Ask: "Who was affected? What would repair look like?" Plan apology, restitution, and boundary- keeping that protects everyone's good. This step turns repentance from feeling to fruit and often unlocks a stalled process by removing lingering guilt and mistrust.

Step 10 — Build mutual submission and accountable community.

Read Ephesians 5:21 (KJV): "Submitting yourselves one to another in the fear of God." Help the counselee identify two people: one peer for weekly check-ins and one mature believer for pastoral oversight. Set a predictable cadence (same day/time), a fixed agenda (truth-telling, Scripture, prayer, action review), and shared visibility (e.g., spouse knows when meetings happen). Isolation keeps sin powerful; light and love break its spell.

Step 11 — Coach body stewardship that supports the soul.

Because change is holistic, fold in basic body care that reinforces sobriety of mind: fixed sleep window, daily outdoor walk, simple meals that avoid known triggers, and media limits. Frame this as Romans 12:1 worship: presenting the body to God for His purposes. Often, modest physical structure reduces the "ambient chaos" that fuels relapse.

Step 12 — Practice daily gratitude and joy as protective habits.

Joy is not fluff; it's fuel (John 15:11). End every session and every homework plan with a short gratitude practice tied to prayer and Scripture (two things God did today; one person to bless tomorrow). This deliberately satisfies the God-given need for joy in godly ways and makes counterfeit comforts less compelling.

Step 13 — Anticipate temptation and plan redemptive responses.

Design a micro-protocol for the next strong urge: *Notice* (name the trigger aloud), *Narrow* (step away from the cue), *Name* (pray a single verse), *Neighbor* (text/call your person), *New action* (pre-chosen replacement). Rehearse it in session. Encourage the counselee to view every temptation as a training moment to love God more.

Step 14 — Measure progress by fruit, not just frequency.

Track wins, not merely abstinence. Use Galatians 5:22–23 (KJV) as a dashboard: "the fruit of the Spirit is love, joy, peace, longsuffering, gentleness, goodness, faith, meekness, temperance." Ask at each follow-up: Where did this fruit show up? Where is it absent? Celebrate small evidences. Correct course when a fruit is consistently missing (that usually points to a heart-level belief you still need to address with Scripture).

Step 15 — Consolidate identity and commission to service.

As stability grows, circle back to identity ("in Christ," 2 Cor. 5:17) and calling. Encourage the counselee to share a testimony in an appropriate setting and to take one small role in serving others

(2 Tim. 2:2). Biblical change matures as it becomes self-giving—what God poured in now flows out.

A sample first-session flow (putting it together quickly)

You frame the work (Step 1), gather story and separate root from symptom with Scripture light (Step 2), sketch the Five Needs/Conflicts map (Step 3), and invite an Awake/Arise decision with prayer (Step 4). You then build one "put off/renew/put on" plan around a single pattern (Step 5), assign a Philippians 4 thought-record and one memorized verse (Step 6), and teach the Spirit- dependence practices (Step 7). You end by setting one redemptive, time-bound goal tied to love of neighbor (Step 8) and scheduling check-ins (Step 10). Keep homework small, specific, and connected to worship, not willpower.

Core Scriptures to read aloud and assign

- **Romans 12:1–2** — consecration and renewal.
- **Ephesians 4:22–24** — put off/renew/put on.
- **Ephesians 5:13–21** — awake, arise, wisdom, Spirit-filling, submission.
- **Romans 8:12–14** — mortify deeds of the body by the Spirit.
- **Philippians 4:6–9** — prayer, peace, and thought focus.
- **Galatians 5:22–23** — fruit as progress markers.

SUMMARY /CONCLUSION

This section presents a comprehensive framework for understanding how Christ Centered Reality Therapy (CCRT) aligns with Biblical truth to address the roots of mental, emotional, and relational problems. At the heart of this section is the contrast between a self-centered life and a Christ-centered life. The opening of the section discussing the difference between the Christ Centered circle and the Self-Centered circle demonstrate that when the self becomes the focus of life—measured by external fulfillment, possessions, or performance—it leads to dysfunction and abnormality. CCRT emphasizes, in agreement with Scripture, that "there is no normal outside the will of God, only degrees of abnormal." Thus, Biblical normality is defined by alignment with God's design rather than human opinion.

The chapter then turns to The Christian's Deception of External Fulfillment and Understanding Your Problem, showing that people often attempt to meet legitimate God-given needs—survival, love, power, freedom, joy, and the need to know God—through abnormal or worldly wants. This produces false solutions such as addiction, self-indulgence, and religious "doing" without true obedience. Here, the Biblical correlation is clear: Scripture consistently warns against laying up treasures on earth (Matthew 6:19–21) and insists that transformation begins with renewing the mind (Romans 12:2). CCRT echoes this truth by asserting that all behavior stems from belief, and faulty belief systems must be replaced with Biblical truth.

The section also explores the vital distinction between Symptoms or Root Causes. CCRT insists that what many clients present as "the problem" (anxiety, addiction, anger) are merely symptoms of deeper root issues—violations of God's law, misplaced priorities, or distorted belief systems. The Root of Mental Illness and Unbiblical Response to Unmet Want diagrams illustrate how self-centered responses spiral into destructive behaviors, guilt, despair, and brokenness. Counselors are taught not to treat surface problems in isolation but to trace them to their spiritual source. This aligns with James 4:17 and 1 John 2:15–17, which expose sin and worldliness as the true roots of dysfunction.

The practical path forward is laid out in Path to Healing and Wholeness, Counseling Intervention, and the Five Step Counseling Model with 2 Timothy 3:16–17. Here, CCRT integrates doctrine, reproof, correction, and instruction with a step-by-step counseling process that mirrors the Biblical mandate for change. The counselor is guided to confront faulty belief systems, call for repentance, and redirect the counselee toward reconciliation with God, restitution with others, and the rebuilding of life on the foundation of Christ. Biblical examples—David's repentance, the prodigal son's return, Zacchaeus' restitution—serve as vivid illustrations of this process.

Finally, the section's closing subsections on Biblical Change and The Biblical Change Process Integrated with CCRT Principles remind both counselor and counselee that transformation is not merely cognitive or emotional, but spiritual. True change requires repentance, responsibility, and obedience empowered by the Holy Spirit, the Word, prayer, and the church community. For the counselor, this chapter becomes both a diagnostic manual and a therapeutic roadmap: it equips them to discern between symptoms and roots, to apply Scripture faithfully, and to walk with the counselee through the steps of repentance and renewal.

To summarize, Section One teaches that mental and emotional health cannot be divorced from spiritual health. CCRT provides the counselor with a Biblically grounded approach that identifies sin and self-centeredness as the root of dysfunction, and reconciliation with Christ as the only path to true healing. The counselor, therefore, is not simply a facilitator of coping strategies, but a shepherd guiding the counselee back to God's truth, God's design, and the abundant life promised in Christ.

STUDY GUIDE QUESTIONS

Directions: Write a 1-2 paragraph answer for each question.

1. What is the difference between a self-centered life and a Jesus-centered life according to CCRT?
2. How does CCRT define 'normality' and what constitutes abnormality?
3. What dangers are illustrated in the 'Self at Center' diagram?
4. Explain the concept of 'The Christian's Deception of External Fulfillment.'
5. What consequences result from living a self-centered life in terms of relationships and family?
6. How does CCRT explain the root causes of human problems compared to secular counseling models?
7. Why does CCRT emphasize the present rather than the past when addressing problems?
8. How does CCRT connect belief systems with behavior?
9. What does CCRT identify as the root cause of mental illness?
10. Explain the difference between symptoms and root causes of problems.
11. What role does reconciliation through Christ play in resolving problems?
12. List and explain the six human needs identified by CCRT.
13. How can these needs be met Biblically rather than abnormally?
14. What tools does CCRT emphasize for Biblical recovery?
15. How does Philippians 4:4–9 provide a mental health framework consistent with CCRT principles?
16. What does CCRT say about misdirected anger and its consequences?
17. How can Biblical examples such as King Saul, Judas, or David illustrate the dangers of self-centeredness?
18. What does CCRT mean by 'false solutions' to problems, and what are some examples?
19. How does CCRT integrate personal responsibility and free will into the counseling process?
20. What is the ultimate goal of CCRT counseling in terms of transformation and healing?

SECTION V
COUNSELING EXAMPLES

SECTION FIVE- TABLE OF CONTENTS

INTRODUCTION TO SECTION 5

Section 5 of this volume represents an essential and highly intentional component of Christ-Centered Reality Therapy (CCRT). Whereas earlier sections establish the theological framework, define key constructs, and outline the structure of the counseling methodology, Section 5 serves as the applied demonstration of the entire CCRT system. It does not merely summarize principles already discussed; rather, it brings those principles to life by presenting a series of counseling examples constructed around well-known biblical characters. These examples are neither fictional embellishments nor attempts to force modern therapy categories onto ancient lives. Instead, each case functions as a pedagogical tool—an illustration of how counselors may approach real human struggles using the CCRT model, especially when those struggles resemble the situations and emotional tensions described in Scripture. In this way, Section 5 becomes an instructional bridge that connects theoretical understanding to practical, real-world application.

One of the defining strengths of Section 5 is that it demonstrates the remarkable continuity of human struggle across time. Although the biblical narratives occur in vastly different cultural, historical, and social contexts, the emotional conflicts, spiritual failures, and relational ruptures they portray remain strikingly familiar. Fear, anger, guilt, pride, rejection, despair, lust, envy, insecurity, rebellion, and broken relationships—these are the same struggles that people bring into counseling today. Section 5 capitalizes on this continuity by showing how CCRT principles may be applied to individuals whose motivations, decisions, and emotional states mirror those we encounter in Scripture. By doing so, it reminds counselors that the core issues faced by people today are rarely new; rather, they are manifestations of the same heart-level conflicts that Scripture has addressed for millennia.

This section also emphasizes a critical truth for counselors: different problems require different approaches. Even though all human dysfunction ultimately stems from sin, distorted belief, unmet needs, or spiritual misalignment, the pathways into those struggles—and the pathways out—vary significantly from person to person. For example, the approaches used with Elijah in his moment of despair would differ from the approaches used with Jonah in his defiance, or with Samson in his impulsivity, or with Peter in his guilt and restoration. Section 5 demonstrates that effective counseling is not formulaic. It requires discernment, flexibility, and a thorough understanding of the unique relational, emotional, and spiritual dynamics at work in each counselee. Through these diverse examples, counselors learn to select different tools from the CCRT model depending on the counselee's mindset, needs, motivations, and stage of repentance.

One of the major contributions of this section is its illustration of how CCRT handles differences in personality and temperament. The biblical record presents an extraordinary spectrum of dispositions—Jonah's stubbornness, David's emotional sensitivity, Elijah's vulnerability, Samson's impulsive strength, Peter's passionate energy, Saul's insecurity, Martha's anxious busyness, and Thomas's doubt. Section 5 highlights that even when individuals share similar emotional outcomes—such as fear or discouragement—their underlying motivations and belief systems can differ dramatically. This diversity forces the counselor to adapt the CCRT methodology to the person in front of them. For instance, confronting a self-righteous or defiant heart requires more direct confrontation than working with someone who is fragile, grieving, or emotionally depleted. These examples train counselors to avoid one-size-fits-all approaches and instead apply CCRT with the precision and discernment that biblical counseling requires.

Another essential emphasis in Section 5 is the counselor's responsibility to correctly identify whether a counselee's struggle arises from unmet needs, distorted wants, false beliefs, rebellion, or legitimate suffering. The way a counselor addresses each of these categories differs significantly. If an individual is experiencing the consequences of sinful rebellion, the primary goal becomes confrontation, repentance, and reorientation to God's authority. In contrast, someone overwhelmed by emotional fatigue or fear may require reassurance, reframing of beliefs, and a renewed understanding of God's presence. Likewise, a person consumed by guilt needs guidance in confession, accountability, and restoration. Section 5's varied examples show how to accurately diagnose not just what a counselee feels, but why they feel it—and how to respond accordingly. This diagnostic nuance is one of the hallmarks of mature CCRT practice.

Section 5 also reinforces the theological conviction that Scripture provides both the framework and the content for effective counseling. Each biblical example demonstrates how human behavior, choices, and emotional reactions reflect underlying spiritual realities. By walking through these narratives with the lens of CCRT, counselors learn how to identify distorted thinking, unbiblical desires, and relational patterns that violate God's design. They also gain insight into how to apply Scripture directly, meaningfully, and responsibly in therapeutic contexts. Rather than using Scripture as a moralistic tool or a collection of isolated verses, Section 5 illustrates how the entire narrative arc of a person's life can be understood and reframed in light of God's ongoing work of sanctification.

This section also highlights one of the most important principles in counseling: emotional reactions are indicators, not final destinations. Whether a counselee presents with anger, guilt, sadness, anxiety, or relational conflict, these emotions serve as signals pointing to deeper spiritual concerns. Section 5's case studies model how counselors can use these emotional indicators to explore underlying beliefs, unmet needs, or patterns of avoidance. For instance, Elijah's despair reveals a distorted perception of himself, others, and God; Jonah's anger unmasks entitlement and self-righteousness; David's guilt illuminates the destructive consequences of sin; Peter's shame demonstrates how fear and failure can be transformed through grace. By examining these emotional patterns in biblical narratives, counselors learn how to engage with their counselees' emotions in a deeper, more spiritually perceptive manner.

Finally, Section 5 serves as a powerful reminder that counseling is fundamentally redemptive. Each example—whether ending in repentance and restoration or in continued rebellion—illustrates the profound spiritual stakes involved in counseling. The counselor's task is not to create temporary emotional relief but to guide individuals toward truth, responsibility, and transformation. This redemptive purpose shapes the tone and content of the section. Through these case studies, counselors witness both the consequences of ignoring God's design and the freedom that comes from submitting to His truth. These examples underscore the central mission of CCRT: to help people move from self-centeredness to Christ-centeredness, from emotional confusion to spiritual clarity, and from destructive patterns to lives shaped by obedience and renewed hope.

In summary, Section 5 stands as the applied laboratory of Christ-Centered Reality Therapy. It brings together biblical insight, psychological understanding, and counseling methodology in a way that demonstrates the richness and adaptability of the CCRT model. By examining diverse biblical characters and their struggles, counselors are equipped to see how differing issues require differing approaches—and how the consistent application of CCRT principles can lead to profound transformation in the lives of those they serve.

COUNSELING EXAMPLES WITH BIBLICAL CHARACTERS

This section presents a series of counseling examples drawn from the lives of well-known biblical characters. While the story foundations come directly from Scripture, the counseling scenarios themselves are made up and are not intended to alter or rewrite the biblical accounts. Instead, they serve as teaching illustrations of how a counselor might approach people today who struggle with similar issues.

It is important to note that the biblical characters themselves did not always require counseling in the way people do today. Their outcomes, struggles, and victories were directly managed by God in His sovereign plan. Cain's judgment, David's restoration, Jonah's repentance, Peter's denial and restoration, Paul's endurance, and others all unfolded under the unique providence of God.

However, these scenarios allow us to see how Christ Centered Reality Therapy (CCRT), when rooted in God's Word, provides a structured and faithful model of counseling. Unlike worldly systems of psychology that rely on human theories, CCRT is built on spiritual principles grounded in Scripture. It emphasizes responsibility, accountability, truth-telling, repentance, forgiveness, and obedience to God's commands. By using biblical truths, CCRT shows how counselors today can guide individuals toward spiritual growth, healing, and Christ-centered change.

Thus, the examples in this chapter are not historical retellings, but practical illustrations: how CCRT and the Bible together can be applied to the issues of sin, conflict, despair, fear, pride, compromise, and reconciliation that people continue to face today.

ANANIAS AND SAPPHIRA
DECEPTION,AND ACCOUNTABILITY

The account of Ananias and Sapphira in Acts 5:1–11 is one of the most sobering examples of deception and lack of integrity in the early church. The couple sold a possession but conspired to withhold part of the proceeds while pretending to donate the full amount. Peter confronted Ananias, saying, 'Why hath Satan filled thine heart to lie to the Holy Ghost, and to keep back part of the price of the land?' (Acts 5:3, KJV). Both Ananias and Sapphira fell dead after their deception was exposed, demonstrating God's judgment on hypocrisy. This passage illustrates the seriousness of dishonesty and the importance of accountability within the body of Christ.

From a CCRT perspective, their actions reflect chosen abnormal behavior. No one forced them to lie; they deliberately chose deception. Their distorted thinking involved the belief that appearances before people mattered more than integrity before God. CCRT emphasizes correcting such misinformation with truth. For counselors, this case highlights how clients may struggle with image management, fear of judgment, or desire for approval, leading them to conceal or distort reality. The role of the counselor is to redirect them toward honesty and responsibility before God and others.

Accountability is central in this story. Peter confronted their deception directly, holding them accountable for their actions. CCRT teaches that accountability is a Reality Key essential to healthy functioning. In counseling, clients must be taught that lying, half-truths, or hypocrisy not only damage relationships but also separate them from God's blessings. Proverbs 12:22 reminds us: 'Lying lips are abomination to the LORD: but they that deal truly are his delight.' Counselors should reinforce that accountability requires truth-telling and transparency, even when it is difficult.

In a modern counseling setting, individuals with patterns of dishonesty may attempt to justify their actions or minimize their wrongdoing. A counselor must adopt CCRT's directive stance of no excuses, no condemnation, only constant redirection. Practical steps for a plan of success could include practicing daily honesty in small matters, confession of specific lies, and accountability partnerships that encourage integrity. Counselors can also use passages like Ephesians 4:25—'Wherefore putting away lying, speak every man truth with his neighbor: for we are members one of another'—to root clients in biblical truth.

For counselor training, several insights emerge from this example: (1) Deception is always a choice, not a mistake; (2) Fear of people often drives dishonesty; (3) Accountability must be firm and uncompromising; (4) Lies must be replaced with the truth of God's Word; (5) Integrity is essential for spiritual and relational health. New counselors must learn to confront dishonesty with clarity and compassion, while also stressing the seriousness of integrity before God.

The expected outcome for counseling individuals like Ananias and Sapphira would be the cultivation of honesty, integrity, and accountability. Clients would learn to reject image management, embrace transparency, and walk in truth. While their biblical story ended in judgment, counseling scenarios built on their example can teach modern believers that God desires integrity and will bless those who walk in truth. For Christian counselors, this case reinforces the necessity of addressing deception quickly and decisively, guiding clients to live in alignment with God's truth.

Counseling Scenario: Ananias & Sapphira

Deceit, Greed, and Integrity

Purpose: To demonstrate how Christ Centered Reality Therapy (CCRT) would address the deceit and greed of Ananias and Sapphira, guiding them toward responsibility, accountability, repentance, and integrity according to God's Word (KJV).

Presenting Problem & Context

Clients: Ananias and Sapphira. Context: In Acts 5:1–11, this couple sold land and deceitfully held back part of the price while pretending to give the full amount to the apostles. Their sin was not in keeping money but in lying to the Holy Ghost, revealing greed, hypocrisy, and lack of accountability. Their deception led to immediate judgment from God.

CCRT Formulation

• Five Needs involved: Survival (money kept back), Power/Self-worth (desire to look generous), Love/Belonging (seeking approval of church), Joy (distorted by dishonesty).

• Five Conflicts involved: Money (withheld funds), Religion (lying in worship), Extended Family/Community (deceiving church fellowship).

• Choice and Responsibility: The couple chose deceit. CCRT emphasizes abnormality begins when a person chooses a lie or unhealthy want over truth and responsibility.

• Accountability: They resisted accountability, conspiring together in secrecy. CCRT stresses that accountability is essential to sustain truth and integrity.

Session Goals

1) Confront deceit and greed as chosen behaviors, not accidental or justified.

2) Lead them to repentance, confession, and restoration of integrity (Proverbs 28:13; 1 John 1:9).

3) Build accountability safeguards to ensure honesty in finances and fellowship.

4) Replace hypocrisy with transparency, aligning with God's holiness.

Counseling Dialogue (Role-Play)

Therapist: Ananias and Sapphira, tell me why you held back part of the money while pretending to give all.

Ananias: We wanted to keep some for ourselves, but we also wanted others to think we were fully generous.

Therapist: That was a choice of deceit. CCRT teaches abnormality is always chosen, and 'We control all of our choices'. How do you see your responsibility?

Sapphira: We lied together. We thought no one would know.

Therapist: But God knows. Acts 5:4 says, 'Thou hast not lied unto men, but unto God.' Proverbs 12:22 says, 'Lying lips are abomination to the LORD: but they that deal truly are his delight.' What needs to change?

Ananias: We must repent and stop lying.

Therapist: Yes. Proverbs 28:13 says, 'He that covereth his sins shall not prosper: but whoso confesseth and forsaketh them shall have mercy.' What steps of accountability could help?

Sapphira: We could involve trusted elders to check our giving and keep us honest.

Therapist: Good. Accountability structures prevent relapse into secrecy. Ephesians 4:25 commands, 'Wherefore putting away lying, speak every man truth with his neighbour.' Let's build a plan for integrity.

Intervention Plan (CCRT Plan of Success)

1) Repentance & Renewal: Confess deceit to God and seek mercy (1 John 1:9; Psalm 32:5).

2) Accountability Structure: Appoint elders for financial accountability; report regularly with honesty (James 5:16; Proverbs 27:17).

3) Replacement Behaviors: Replace secrecy with transparency—share truthfully with the church body (Ephesians 4:25). Replace greed with generosity (2 Corinthians 9:7).

4) Measurable Goals: Maintain written record of giving and financial choices; review with accountability partner monthly.

5) Long-term Maintenance: Celebrate milestones of integrity; watch for relapse signs—secrecy, hypocrisy, rationalization.

CCRT Principles Applied

• Abnormal behavior is a chosen pattern; responsibility is personal.

• Accountability is a Reality Key to normality; supportive accountability ensures honesty.

• Plans must be specific, realistic, and measurable.

• Directive, no-excuses stance: accountability and redirection without condemnation.

• Early tracking: name the problem, recognize recurrence, act quickly.

Key KJV Scriptures Used

Acts 5:1–11; Acts 5:4; Proverbs 12:22; Proverbs 28:13; 1 John 1:9; Psalm 32:5; Ephesians 4:25; 2 Corinthians 9:7; James 5:16; Proverbs 27:17.

Expected Outcomes

Ananias and Sapphira recognize deceit and greed as sin, repent, and commit to transparency. Through accountability and renewed integrity, they replace hypocrisy with honesty and greed with generosity, aligning their actions with God's holiness and the Spirit's truth.

CAIN
ANGER, AND REPENTANCE

The account of Cain in Genesis 4 provides one of the clearest biblical pictures of how unresolved anger, distorted thinking, and a refusal to accept responsibility can lead to destructive choices. Cain and his brother Abel both brought offerings to the Lord, but Abel's was accepted while Cain's was rejected. Scripture records Cain's emotional response: 'Cain was very wroth, and his countenance fell' (Genesis 4:5, KJV). Rather than examining his own heart, Cain allowed jealousy and resentment to grow. The Lord confronted Cain with accountability and hope, saying, 'If thou doest well, shalt thou not be accepted? and if thou doest not well, sin lieth at the door. And unto thee shall be his desire, and thou shalt rule over him' (Genesis 4:7). This statement demonstrates both responsibility and choice—Cain had the ability to redirect his emotions and behavior. Tragically, instead of responding to God's invitation, Cain surrendered to sin and murdered his brother.

From a CCRT perspective, Cain illustrates the principle that all abnormal behavior is chosen. Anger in itself is not sin, but what Cain chose to do with it became destructive. He refused accountability and projected blame outward rather than inward. CCRT emphasizes accountability as a Reality Key to normality, yet Cain rejected the accountability offered by God Himself. A counselor working with someone like Cain would focus on clarifying the difference between feelings and choices. Emotions may be intense, but responsibility lies in how a person chooses to act upon them. Counselors must help clients see that excuses, blame-shifting, and denial are obstacles to growth.

Cain's thinking also demonstrates how misinformation can dominate decision-making. He believed that Abel was the source of his frustration, when in reality the true issue was his own heart before God. CCRT stresses correcting misinformation with truth. For new counselors, the lesson is clear: when clients externalize blame, it is essential to bring them back to personal responsibility. Scripture such as James 1:20— 'For the wrath of man worketh not the righteousness of God'—helps anchor clients in truth, showing that anger does not justify destructive behavior. The counselor's role is to guide clients toward repentance and confession, reminding them that God's correction is an act of love, not rejection.

In practical counseling, Cain's case shows the importance of early intervention. God warned him before the sin occurred, demonstrating the principle of prevention. CCRT also teaches that plans of success must be specific, measurable, and achievable. For someone like Cain, a counselor would encourage specific steps such as acknowledging feelings honestly in prayer, seeking constructive outlets for frustration, and replacing lies with affirmations of God's truth. Accountability could be built through community support or spiritual mentors who reinforce positive choices. The emphasis is on redirection rather than condemnation.

For training purposes, new counselors should note several key insights from Cain's example: (1) Always distinguish between feelings and choices; (2) Address blame-shifting quickly and firmly with truth; (3) Use Scripture to expose lies and guide repentance; (4) Establish accountability structures that reinforce obedience; (5) Remind counselees that responsibility and repentance lead to restoration, while denial and rebellion lead to further bondage. Cain refused God's invitation to change, but counselees today can be guided to respond differently.

The expected outcome of counseling someone like Cain would be a redirection of emotions toward repentance and obedience. Instead of blaming others, the counselee would learn to accept responsibility, replace misinformation with biblical truth, and live under accountability to God and trusted spiritual mentors. For Christian counselors, the key lesson is that God always provides an open door for change. The counselor's task is to help clients see that door, step through it, and choose responsibility in obedience to Christ.

Counseling Scenario: Cain

Anger, Envy, and Personal Responsibility

Purpose: Demonstrate how Christ Centered Reality Therapy (CCRT) operates in-session to move a client from blame and envy to responsibility, accountability, repentance, and obedience to God's Word (KJV).

Presenting Problem & Context

Client: Cain. Context: God regarded Abel's offering but did not regard Cain's. Cain is angry and downcast (Genesis 4:5–7, KJV). He frames his distress as Abel's fault and God's unfairness, fixating on perceived injustice.

CCRT Formulation

• Five Needs involved: Power/Self-worth (threatened), Love/Belonging (sibling rupture), Freedom (asserting will vs. God's will), Joy (stolen by envy).

• Five Conflicts involved: Extended Family (brother), Religion (offerings/obedience to God), possibly Money/Provision (offering quality), Children/Sex (future family fallout risk).

• Choice and Responsibility: CCRT teaches that abnormal behavior is a matter of choice and that we control our choices; thus Cain must own his responses rather than externalize blame.

• Accountability: A CCRT Reality Key. Accountability structures (family/faith community) support change without control or condemnation.

Session Goals

1) Help Cain accept responsibility for his attitudes (anger/envy) and choices before God.

2) Establish accountability supports and a specific plan of success to replace envy with obedience and right worship.

3) Lead Cain to repentance and renewed obedience (Genesis 4:7; Acts 3:19; 1 John 1:9).

Counseling Dialogue (Role-Play)

Therapist: Cain, tell me what happened with your offering and how you're feeling now.

Cain: God took Abel's gift, not mine. It's not right. Abel makes me look bad. I'm angry.

Therapist: Your feelings are real, but feelings don't have to rule choices. In CCRT we look at choices and responsibility. What choices are you making with this anger? (cf. Romans 14:12; Galatians 6:5).

Cain: I can't help it. This is on Abel and on God's unfairness.

Therapist: Scripture records God's counsel to you: 'If thou doest well, shalt thou not be accepted? and if thou doest not well, sin lieth at the door…' (Genesis 4:7). God puts the decision in front of you. What would 'doing well' look like today?

Cain: Maybe I should fix my offering? But I still feel envy.

Therapist: Envy corrodes the heart: 'A sound heart is the life of the flesh: but envy the rottenness of the bones' (Proverbs 14:30). 'He that is slow to anger is better than the mighty…' (Proverbs 16:32). Let's own the envy and anger, not excuse them.

Cain: So I'm responsible for how I respond, even if I feel wronged.

Therapist: Yes. CCRT says abnormal patterns are chosen and can be replaced with new choices. We also build accountability so you're not alone. God invited you to master the sin at the door (Genesis 4:7). What step aligns with obedience right now?

Cain: I need to repent of envy and anger, and bring an acceptable offering in faith (cf. Hebrews 11:4).

Therapist: Good. Repentance means turning from sin to God. We'll create a plan: confession to God (1 John 1:9), reconciliation steps with Abel if safe and appropriate (Matthew 5:23–24), and a new pattern of worship that honors God's instruction.

Cain: I'll do it. But I'll need help staying on track.

Therapist: That's accountability—one of CCRT's keys to normality. Choose a godly mentor or elder to check in with you (Ecclesiastes 4:9–12; Proverbs 27:17). We'll set achievable goals and celebrate obedience, not punish lapses.

Intervention Plan (CCRT Plan of Success)

1) Repentance & Worship Reset (Today): Confess envy/anger before God (Psalm 139:23–24; 1 John 1:9). Offer an acceptable sacrifice in obedience and faith (Genesis 4:7; Hebrews 11:4).

2) Accountability Structure (Within 24 hours): Identify a same-sex mentor/elder as an accountability partner; daily check-in for two weeks; weekly in-person review (James 5:16; Hebrews 10:24–25).

3) Replacement Behaviors for Anger/Envy (Immediate): When triggered, pause–pray–choose. Recite James 1:19–20; Proverbs 16:32. Offer thanks for Abel's faithfulness (Romans 12:10).

4) Reconciliation Steps (As soon as possible and safe): Seek peace with Abel; acknowledge resentment; express commitment to obedience (Matthew 5:23–24; Romans 12:18).

5) Measurement & Review (Weekly, 4 weeks): Track triggers, choices, outcomes; celebrate obedience milestones; adjust plan quickly if relapse indicators appear.

CCRT Principles Applied

• Choice & Responsibility: 'We control all of our choices'; abnormal behavior is a chosen pattern.

• Accountability: 'Accountability is a Reality Key to normality' and should focus on celebration of goals, not punishment.

• Specific Plan: 'The plan of success is always very specific and includes achievable goals'.

• Directive, No-Excuses Stance with No Condemnation: 'Reality Therapy stresses accountability and no excuses… no condemnation, only constant redirection.

• Early Tracking & Warning Signs: Name the problem, recognize recurrence, know what to watch; intervene early.

Key KJV Scriptures Used

Genesis 4:5–7; Proverbs 14:30; Proverbs 16:32; James 1:19–20; Romans 14:12; Galatians 6:5; Psalm 139:23–24; 1 John 1:9; Matthew 5:23–24; Romans 12:18; Hebrews 11:4; Ecclesiastes 4:9–12; Proverbs 27:17; Hebrews 10:24–25.

Expected Outcomes

Cain practices obedience through an acceptable offering, replaces envy with gratitude and self-control, repairs relationship rupture, and sustains change through accountability. Progress is measured by concrete behaviors, not feelings alone.

DAVID
SIN, REPENTANCE, AND RESTORATION

The story of King David demonstrates both the depths of human failure and the possibility of restoration through repentance. David, described as a man after God's own heart, nevertheless fell into grievous sin by committing adultery with Bathsheba and orchestrating the death of her husband, Uriah (2 Samuel 11). For a time, David concealed his sin, attempting to maintain appearances, but inwardly he was wasting away. Later, in Psalm 32:3–4, David confessed, 'When I kept silence, my bones waxed old through my roaring all the day long. For day and night thy hand was heavy upon me: my moisture is turned into the drought of summer.' His experience illustrates how guilt and unconfessed sin create psychological, emotional, and spiritual distress.

From a CCRT perspective, David's situation shows how choices, not circumstances, determine outcomes. Abnormal behavior is chosen, and responsibility must be accepted. David chose lust, deception, and violence, but he also chose repentance when confronted by Nathan the prophet. In Psalm 51, David's prayer reveals the heart of confession: 'Have mercy upon me, O God, according to thy lovingkindness: according unto the multitude of thy tender mercies blot out my transgressions' (Psalm 51:1). For new counselors, this shows that even those with strong faith can fall, but recovery depends on accepting responsibility rather than hiding sin.

A central theme of David's restoration is accountability. Nathan provided the confrontation David needed by telling him, 'Thou art the man' (2 Samuel 12:7). CCRT teaches that accountability is a Reality Key to normality. In counseling, the role of accountability is to provide truth and direction without condemnation. The counselor's responsibility is to create an environment where the client can admit wrongdoing and choose a new path. Just as Nathan directed David toward repentance, so too must counselors guide clients from denial and excuses to confession and change.

David also illustrates the principle of correcting misinformation with truth. At first, David believed the lie that his sin could be covered up, but the truth was that 'be sure your sin will find you out' (Numbers 32:23). A counselor today would need to confront the lie of concealment and show that forgiveness and healing come only through confession (1 John 1:9). For new counselors, David's case is a reminder that people often come to counseling weighed down by hidden guilt, and the task is to help them bring sin into the light of God's Word.

Practical counseling with someone like David would involve leading them through confession, repentance, and a plan for restoration. The counselor might encourage journaling prayers of confession, memorizing passages such as Psalm 51, and establishing accountability partners to avoid repeated failure. The plan of success must be specific and achievable, with clear spiritual practices that rebuild integrity. For example, daily Scripture meditation, accountability meetings, and prayer focused on purity and honesty can provide measurable steps toward growth.

For training purposes, new counselors should note several lessons: (1) Sin brings inner turmoil until confessed; (2) Confrontation, when done biblically, can bring repentance; (3) Accountability is essential for lasting change; (4) Lies of concealment must be replaced with truth; (5) Restoration requires ongoing spiritual practices. These insights equip counselors to walk with clients through failure and into restoration, always pointing them to Christ's mercy.

The expected outcome for counseling someone like David would be deep repentance, renewed joy in God's presence, and accountability that guards against relapse. Psalm 51:12 records David's cry, 'Restore unto me the joy of thy salvation; and uphold me with thy free spirit.' When counselees follow this path, they move from guilt and shame into freedom and restoration. For Christian counselors, David's example is a powerful reminder that even grievous sin can be forgiven, and God can bring beauty from brokenness when responsibility, accountability, and repentance are embraced.

Counseling Scenario: King David

Lust, Deceit, and Repentance

Purpose: To demonstrate how Christ Centered Reality Therapy (CCRT) addresses King David's fall into lust, deceit, and cover-up, guiding him toward responsibility, accountability, repentance, and renewed obedience to God's Word (KJV).

Presenting Problem & Context

Client: King David. Context: In 2 Samuel 11, David lusts after Bathsheba, commits adultery, and arranges the death of her husband Uriah to conceal his sin. These choices reflect unchecked desire, abuse of power, and deceit. Though a man after God's heart, David fell gravely and needed confrontation and repentance (see 2 Samuel 12).

CCRT Formulation

• Five Needs involved: Love/Belonging (distorted into lust), Power/Self-worth (abuse of authority), Joy (seeking pleasure over righteousness).

• Five Conflicts involved: Sex (adultery), Extended Family (impact on Uriah, household), Religion (defying God's commands).

• Choice and Responsibility: David must own his choices. CCRT stresses that abnormal wants (lust, deceit) are learned and chosen behaviors.

• Accountability: David initially avoided accountability by covering sin. In CCRT, accountability is a Reality Key that fosters confession, measurable goals, and encouragement.

Session Goals

1) Help David admit lust and deceit as personal responsibility, not circumstances or power privilege.

2) Guide him to repentance, confession, and reconciliation with God (Psalm 51).

3) Establish accountability safeguards to prevent relapse into lustful choices.

4) Build a specific plan for obedience, replacing lust with purity and deceit with integrity.

Counseling Dialogue (Role-Play)

Therapist: David, tell me about the events with Bathsheba and Uriah.

David: I saw her, I desired her, and I took her. Then I tried to cover it up by sending Uriah to the front lines (2 Samuel 11:2–17).

Therapist: These were choices. CCRT teaches, 'We control all of our choices'. How do you see your responsibility?

David: I misused my power. I let lust guide me.

Therapist: Yes. James 1:14–15 warns, 'But every man is tempted, when he is drawn away of his own lust, and enticed. Then when lust hath conceived, it bringeth forth sin…' How has lust enticed you?

David: It blinded me. I thought only of myself.

Therapist: That blindness also led to deceit. Proverbs 28:13 says, 'He that covereth his sins shall not prosper: but whoso confesseth and forsaketh them shall have mercy.' What needs to change today?

David: I must repent before God and confess my sin, like Nathan confronted me (2 Samuel 12:7–13).

Therapist: Good. Accountability helps sustain repentance. Who will help keep you from secret sin? Trusted men of faith?

David: Yes, I need faithful accountability partners. I can't hide sin any longer.

Therapist: Excellent. Repentance is not just confession but turning. Psalm 51:10–12 records your prayer: 'Create in me a clean heart, O God; and renew a right spirit within me.' Let's set a plan for obedience and accountability.

Intervention Plan (CCRT Plan of Success)

1) Repentance & Renewal: Confess sins openly to God (Psalm 32:5; 1 John 1:9). Pray Psalm 51 daily for renewal.

2) Accountability Structure: Commit to trusted spiritual elders for weekly accountability check-ins (James 5:16; Proverbs 27:17).

3) Replacement Behaviors: Replace lust with disciplined worship and focus on God's Word (Job 31:1; Matthew 5:8). Replace deceit with truth-telling (Ephesians 4:25).

4) Measurable Goals: Record moments of temptation and responses daily. Share with accountability partner for review.

5) Long-term Maintenance: Celebrate obedience milestones. Track relapse indicators such as secrecy, isolation, or rationalization.

CCRT Principles Applied

• Abnormal wants/behaviors are chosen; responsibility is personal.

• Accountability is a Reality Key to normality; celebrate obedience, not punish failure.

• Plans must be specific and realistic with achievable goals.

• Directive, no-excuses stance: accountability and redirection without condemnation.

• Early intervention and tracking: name the problem, recognize recurrence, watch for relapse signs.

Key KJV Scriptures Used

2 Samuel 11:2–17; 2 Samuel 12:7–13; James 1:14–15; Proverbs 28:13; Psalm 51:10–12; Psalm 32:5; 1 John 1:9; Job 31:1; Matthew 5:8; Ephesians 4:25; Proverbs 27:17; James 5:16.

Expected Outcomes

David takes ownership of his sin, repents sincerely, and begins rebuilding integrity. Through accountability and spiritual renewal, he learns to replace lust with purity, deceit with truth, and relapse patterns with obedience and joy in God.

DEMAS
WORLDLINESS AND LOST FOCUS

The story of Demas is a sobering reminder of how love for the world can draw believers away from faithful service. Demas is mentioned positively as a fellow laborer with Paul in Colossians 4:14 and Philemon 1:24, where he is listed among a circle of faithful companions that included Luke and Mark. However, in 2 Timothy 4:10 Paul lamented, 'For Demas hath forsaken me, having loved this present world, and is departed unto Thessalonica' (KJV). Demas' trajectory—from faithful service alongside great leaders to abandoning the mission—illustrates the danger of divided loyalty and misplaced affection.

From a CCRT perspective, Demas' departure reveals a choice rooted in misplaced values. Christ Centered Reality Therapy emphasizes that behavior is always chosen. Demas chose the temporary pleasures of the world over the hardship and sacrifice of ministry. His distorted thinking equated worldly security and comfort with greater value than eternal reward. CCRT stresses correcting such misinformation with truth. For counselors, Demas represents clients who rationalize compromise by convincing themselves that worldly pursuits will bring satisfaction, when in fact such choices erode spiritual integrity.

Accountability is a critical lesson from Demas' fall. While he once thrived in the company of faithful believers, he ultimately abandoned accountability to Paul, to the mission, and to Christ. CCRT identifies accountability as a Reality Key necessary for maintaining direction and spiritual health. In counseling, clients drifting toward worldliness must be challenged to re-establish accountability relationships that encourage obedience and perseverance. Scriptures such as 1 John 2:15— 'Love not the world, neither the things that are in the world'—remind counselees that worldly affections are incompatible with devotion to Christ.

In a counseling session, a client like Demas might confess feelings of exhaustion, disillusionment, or attraction to worldly pleasures. A counselor guided by CCRT would validate the struggle but redirect focus toward eternal priorities. Questions such as, 'What are you seeking in the world that you feel God is not providing?' can expose faulty beliefs. Scripture like Matthew 6:33— 'But seek ye first the kingdom of God, and his righteousness; and all these things shall be added unto you'—anchors the client in God's provision. The plan of success must include specific and measurable steps such as reducing worldly influences, engaging in daily spiritual disciplines, and reconnecting with accountability partners. CCRT insists on achievable, measurable plans for lasting change.

For counselor training, Demas' example provides several insights: (1) Even faithful workers can drift when worldly love grows unchecked; (2) Distorted values must be confronted with truth; (3) Accountability structures are essential to sustain long-term faithfulness; (4) Counselors must recognize the subtle appeal of comfort and help clients redirect their desires; (5) Restoration requires repentance and re-engagement in Christ's mission. By integrating truth and accountability, counselors can guide clients away from compromise and back toward obedience.

The expected outcome for counseling someone like Demas would be recognition of misplaced values, repentance from worldliness, and renewed focus on eternal priorities. With accountability and truth, such a counselee could be restored to faithful service. For Christian counselors, Demas' example serves as a warning but also an opportunity: to guide those drifting toward the world back to Christ-centered commitment.

Counseling Scenario: Demas

Worldliness, Abandonment, and Restoration

Purpose: To demonstrate how Christ Centered Reality Therapy (CCRT) would address Demas' decision to forsake Paul because of love for the present world (2 Timothy 4:10), guiding him toward responsibility, accountability, repentance, and restoration in obedience to God's Word (KJV).

Presenting Problem & Context

Client: Demas. Context: Demas was once a trusted companion of Paul, mentioned with Luke and Mark as part of Paul's inner circle (Colossians 4:14; Philemon 1:24). Despite his privileged ministry role, Demas abandoned Paul and the mission, 'having loved this present world' (2 Timothy 4:10). His problem was worldliness, misplaced values, and forsaking accountability within a strong spiritual community.

CCRT Formulation

• Five Needs involved: Love/Belonging (desire for worldly acceptance), Power/Self-worth (seeking status apart from sacrifice), Joy (seeking comfort/pleasure over mission).

• Five Conflicts involved: Religion (forsaking mission), Extended Family/Community (leaving Paul and fellow workers).

• Choice and Responsibility: Demas chose to depart. CCRT teaches that abnormal patterns are chosen and must be owned.

• Accountability: Demas rejected the accountability of Paul's circle. CCRT emphasizes accountability as a Reality Key to normality, requiring fellowship and encouragement.

Session Goals

1) Help Demas acknowledge responsibility for loving the world and forsaking the mission.

2) Lead him to repentance and restoration in obedience to Christ's call (Luke 9:62).

3) Reestablish accountability within faithful fellowship rather than isolation.

4) Replace worldliness with eternal perspective and faithfulness to ministry.

Counseling Dialogue (Role-Play)

Therapist: Demas, you once traveled with Paul, Luke, and Mark—faithful men of God (Colossians 4:14; Philemon 1:24). What happened?

Demas: I grew weary of sacrifice. I longed for comfort. I loved the present world more (2 Timothy 4:10).

Therapist: That was a choice. CCRT teaches, 'We control all of our choices'. How do you see your responsibility in leaving the mission?

Demas: I chose to walk away. I left my calling and my accountability.

Therapist: Yes. James 4:4 warns, 'Whosoever therefore will be a friend of the world is the enemy of God.' How has worldliness affected your faith?

Demas: It weakened me. I became distant from God and my brothers.

Therapist: Exactly. Worldliness promises comfort but robs calling. 1 John 2:15 says, 'Love not the world, neither the things that are in the world.' What steps of repentance do you need to take?

Demas: I must repent and return to fellowship, choosing eternal priorities.

Therapist: Good. Repentance is turning from love of the world to love for God. Accountability will help you stay faithful. Who could walk with you in restoration?

Demas: Faithful brothers like Luke or Mark could hold me accountable.

Therapist: Yes. Accountability is a Reality Key. Fellowship strengthens perseverance (Hebrews 10:24–25). Let's set a plan to rebuild integrity and faithfulness.

Intervention Plan (CCRT Plan of Success)

1) Repentance & Renewal: Confess love of the world; recommit to God's mission (1 John 1:9; Luke 9:62).

2) Accountability Structure: Rejoin fellowship with faithful believers like Luke and Mark; weekly check-ins (Proverbs 27:17; James 5:16).

3) Replacement Behaviors: Replace worldly pursuits with spiritual disciplines (Colossians 3:1–2; Matthew 6:33).

4) Measurable Goals: Track daily prayer, scripture meditation, and ministry acts; review with accountability partners.

5) Long-term Maintenance: Celebrate obedience and perseverance; watch for relapse signs such as isolation, distraction, or desire for worldly approval.

CCRT Principles Applied

• Abnormal behaviors are chosen; responsibility is personal.

• Accountability is a Reality Key to normality; faithful fellowship ensures perseverance.

• Plans must be specific, measurable, and achievable.

• Directive, no-excuses stance: accountability and redirection without condemnation.

• Early tracking: name the problem, recognize recurrence, act quickly to prevent relapse.

Key KJV Scriptures Used

Colossians 4:14; Philemon 1:24; 2 Timothy 4:10; James 4:4; 1 John 2:15; Luke 9:62; Colossians 3:1–2; Matthew 6:33; Hebrews 10:24–25; Proverbs 27:17; James 5:16; 1 John 1:9 1 John 2:15-17.

Expected Outcomes

Demas admits responsibility for forsaking the mission out of worldliness, repents, and restores fellowship. Through accountability with faithful brothers and renewed focus on eternal priorities, he learns to resist worldly distractions and persevere in God's call.

ELIJAH
FEAR, DEPRESSION, AND RESTORATION

The prophet Elijah provides a powerful example of how even strong spiritual leaders can fall into despair when fatigue, fear, and misinformation overwhelm their perspective. After his dramatic victory over the prophets of Baal on Mount Carmel (1 Kings 18), Elijah fled into the wilderness when Jezebel threatened his life. Exhausted and discouraged, he sat under a juniper tree and prayed that he might die: 'It is enough; now, O LORD, take away my life; for I am not better than my fathers' (1 Kings 19:4, KJV). Despite having experienced God's power, Elijah's faulty thinking led him to believe that he was utterly alone and that his work was in vain. This downward spiral reveals how misinformation and abandonment of God's placement can distort perspective.

From a CCRT perspective, Elijah demonstrates the need to address misinformation and correct distorted thinking. Elijah believed lies such as, 'I am alone,' and 'My work has accomplished nothing.' In reality, God reminded him that 7,000 in Israel had not bowed to Baal (1 Kings 19:18). CCRT teaches that counselors must help clients replace lies with truth, recognizing that despair often stems from false beliefs. For counselors, Elijah's case shows the importance of listening carefully for underlying misinformation that drives hopelessness.

Another significant lesson from Elijah's story is the role of exhaustion and misplaced focus. Elijah abandoned the place God had put him and distanced himself from others, fueling his isolation. God responded with physical care—sending food, water, and rest through an angel (1 Kings 19:5–8). This illustrates the CCRT principle of addressing practical needs as part of restoring normal functioning. For new counselors, it is important to note that spiritual despair is often intertwined with physical depletion, and addressing both can lead to renewal.

Accountability and reorientation also played a key role in Elijah's restoration. God spoke to him not in the wind, earthquake, or fire, but in a still small voice (1 Kings 19:12), reminding him of His presence and guidance. Elijah was then given new assignments, including anointing kings and a successor, Elisha. This demonstrates CCRT's Reality Key of accountability and goal-setting. In counseling, a client experiencing despair must be redirected to purposeful, God-given tasks that restore meaning and accountability.

In practical counseling, Elijah's case encourages the counselor to ask questions such as: 'What lies are you believing about your situation?' and 'What truths from Scripture counter those lies?' Passages like Isaiah 41:10— 'Fear thou not; for I am with thee: be not dismayed; for I am thy God: I will strengthen thee; yea, I will help thee; yea, I will uphold thee with the right hand of my righteousness'—help anchor clients in truth. A plan of success for someone like Elijah would include restoring healthy routines (sleep, nourishment, prayer), reconnecting with accountability partners, and setting achievable spiritual goals to redirect focus. CCRT emphasizes that these plans be specific and measurable.

For counselor training, Elijah's experience highlights several insights: (1) Even faithful leaders can experience despair; (2) Misinformation must be corrected with biblical truth; (3) Physical and emotional care is part of counseling; (4) Accountability and new goals restore purpose; (5) God's presence and Word are the ultimate anchors for renewal. Counselors must be alert to signs of hopelessness, yet always guide clients to the reality of God's presence and the hope found in His promises.

The expected outcome for counseling someone like Elijah would be a renewed sense of hope, restored physical and emotional strength, and re-engagement in meaningful service. Through correction of lies, restoration of accountability, and reassurance of God's presence, clients can move from despair to renewed purpose. Elijah's story assures both counselors and counselees that God does not abandon His servants in their weakness, but restores them for continued ministry.

Counseling Scenario: Elijah

Fear, Depression, and Restoration

Purpose: To demonstrate how Christ Centered Reality Therapy (CCRT) addresses Elijah's fear, discouragement, and distorted thinking in 1 Kings 19, guiding him toward responsibility, accountability, repentance, and restoration through God's truth (KJV).

Presenting Problem & Context

Client: Elijah. Context: After the victory at Mount Carmel (1 Kings 18), Elijah fled into the wilderness in fear of Jezebel's threat. He became discouraged, isolated himself, abandoned his post, and asked God to take his life (1 Kings 19:4). He also misinformed himself, claiming he was the only faithful one left (1 Kings 19:10), reflecting faulty thinking, self-pity, and despair. God confronted him, provided for his needs, corrected his misinformation, and restored him to his mission.

CCRT Formulation

• Five Needs involved: Survival (fear of Jezebel's threat), Love/Belonging (feeling isolated), Power/Self-worth (feeling ineffective), Joy (lost in despair).

• Five Conflicts involved: Religion (loss of perspective in ministry), Extended Family/Community (feeling abandoned by Israel).

• Choice and Responsibility: Elijah fled his post and indulged lies about being alone. CCRT stresses that even in discouragement, choices must be owned.

• Accountability: Elijah abandoned his place and support. CCRT emphasizes accountability as a Reality Key to normality—restoring perspective through God's Word, community, and achievable steps.

Session Goals

1) Help Elijah identify and confront faulty thinking and lies he told himself.

2) Restore truth: he was not alone, God still had a remnant, and his mission remained.

3) Rebuild accountability with God's direction, proper placement, and supportive partnerships (Elisha).

4) Replace fear and discouragement with renewed perspective, obedience, and joy in God's mission.

Counseling Dialogue (Role-Play)

Therapist: Elijah, after such a great victory on Mount Carmel, why did you run into the wilderness?

Elijah: Jezebel threatened to kill me. I was afraid. I left my servant and went alone (1 Kings 19:3–4).

Therapist: That was a choice. CCRT teaches that abnormal responses are chosen, and 'We control all of our choices'. What responsibility do you see in leaving your post and isolating yourself?

Elijah: I abandoned the place God put me. I felt overwhelmed.

Therapist: Yes. You also told yourself, 'I, even I only, am left' (1 Kings 19:10). That was misinformation. In truth, God had preserved 7,000 who had not bowed to Baal (1 Kings 19:18). How does that correction change your outlook?

Elijah: I wasn't as alone as I thought. I had believed a lie.

Therapist: Exactly. Faulty thinking leads to despair. Proverbs 23:7 says, 'For as he thinketh in his heart, so is he.' How might renewed thinking bring hope?

Elijah: If I remember God's truth, I can endure. He is still in control.

Therapist: Right. God restored you with nourishment and a gentle voice (1 Kings 19:5–12). He reassigned you and provided Elisha as a companion. Accountability structures restore perspective and prevent relapse. Who can help hold you accountable now?

Elijah: Elisha. God placed him with me to continue the mission together.

Therapist: Good. Accountability is a Reality Key. With restored placement, partnership, and God's truth, you can walk in renewed strength and obedience (Isaiah 40:31).

Intervention Plan (CCRT Plan of Success)

1) Repentance & Renewal: Confess faulty thinking and despair; embrace God's truth (Psalm 42:5; 1 John 1:9).

2) Accountability Structure: Reconnect with Elisha as partner; stay aligned with God's mission (Ecclesiastes 4:9–10; Proverbs 27:17).

3) Replacement Behaviors: Replace lies ('I am alone') with truth (Romans 11:4). Replace fear with trust in God's power (Psalm 27:1).

4) Measurable Goals: Journal daily truths countering lies; share weekly with accountability partner.

5) Long-term Maintenance: Celebrate restored mission steps; watch for relapse signs—self-pity, misinformation, abandonment of God's post.

CCRT Principles Applied

• Abnormal responses are chosen; responsibility is personal.

• Accountability is a Reality Key to normality; supportive accountability restores placement and perspective.

• Plans must be specific, realistic, and achievable.

• Directive, no-excuses stance: accountability and redirection without condemnation.

• Early intervention: name the problem, recognize recurrence, correct misinformation quickly.

Key KJV Scriptures Used

1 Kings 19:3–18; Proverbs 23:7; Psalm 42:5; Isaiah 40:31; Psalm 27:1; Romans 11:4; Ecclesiastes 4:9–10; Proverbs 27:17; 1 John 1:9.

Expected Outcomes

Elijah recognizes fear, discouragement, and misinformation as distortions, repents, and embraces God's truth. With accountability through Elisha, restored placement, and renewed perspective, he overcomes despair and continues faithfully in God's mission.

HAGAR
REJECTION, DESPAIR, AND GOD WHO SEES

The story of Hagar, found in Genesis 16 and 21, illustrates the struggles of rejection, despair, and abandonment, as well as the hope that comes from God's presence. Hagar, an Egyptian servant, bore Abraham a son after Sarah's suggestion. However, once Isaac was born, Sarah demanded that Abraham cast Hagar and her son Ishmael out. In the wilderness, overwhelmed and hopeless, Hagar placed Ishmael under a shrub and wept, unable to watch him die. At that moment, God intervened. Genesis 21:17 records, 'And God heard the voice of the lad; and the angel of God called to Hagar out of heaven, and said unto her, what aileth thee, Hagar? fear not; for God hath heard the voice of the lad where he is' (KJV). God revealed Himself to Hagar as El Roi, the God who sees, offering comfort and provision.

From a CCRT perspective, Hagar's story reflects how despair often arises from misinformation and distorted thinking. Hagar believed the lie that she and her son were abandoned to die, when in truth God was present and had a plan for them. CCRT emphasizes the need to correct such lies with truth. In counseling, clients who feel rejected or hopeless must be reminded of God's promises and presence. Verses such as Deuteronomy 31:8— 'And the LORD, he it is that doth go before thee; he will be with thee, he will not fail thee, neither forsake thee'—anchor clients in hope when feelings of abandonment overwhelm them.

Hagar's case also demonstrates the principle of accountability. Though a victim of circumstances, she was still responsible for her responses. CCRT teaches that abnormal responses are chosen, even in difficult situations. A counselor would help Hagar see that while she could not control Sarah's actions or Abraham's decision, she could choose how to respond in faith rather than despair. This shift from focusing on what is uncontrollable to embracing personal responsibility is central to healing.

In a counseling session, a client like Hagar might say, 'I feel abandoned, unwanted, and forgotten.' The counselor could respond by acknowledging the pain while gently asking, 'What does God's Word say about His presence with you?' By using CCRT's directive stance of no excuses and constant redirection, the counselor would guide her to replace despair with truth. Practical steps might include writing down Scriptures of God's presence, practicing daily affirmations of His care, and establishing accountability with trusted believers who remind her that she is seen and valued. CCRT emphasizes that plans must be specific and measurable.

For counselor training, Hagar's example offers several insights: (1) Feelings of abandonment can create despair if left unchecked; (2) Lies of rejection must be replaced with the truth of God's presence; (3) Even in victimhood, responsibility for one's response remains; (4) Accountability and support from others can reinforce hope; (5) Counselors must use both empathy and redirection to anchor clients in God's promises. Hagar's encounter with God teaches that He sees and hears the rejected, offering comfort and purpose.

The expected outcome for counseling someone like Hagar would be a shift from despair to hope, from feeling unseen to embracing God's presence. The counselee would learn to accept responsibility for her responses, correct lies with truth, and live in the assurance that God sees and cares. This case reassures both counselors and counselees that no one is beyond the gaze of El Roi—the God who sees.

Counseling Scenario: Hagar

Rejection, Despair, and Hope in God

Purpose: To demonstrate how Christ Centered Reality Therapy (CCRT) would address Hagar's emotional roller coaster of rejection, abandonment, and despair after being cast out by Abraham and Sarah, guiding her toward responsibility, accountability, renewed faith, and hope in God's promises (KJV).

Presenting Problem & Context

Client: Hagar. Context: Hagar, Sarah's maid, bore Abraham a son, Ishmael (Genesis 16). Later, Sarah demanded that Abraham send her and Ishmael away (Genesis 21:9–10). Cast out into the wilderness, Hagar despaired, placing Ishmael under a shrub and sitting away, saying, 'Let me not see the death of the child' (Genesis 21:16). In this moment, she believed she and her son were abandoned to die. Yet God heard Ishmael's cry, opened Hagar's eyes to a well of water, and reaffirmed His promise to make Ishmael a great nation (Genesis 21:17–18).

CCRT Formulation

• Five Needs involved: Survival (fear of death in wilderness), Love/Belonging (rejection by Abraham and Sarah), Power/Self-worth (feeling discarded), Joy (lost in despair).

• Five Conflicts involved: Extended Family (strife with Sarah), Religion (trust in God's promises vs. despair).

• Choice and Responsibility: Though cast out unjustly, Hagar chose despair, saying she could not watch her son die. CCRT teaches that abnormal responses are choices—even in pain—and new responses must be owned.

• Accountability: Hagar felt abandoned, but God provided accountability through His Word and promise. CCRT emphasizes that accountability is a Reality Key to normality, sustaining faith and hope through encouragement and structure.

• Distorted Thinking: Hagar believed death was certain, when in truth God had promised a future for Ishmael. CCRT stresses replacing misinformation and lies with truth.

Session Goals

1) Help Hagar process rejection and despair without succumbing to hopelessness.

2) Restore perspective by correcting faulty thinking ('we will die') with God's truth ('I will make him a great nation').

3) Establish accountability by relying on God's Word, promises, and commitment to Ishmael's future.

4) Replace despair with hope, and abandonment with confidence in God's presence and provision.

Counseling Dialogue (Role-Play)

Therapist: Hagar, what were you feeling when you placed Ishmael under the shrub?

Hagar: I was overwhelmed. I said, 'Let me not see the death of the child' (Genesis 21:16). I believed we were abandoned.

Therapist: Your feelings were real, but your thinking was faulty. CCRT teaches that emotions are neutral, but choices and beliefs guide actions. What lie were you telling yourself?

Hagar: That God had abandoned me. That my son would die.

Therapist: Yes, but God had promised: 'I will make him a great nation' (Genesis 21:18). Psalm 34:18 says, 'The LORD is nigh unto them that are of a broken heart.' How does knowing God sees you change your perspective?

Hagar: It means I am not forsaken. He is El Roi—the God who sees me (Genesis 16:13).

Therapist: Exactly. God opened your eyes to water in the desert (Genesis 21:19). In CCRT, we replace misinformation with truth. What truth will sustain you now?

Hagar: That God hears Ishmael's cry and has a future for him. We are not abandoned.

Therapist: Good. Accountability means living by that truth daily—providing for Ishmael and raising him in faith. Who could help you walk in this truth?

Hagar: I must depend fully on God's presence and promises.

Therapist: Yes. Isaiah 41:10 says, 'Fear thou not; for I am with thee… I will strengthen thee; yea, I will help thee.' Let's make a plan for hope and faithfulness.

Intervention Plan (CCRT Plan of Success)

1) Repentance & Renewal: Confess despair and fear to God; embrace His promise of life and future (Genesis 21:18; 1 John 1:9).

2) Accountability Structure: Commit to prayer and daily remembrance of God's promises; teach Ishmael faithfulness (Proverbs 22:6).

3) Replacement Behaviors: Replace despair with thanksgiving (Philippians 4:6–7). Replace lies ('we will die') with truth ('God has a future for us').

4) Measurable Goals: Journal daily answered prayers and provisions. Share testimony with others when possible (Psalm 105:1).

5) Long-term Maintenance: Celebrate God's provisions. Watch for relapse into misinformation or self-pity; replace with prayer and gratitude.

CCRT Principles Applied

• Abnormal responses are chosen; responsibility is personal.

• Accountability is a Reality Key to normality; God's promises provide sustaining accountability.

• Plans must be specific, measurable, and achievable,

• Directive, no-excuses stance: accountability and redirection without condemnation.

• Early intervention: correct misinformation and lies with truth.

Key KJV Scriptures Used

Genesis 16:13; Genesis 21:16–19; Genesis 21:18; Psalm 34:18; Isaiah 41:10; Proverbs 22:6; Philippians 4:6–7; Psalm 105:1; 1 John 1:9.

Expected Outcomes

Hagar acknowledges her despair and misinformation, repents, and embraces God's truth. Through accountability to God's promises and daily renewal, she replaces despair with hope, raising Ishmael with faith and gratitude in the God who sees and provides.

JOHN MARK
FAILURE, MENTORSHIP, AND RESTORATION

John Mark provides a meaningful example of failure, rejection, and eventual restoration. During Paul and Barnabas' first missionary journey, Mark departed from them and returned to Jerusalem (Acts 13:13). Later, when Barnabas proposed taking Mark again, Paul refused, resulting in a sharp disagreement that divided the two leaders (Acts 15:37–39). For a time, Mark lived under the shadow of failure and rejection. Yet through Barnabas' mentorship and God's grace, Mark matured. Eventually, Paul himself testified of Mark's restoration, writing in 2 Timothy 4:11, 'Take Mark, and bring him with thee: for he is profitable to me for the ministry' (KJV).

From a CCRT perspective, Mark's departure reflects a poor choice that carried real consequences. Christ Centered Reality Therapy emphasizes that behavior is always chosen. Mark's choice to withdraw was his responsibility, even if motivated by fear, immaturity, or discouragement. CCRT insists that counselees accept responsibility without excuses. Yet Mark's story also demonstrates the value of accountability and mentoring. Barnabas provided the support and guidance that Mark needed, embodying CCRT's Reality Key of Through accountability, Mark grew into maturity and usefulness.

Mark's thinking could have been distorted by lies such as, 'I am a failure,' or 'I am unfit for ministry.' CCRT teaches that misinformation must be corrected with truth. For new counselors, this highlights the importance of listening for internalized lies after failure and helping clients replace them with God's truth. In Mark's case, the truth was that God's calling is not revoked by one mistake, and His mercy provides opportunity for restoration. Scriptures such as Proverbs 24:16—'For a just man falleth seven times, and riseth up again'—affirm this hope.

In a counseling session, a client like John Mark might express regret, shame, and fear of rejection. A counselor could ask, 'What do you believe about your usefulness after failure?' and 'What does God's Word say about His mercy and calling?' By integrating passages such as Philippians 1:6—'Being confident of this very thing, that he which hath begun a good work in you will perform it until the day of Jesus Christ'—the counselor would redirect the client from despair to hope. A plan of success might include identifying past failures, confessing them to God, seeking accountability through mentors, and re-engaging in service opportunities. CCRT insists on specific and measurable steps.

For counselor training, Mark's example teaches several key lessons: (1) Failure must be owned as a choice without excuses; (2) Accountability and mentorship are vital for restoration; (3) Lies of disqualification must be confronted with biblical truth; (4) Restoration includes both forgiveness and renewed service; (5) Counselors must help clients reframe failure as an opportunity for growth. Mark's story illustrates that a counselee who embraces responsibility and accountability can be restored to meaningful ministry.

The expected outcome for counseling someone like John Mark would be freedom from shame, renewed confidence in God's calling, and restoration to usefulness. Instead of being paralyzed by past mistakes, the counselee would learn to embrace responsibility, accept accountability, and walk in truth. For Christian counselors, Mark's story provides a model of hope: failure is not final when God's grace and accountability bring restoration.

Counseling Scenario: John Mark

Guilt, Rejection, and Restoration

Purpose: To demonstrate how Christ Centered Reality Therapy (CCRT) would address John Mark's feelings of guilt, rejection, and discouragement after leaving the mission field and experiencing Paul's anger, while guiding him toward responsibility, accountability, restoration, and renewed usefulness in ministry (KJV).

Presenting Problem & Context

Client: John Mark. Context: Mark left Paul and Barnabas during their first missionary journey (Acts 13:13). Later, Paul refused to take him on the second journey, leading to sharp contention with Barnabas (Acts 15:36–40). This left Mark feeling rejected, guilty, and possibly unfit for ministry. Yet later Paul wrote, 'Take Mark, and bring him with thee: for he is profitable to me for the ministry' (2 Timothy 4:11). This arc demonstrates failure, growth, accountability, and restoration.

CCRT Formulation

• Five Needs involved: Love/Belonging (feeling rejected by Paul), Power/Self-worth (loss of confidence), Freedom (desire to leave mission), Joy (lost through rejection).

• Five Conflicts involved: Mission (leaving the work), Extended Family/Community (disagreement between Paul and Barnabas).

• Choice and Responsibility: Mark chose to leave the mission. CCRT emphasizes abnormal behavior is a matter of choice, and he must take responsibility to grow from it.

• Accountability: Barnabas supported Mark, offering mentoring and encouragement. CCRT stresses accountability as a Reality Key to rebuild integrity and perseverance.

• Faulty Thinking Risk: Mark may have believed he was a permanent failure. CCRT insists on replacing misinformation with truth, reminding him that failure is not final.

Session Goals

1) Help Mark accept responsibility for leaving the mission without excusing himself.

2) Guide him to reject lies of permanent failure and embrace restoration through God's grace.

3) Encourage accountability relationships (Barnabas, later reconciliation with Paul).

4) Build perseverance for future ministry usefulness.

Counseling Dialogue (Role-Play)

Therapist: Mark, how did you feel when Paul refused to take you on the second journey?

Mark: Rejected and ashamed. I left before, and he would not forgive me (Acts 15:38–39).

Therapist: Yes, but CCRT teaches that while choices have consequences, they do not define your future. Proverbs 24:16 says, 'For a just man falleth seven times, and riseth up again.' What responsibility do you take for leaving?

Mark: I was immature. I gave up when I should have persevered.

Therapist: Good. Responsibility is the first step. But failure is not final. Philippians 1:6 reminds us, 'He which hath begun a good work in you will perform it.' How does that give you hope?

Mark: It means God isn't finished with me. I can grow and be useful again.

Therapist: Yes. Later Paul himself said you were 'profitable' (2 Timothy 4:11). Accountability with Barnabas helped you grow. Who can help you remain faithful now?

Mark: Barnabas has always supported me, and now I want to prove myself faithful to Paul as well.

Therapist: Excellent. Accountability and perseverance will rebuild your usefulness in ministry.

Intervention Plan (CCRT Plan of Success)

1) Repentance & Renewal: Confess discouragement and fear; embrace God's grace (1 John 1:9; Philippians 1:6).

2) Accountability Structure: Continue mentoring under Barnabas; seek reconciliation with Paul (Proverbs 27:17).

3) Replacement Behaviors: Replace quitting with perseverance; replace shame with hope in God's promises (Romans 8:1).

4) Measurable Goals: Journal ministry progress; share weekly with Barnabas or other mentors.

5) Long-term Maintenance: Celebrate growth and restoration; watch for relapse indicators such as fear or avoidance.

CCRT Principles Applied

- Abnormal behaviors are chosen; responsibility is personal.
- Accountability is a Reality Key to normality; supportive mentors foster growth.
- Plans must be specific, measurable, and achievable.
- Directive, no-excuses stance: accountability and redirection without condemnation.

• Early tracking: replace lies of failure with truth about God's promises.

Key KJV Scriptures Used

Acts 13:13; Acts 15:36–40; 2 Timothy 4:11; Proverbs 24:16; Philippians 1:6; Romans 8:1; 1 John 1:9; Proverbs 27:17.

Expected Outcomes

Mark accepts responsibility for leaving the mission, rejects lies of permanent failure, and embraces accountability. Through growth, perseverance, and God's grace, he is restored to ministry usefulness, even gaining Paul's affirmation.

JONAH
DISOBEDIENCE, FEAR, AND GOD'S MERCY

The prophet Jonah provides a vivid example of how fear, disobedience, and avoidance can create inner turmoil. When God commanded him to go to Nineveh and preach repentance, Jonah fled in the opposite direction (Jonah 1:3). His attempt to escape God's call led him onto a ship, into a storm, and finally into the belly of a great fish. Jonah admitted to the sailors, 'I know that for my sake this great tempest is upon you' (Jonah 1:12, KJV). His story reveals the consequences of rebellion but also the depth of God's mercy in giving him a second chance. When Jonah finally obeyed, the city of Nineveh repented, yet even then Jonah struggled with anger and resentment that God had spared the people he despised (Jonah 4:1–2).

From a CCRT perspective, Jonah's struggles illustrate the principle of choice and responsibility. Rather than obeying God, Jonah chose avoidance. His abnormal response—rebellion—was not forced upon him; it was chosen. CCRT stresses that counselees must recognize their responsibility in choosing disobedience or withdrawal. Jonah also demonstrates how misinformation shapes behavior. He believed that avoiding Nineveh would remove him from responsibility, but the truth was that God's call was inescapable. For new counselors, Jonah's case underscores the importance of helping clients recognize avoidance patterns and confront the lies they believe about escaping responsibility.

Accountability is another key element in Jonah's story. God held Jonah accountable by sending the storm, the fish, and ultimately the rebuke about his anger when Nineveh repented. In counseling, accountability structures help clients stay aligned with truth. CCRT describes accountability as a Reality Key that restores balance. For a client like Jonah, a counselor would need to emphasize the difference between God's justice and human prejudice, helping the client see that obedience leads to peace while rebellion brings turmoil.

In a modern counseling session, the counselor might ask probing questions such as: 'What fears drive your avoidance?' or 'How has running from responsibility affected your peace?' By integrating Scripture, the counselor can point to truths such as Psalm 139:7–8— 'Whither shall I go from thy spirit? or whither shall I flee from thy presence? If I ascend up into heaven, thou art there: if I make my bed in hell, behold, thou art there.' These reminders confront the lie of escape and ground the counselee in God's presence. The plan of success must include concrete steps such as journaling areas of avoidance, confessing disobedience, and practicing immediate obedience in smaller daily matters to build discipline. CCRT insists that such plans be specific and measurable.

For counselor training, Jonah's case provides several lessons: (1) Avoidance is a chosen behavior, not an accident; (2) Disobedience creates turmoil, while obedience brings peace; (3) Prejudice and resentment can distort thinking even after obedience; (4) Accountability is necessary to sustain obedience; (5) God's mercy provides second chances, but responsibility must be embraced. Counselors must be alert to signs of avoidance in their clients and use Scripture to draw them back to obedience and truth.

The expected outcome for counseling someone like Jonah would be recognition of avoidance patterns, acceptance of responsibility, and peace through obedience. Jonah's story shows that even reluctant servants can be used by God when they surrender to His will. For Christian counselors, the application is clear: help clients face their fears, accept their responsibilities, and trust God's mercy to restore them to fruitful service.

Counseling Scenario: Jonah

Rebellion, Bitterness, and Surrender to God's Will

Purpose: To demonstrate how Christ Centered Reality Therapy (CCRT) addresses Jonah's rebellion, resentment, and bitterness toward God's will, guiding him toward responsibility, accountability, repentance, and obedience to God's Word (KJV).

Presenting Problem & Context

Client: Jonah. Context: God commanded Jonah to preach to Nineveh (Jonah 1:1–2), but Jonah fled in the opposite direction. Later, though Jonah preached, he became angry at God's mercy toward Nineveh (Jonah 4:1–3). His rebellion and bitterness reveal unwillingness to align with God's will and misplaced values, prioritizing personal prejudice over divine command.

CCRT Formulation

• Five Needs involved: Freedom (resisting God's direction), Power/Self-worth (pride in his own judgment), Joy (distorted by bitterness).

• Five Conflicts involved: Religion (rejecting God's command), Extended Family/Nation (resentment against Assyrians).

• Choice and Responsibility: Jonah chose rebellion. CCRT emphasizes abnormal behavior is chosen; we are always responsible for our responses.

• Accountability: Jonah avoided accountability by fleeing. In CCRT, accountability with God and trusted community is essential to sustain obedience.

Session Goals

1) Help Jonah admit rebellion and bitterness as personal responsibility, not justified by circumstances or enemies.

2) Guide him to repent of resisting God's will and surrender in obedience (Jonah 2:9; Acts 9:6).

3) Establish accountability safeguards to ensure continued obedience to God's Word.

4) Replace bitterness with compassion, aligning Jonah's heart with God's mercy.

Counseling Dialogue (Role-Play)

Therapist: Jonah, why did you flee from God's call to Nineveh?

Jonah: I didn't want to go. They didn't deserve mercy. I ran away (Jonah 1:3).

Therapist: That was a choice. CCRT teaches 'We control all of our choices'. Running was rebellion. How do you see your responsibility?

Jonah: I disobeyed. I wanted my way, not God's.

Therapist: Yes. God's Word says, 'Obedience is better than sacrifice' (1 Samuel 15:22). Your calling was clear. Why did you resist?

Jonah: I was angry at God's mercy. When Nineveh repented, I felt bitter (Jonah 4:1–2).

Therapist: Bitterness blinds us. Hebrews 12:15 warns, 'lest any root of bitterness springing up trouble you, and thereby many be defiled.' How is bitterness affecting your joy?

Jonah: I have no joy. Even when the city was saved, I was angry.

Therapist: That reveals misplaced values. God values mercy. Micah 6:8 says, '…what doth the LORD require of thee, but to do justly, and to love mercy, and to walk humbly with thy God?' How can you realign with God's values?

Jonah: I must surrender to His will and let go of bitterness.

Therapist: Good. Repentance means turning from rebellion to obedience. You prayed in the fish: 'Salvation is of the LORD' (Jonah 2:9). Let's strengthen accountability—who could support your obedience?

Jonah: Other prophets, elders, or a faith community could keep me accountable.

Therapist: Excellent. Accountability is a Reality Key that supports obedience. Let's set a plan of success to replace rebellion with obedience and bitterness with compassion.

Intervention Plan (CCRT Plan of Success)

1) Repentance & Renewal: Confess rebellion and bitterness to God; pray for a surrendered heart (Jonah 2:9; Psalm 51:10).

2) Accountability Structure: Commit to sharing obedience steps with trusted spiritual leaders; weekly review for encouragement (Proverbs 27:17; Hebrews 10:24–25).

3) Replacement Behaviors: Replace flight with immediate obedience (Psalm 119:60). Replace bitterness with prayer for enemies (Matthew 5:44).

4) Measurable Goals: Record decisions of obedience; track attitude shifts toward compassion. Share with accountability partner weekly.

5) Long-term Maintenance: Celebrate acts of obedience. Watch for relapse indicators: resentment, avoidance, or isolation.

CCRT Principles Applied

• Abnormal behavior is chosen; responsibility is personal.

• Accountability is a Reality Key to normality; build supportive structures

• Plans must be specific, measurable, and achievable

• Directive, no-excuses stance: accountability and redirection without condemnation.

• Early intervention and tracking: name problem, watch for recurrence, act quickly.

Key KJV Scriptures Used

Jonah 1:1–3; Jonah 2:9; Jonah 4:1–2; 1 Samuel 15:22; Hebrews 12:15; Micah 6:8; Psalm 51:10; Psalm 119:60; Matthew 5:44; Proverbs 27:17; Hebrews 10:24–25.

Expected Outcomes

Jonah recognizes rebellion and bitterness as sin, repents, and surrenders to God's will. With accountability and renewed perspective, he replaces resistance with obedience and resentment with compassion, aligning with God's mercy and mission.

JONATHAN
DIVIDED LOYALTIES AND INTEGRITY

Jonathan, the son of King Saul, provides a powerful example of inner conflict created by divided loyalties. On one hand, Jonathan was bound to his father, Saul, who increasingly acted in jealousy and hatred toward David. On the other, Jonathan shared a covenantal friendship with David, recognizing that God's hand was upon him to be Israel's next king. Scripture records Jonathan's devotion to David: 'And Jonathan caused David to swear again, because he loved him: for he loved him as he loved his own soul' (1 Samuel 20:17, KJV). Jonathan's dilemma illustrates the painful tension between family loyalty and obedience to God's revealed plan.

From a CCRT perspective, Jonathan's conflict reveals how responsibility and accountability provide direction in situations of divided loyalty. Christ Centered Reality Therapy emphasizes that individuals cannot control the actions of others but must accept responsibility for their own choices. Jonathan could not change Saul's hatred of David, but he was responsible for acting with integrity and faithfulness. His accountability was not only to David but ultimately to God, who had chosen David to be king. CCRT identifies accountability as a Reality Key necessary to remain anchored in truth and responsibility.

Jonathan's thinking could have been distorted by fear of betraying his father, yet he corrected misinformation by clinging to God's truth. Rather than believing the lie that loyalty to Saul required opposing David, Jonathan recognized that true loyalty involved obedience to God's will. CCRT teaches that counselors must help clients distinguish between misplaced loyalty and godly obedience by correcting misinformation with truth. For Jonathan, this meant supporting David while still honoring his father as much as possible without participating in Saul's sin.

In a counseling session, a client like Jonathan might say, 'I feel torn between my family's expectations and my conviction about what God wants.' The counselor could guide them with Scripture such as Acts 5:29— 'We ought to obey God rather than men.' Practical steps in a plan of success would include clarifying God's will through Scripture, seeking accountability with faithful believers, and committing to truth and obedience even when costly. CCRT insists that these plans be specific and measurable. For example, journaling decisions made out of obedience versus compromise could provide accountability and reflection.

For counselor training, Jonathan's example provides important lessons: (1) Divided loyalties are common but must be resolved by prioritizing obedience to God; (2) Integrity requires standing with truth even when family or friends oppose it; (3) Accountability structures strengthen the resolve to obey God; (4) Lies about loyalty must be replaced with biblical truth; (5) Counselors must help clients process guilt, fear, and conflict while leading them toward courage in obedience. Jonathan's story shows that it is possible to remain faithful to God's plan even in the midst of family conflict and divided loyalties.

The expected outcome for counseling someone like Jonathan would be peace of mind through obedience to God, even if relationships remain difficult. The counselee would learn to accept responsibility for choices, correct lies about loyalty, and establish accountability that supports faithfulness. For Christian counselors, Jonathan's story is a reminder that integrity means choosing God's will above all, and that such obedience leads to lasting peace.

Counseling Scenario: Jonathan

Divided Loyalties, Integrity, and Faithfulness

Purpose: To demonstrate how C Centered Reality Therapy (CCRT) would address Jonathan's dilemma of divided loyalties—between his father Saul, who unjustly persecuted David, and his covenant friendship with David—guiding him toward responsibility, accountability, and peace through integrity and obedience to God's will (KJV).

Presenting Problem & Context

Client: Jonathan. Context: Jonathan was the son of King Saul, who became increasingly hostile toward David, seeking to kill him out of jealousy (1 Samuel 18–20). At the same time, Jonathan shared a covenant friendship with David, loving him as his own soul (1 Samuel 20:17). Jonathan's dilemma was divided loyalty—his duty to honor his father clashed with his commitment to protect David, God's chosen future king. This created deep emotional, familial, and spiritual conflict, leaving Jonathan burdened and in need of clarity, accountability, and peace.

CCRT Formulation

• Five Needs involved: Love/Belonging (father/son bond; covenant with David), Power/Self-worth (identity as prince), Freedom (ability to choose integrity), Joy (robbed by conflict).

• Five Conflicts involved: Extended Family (father vs. friend), Religion (obeying God's anointing vs. father's wishes), Power (between Saul and David's future reign).

• Choice and Responsibility: Jonathan could not control Saul's hatred, but he was responsible for his own choices—supporting David in truth while remaining respectful toward Saul.

• Accountability: Jonathan's covenant with David created mutual accountability in truth, trust, and loyalty (1 Samuel 20:16–17). CCRT emphasizes accountability as a Reality Key to normality, supporting faithfulness and courage under pressure.

• Conflict Management: Jonathan embodies multiple conflicts—family loyalty, spiritual obedience, and personal integrity—which require CCRT's focus on identifying and resolving core conflicts where possible, and choosing integrity when reconciliation is impossible.

Session Goals

1) Help Jonathan process the weight of divided loyalties without succumbing to despair or paralysis.

2) Guide him to accept responsibility for supporting David while still honoring Saul respectfully.

3) Establish accountability through his covenant with David and reliance on God's larger plan.

4) Replace guilt and fear with peace through integrity, prioritizing obedience to God above man.

Counseling Dialogue (Role-Play)

Therapist: Jonathan, how are you experiencing the tension between your father and David?

Jonathan: It tears me apart. My father is the king and my father, but David is my friend—and God's chosen. Saul wants him dead, yet I love him as my own soul (1 Samuel 20:17).

Therapist: That is a painful conflict. CCRT teaches that while you cannot control Saul's jealousy, you are responsible for your own choices. What choices have you made?

Jonathan: I warned David, protected him, and affirmed our covenant (1 Samuel 20:16). But I feel guilty opposing my father.

Therapist: Yes. Exodus 20:12 calls us to honor our parents, but Acts 5:29 says, 'We ought to obey God rather than men.' How can you honor Saul without joining his sin?

Jonathan: By respecting him as my father and king, but refusing to harm David.

Therapist: Exactly. Proverbs 27:17 reminds us, 'Iron sharpeneth iron; so a man sharpeneth the countenance of his friend.' David is your accountability partner. How has your covenant with him helped you?

Jonathan: It gives me courage. I know I'm not alone.

Therapist: Good. That covenant is accountability in action—mutual support in obedience to God. What new steps will help you endure this conflict with peace?

Jonathan: I will remain faithful to God's will, support David, and treat my father with respect, even if he rejects me.

Therapist: That integrity honors God. Psalm 37:5 says, 'Commit thy way unto the LORD; trust also in him; and he shall bring it to pass.' Faithfulness, not compromise, defines your legacy.

Intervention Plan (CCRT Plan of Success)

1) Repentance & Renewal: Confess guilt and fear to God; embrace His peace and plan (Psalm 37:5; Philippians 4:6–7).

2) Accountability Structure: Continue covenant accountability with David; seek God's strength through prayer (1 Samuel 20:16–17; Ecclesiastes 4:9–10).

3) Replacement Behaviors: Replace guilt with peace (John 14:27). Replace fear with courage through trust in God (Joshua 1:9).

4) Measurable Goals: Meet regularly with David for encouragement; pray daily for Saul while refusing to join his sin (1 Samuel 20:42).

5) Long-term Maintenance: Celebrate acts of integrity; guard against relapse into despair or paralysis; keep eyes on God's sovereignty.

CCRT Principles Applied

• Abnormal behaviors are chosen; responsibility is personal.

• Accountability is a Reality Key to normality; Jonathan's covenant with David models supportive accountability.

• Plans must be specific, measurable, and achievable.

• Directive, no-excuses stance: accountability and redirection without condemnation,

• Conflict management: Identify conflicts, recognize irreconcilable tensions, and choose integrity aligned with God's will.

Key KJV Scriptures Used

1 Samuel 18–20; 1 Samuel 20:16–17; 1 Samuel 20:42; Exodus 20:12; Acts 5:29; Proverbs 27:17; Ecclesiastes 4:9–10; Psalm 37:5; Philippians 4:6–7; John 14:27; Joshua 1:9.

Expected Outcomes

Jonathan accepts responsibility for his choices, embraces accountability with David, and finds peace in prioritizing obedience to God. Though torn between divided loyalties, he learns that integrity, faithfulness, and covenant accountability provide strength and courage to endure conflict while leaving a legacy of godly friendship and honor.

KING SAUL
JEALOUSY AND RBELLION

The life of King Saul illustrates the destructive nature of jealousy, insecurity, and disobedience when responsibility is rejected. Saul began his reign with humility, but over time he allowed fear of people and jealousy of David to dominate his thinking. When David's victories were praised more than his own, Saul's anger flared: 'Saul hath slain his thousands, and David his ten thousand (1 Samuel 18:7, KJV). Rather than finding security in God's calling, Saul compared himself to David and fell into a cycle of envy, fear, and rebellion against God's instructions. His disobedience in sparing King Agag and the Amalekite livestock, against God's command, led Samuel to rebuke him: 'Behold, to obey is better than sacrifice, and to hearken than the fat of rams' (1 Samuel 15:22).

From a CCRT perspective, Saul's struggles reveal how distorted thinking and misplaced priorities drive abnormal behavior. Christ Centered Reality Therapy emphasizes that behavior is always chosen. Saul consistently chose to please people and protect his pride rather than obey God. His jealousy of David was based on a lie—that David sought his throne—when in fact David honored him. CCRT highlights the necessity of correcting misinformation with truth. A counselor working with someone like Saul would need to expose the faulty belief that worth is measured by comparison or applause. Instead, the truth is that worth comes from obedience and accountability to God.

Another central principle demonstrated in Saul's story is accountability. Rather than submitting to God's Word through Samuel, Saul deflected blame, excused his actions, and justified disobedience. CCRT stresses accountability as a Reality Key to normality. In a counseling setting, a modern client with Saul's issues might shift blame onto others or minimize personal fault. For new counselors, the lesson is clear: excuses must not be accepted. Instead, counselors should direct the client back to responsibility and truth, pointing them toward passages such as Galatians 6:7, 'Be not deceived; God is not mocked: for whatsoever a man soweth, that shall he also reap.'

Practically, counseling someone like Saul would involve addressing his insecurity and fear of others' opinions. The counselor might ask questions to uncover the source of this insecurity: 'Whose approval are you seeking? What does God say about obedience and worth?' By integrating Scripture, such as Proverbs 29:25— 'The fear of man bringeth a snare: but whoso putteth his trust in the LORD shall be safe'—the counselor can guide the client to replace people-pleasing with God-pleasing. The plan of success must include concrete steps, such as journaling instances where choices are made for people's approval, confessing them in prayer, and replacing them with faith-based affirmations. CCRT insists that these steps be specific and measurable.

For training purposes, new counselors should observe Saul's patterns: (1) Jealousy often arises from comparison; (2) Fear of man undermines obedience to God; (3) Excuses and blame-shifting reveal resistance to accountability; (4) Distorted beliefs must be confronted with truth; (5) Plans must redirect the client toward obedience and spiritual accountability. By applying these insights, counselors can help clients overcome insecurity, avoid destructive jealousy, and walk in obedience to God's Word.

The expected outcome for counseling someone like Saul would be a renewed focus on obedience rather than comparison, security in God's calling instead of fear of others, and acceptance of accountability. If these principles are applied, the counselee can move from rebellion and insecurity to peace and faithful service. For Christian counselors, the key lesson from Saul's example is that disobedience always carries consequences, but redirecting clients to responsibility and truth provides the opportunity for restoration.

Counseling Scenario: King Saul

Insecurity, Pride, and Disobedience

Purpose: To demonstrate how Christ Centered Reality Therapy (CCRT) addresses King Saul's struggles with insecurity, pride, and disobedience, guiding him toward responsibility, accountability, repentance, and obedience to God's Word (KJV).

Presenting Problem & Context

Client: King Saul. Context: In 1 Samuel 13–15, Saul disobeys God by offering a sacrifice instead of waiting for Samuel and later by sparing King Agag and the best livestock, directly violating God's command. His insecurity and pride lead to disobedience, blame-shifting, and eventual rejection as king.

CCRT Formulation

• Five Needs involved: Power/Self-worth (fear of losing authority), Love/Belonging (fear of people's opinion), Freedom (acting outside God's command), Joy (seeking approval vs. God's pleasure).

• Five Conflicts involved: Religion (obedience vs. ritual), Extended Family/Nation (relationship with Israel and Samuel), Money/Provision (keeping spoil of Amalekites).

• Choice and Responsibility: Saul must own his choices—disobedience is not forced by circumstance or people's pressure. CCRT teaches abnormality is always a chosen pattern.

• Accountability: Saul avoids accountability by blaming people (1 Samuel 15:15). CCRT emphasizes accountability as a key to normality, involving honest acknowledgment and measurable goals.

Session Goals

1) Help Saul acknowledge insecurity and pride as root issues fueling disobedience.

2) Lead him to accept responsibility for his sinful choices and stop blaming others.

3) Establish accountability structures to prevent relapse into fear-driven decision making.

4) Guide him to repentance and obedience to God's Word (1 Samuel 15:22; Acts 5:29).

Counseling Dialogue (Role-Play)

Therapist: Saul, let's talk about why you offered the sacrifice before Samuel arrived.

Saul: The people were scattering. I felt pressured, so I forced myself to act (1 Samuel 13:11–12).

Therapist: That choice revealed insecurity. CCRT teaches that even under pressure, responsibility for choices remains with you.

Saul: But the people demanded it. Later, they also wanted to keep the best sheep (1 Samuel 15:15).

Therapist: Blame-shifting is avoidance of accountability. God's Word says, 'To obey is better than sacrifice, and to hearken than the fat of rams' (1 Samuel 15:22). How do you see your responsibility here?

Saul: I see I disobeyed. My fear of people mattered more than obeying God.

Therapist: Exactly. Proverbs 29:25 warns, 'The fear of man bringeth a snare: but whoso putteth his trust in the LORD shall be safe.' What new choice could you make next time fear rises?

Saul: I could choose trust and obedience, even if unpopular.

Therapist: That's accountability in action. In CCRT, accountability is a Reality Key that ensures success by involving others and celebrating obedience. Who could hold you accountable—Samuel, perhaps?

Saul: Yes, Samuel could guide me. I must also repent before God for disobedience.

Therapist: Good. Repentance is key: 'Repent ye therefore, and be converted, that your sins may be blotted out' (Acts 3:19). Let's set a plan for accountability, obedience, and trust in God's direction rather than human opinion.

Intervention Plan (CCRT Plan of Success)

1) Repentance & Renewal: Confess disobedience before God (Psalm 51:10–12; Acts 3:19). Pray for a renewed spirit of obedience and trust.

2) Accountability Structure: Establish Samuel or a spiritual elder as accountability partner to review decisions before action (Proverbs 27:17; Hebrews 10:24–25).

3) Replacement Behaviors: When tempted by fear of people, pause and recall Acts 5:29— 'We ought to obey God rather than men.'

4) Measurable Goals: Document each key decision; note if obedience or fear guided it; review weekly with accountability partner.

5) Long-term Maintenance: Celebrate milestones of obedience; track early relapse indicators such as self-justification or blame-shifting.

CCRT Principles Applied

• Abnormal behavior is a chosen pattern; responsibility is personal.

• Accountability is a Reality Key to normality, focusing on encouragement and achievable goals.

• Directive, no-excuses stance: 'Reality Therapy stresses accountability and no excuses... no condemnation, only constant redirection'.

• Early intervention: name the problem, recognize recurrence, know what to watch.

• Plans must be specific and realistic: 'The plan of success is always very specific and includes achievable goals'.

Key KJV Scriptures Used

1 Samuel 13:11–12; 1 Samuel 15:15, 22; Proverbs 29:25; Acts 5:29; Acts 3:19; Psalm 51:10–12; Proverbs 27:17; Hebrews 10:24–25.

Expected Outcomes

Saul learns to identify insecurity and pride, accepts responsibility for his choices, and repents of disobedience. With accountability through spiritual leadership, he practices obedience to God above fear of man. Success is measured by faithful obedience and rejection of blame-shifting.

MARY, THE MOTHER OF JESUS
REPUTATION AND TRUST IN GOD

Mary, the mother of Jesus, provides a profound example of enduring faith in the face of misunderstanding and false accusations. Though chosen by God to bear the Messiah, Mary faced the reality of living under suspicion in her community. The Gospels record hints of ridicule aimed at Jesus' birth: 'We be not born of fornication' (John 8:41, KJV), a statement implying that Mary's pregnancy outside of marriage was sinful. While Joseph had been assured by the angel of Mary's innocence (Matthew 1:20–21), the gossip and judgment of others likely persisted. Mary had to bear the weight of misrepresentation while holding fast to God's calling on her life.

From a CCRT perspective, Mary's situation highlights how responsibility, accountability, and truth sustain a believer through unjust suffering. Christ Centered Reality Therapy emphasizes that while individuals cannot control others' perceptions, they are responsible for their own responses. Mary could not silence every rumor, but she could choose to respond with dignity and faithfulness. Her accountability was to God's call and to Joseph, who stood by her in obedience to God's Word. CCRT identifies accountability as a Reality Key that anchors believers in their commitments despite external pressures.

Mary's potential struggle with misinformation is clear: she might have been tempted to believe the lie that her reputation defined her worth. But the truth was that her worth came from God's favor, not human opinion. Gabriel had said, 'Hail, thou that art highly favored, the Lord is with thee: blessed art thou among women' (Luke 1:28). CCRT teaches that counselors must help clients reject lies rooted in fear of people and replace them with the truth of God's Word. In Mary's case, the counselor would emphasize that obedience to God always outweighs the court of public opinion.

In a counseling session, a client like Mary might express pain over slander, gossip, or social rejection. The counselor could validate her grief but also redirect her toward God's promises, asking questions such as: 'What does God's Word say about your identity?' and 'How can you focus on His approval rather than people's opinions?' Scripture such as Galatians 1:10— 'For do I now persuade men, or God? or do I seek to please men? for if I yet pleased men, I should not be the servant of Christ'— would provide grounding. A plan of success might include rehearsing affirmations of God's favor, journaling answered prayers that confirm His presence, and seeking fellowship with trusted believers who reinforce God's truth. CCRT insists that such steps be specific and measurable.

For counselor training, Mary's example offers several lessons: (1) Reputation struggles can weigh heavily even on the faithful; (2) Fear of people's opinions must be confronted with God's truth; (3) Accountability to God's call brings stability amid criticism; (4) Lies about worth and reputation must be replaced with God's perspective; (5) Counselors must balance empathy with encouragement, helping clients endure slander with dignity. Mary's endurance demonstrates that faith in God's calling is sufficient to sustain believers through misunderstanding and gossip.

The expected outcome for counseling someone like Mary would be a deeper trust in God's favor and calling, freedom from bondage to reputation, and peace in knowing that obedience matters more than approval. For Christian counselors, Mary's story is a reminder that clients facing slander or false accusations must be guided to rest in God's truth. Endurance under criticism not only honors God but also provides a testimony of faith to others.

Counseling Scenario: Mary, Mother of Jesus

Bearing False Accusations with Faith

Purpose: To demonstrate how Christ Centered Reality Therapy (CCRT) would address Mary's burden of false accusations, social shame, and misunderstanding, guiding her toward responsibility, accountability, and peace through faith in God's Word (KJV).

Presenting Problem & Context

Client: Mary, mother of Jesus. Context: Mary knew she had been chosen by God and that her pregnancy was miraculous (Luke 1:26–38). Joseph was reassured by an angel and remained faithful to her (Matthew 1:18–25). However, neighbors and community members gossiped, taunting her son with accusations such as, 'We be not born of fornication' (John 8:41). Though innocent, Mary bore the weight of slander and social shame for years. The emotional burden involved rejection, false judgment, and enduring lies while holding on to the truth of God's calling.

CCRT Formulation

• Five Needs involved: Love/Belonging (rejected by community), Power/Self-worth (misjudged as immoral), Freedom (limited by gossip), Joy (robbed by slander).

• Five Conflicts involved: Extended Family/Community (gossip and rejection), Religion (bearing God's Son yet treated as sinful).

• Choice and Responsibility: Mary could not control gossip but she could choose her response. CCRT stresses that abnormal responses are chosen, and faithfulness is also a choice.

• Accountability: Mary's accountability was to God and His Word. She also drew support from Joseph, Elizabeth, and later the disciples. CCRT emphasizes accountability as a Reality Key to sustain hope and courage.

• Faulty Thinking Risk: Believing lies could have led to despair. Instead, Mary clung to God's truth in her song of faith (Luke 1:46–55). CCRT stresses replacing misinformation with truth.

Session Goals

1) Help Mary process the pain of false accusations without internalizing them.

2) Encourage her to remain grounded in God's promises, not in people's opinions.

3) Build accountability through supportive relationships with Joseph, Elizabeth, and the faith community.

4) Replace shame with joy in her calling, focusing on obedience to God's will.

Counseling Dialogue (Role-Play)

Therapist: Mary, how have the community's words affected you?

Mary: They whisper and taunt, saying I was immoral. They even insult my son (John 8:41). It is painful.

Therapist: Yes, rejection is painful. But CCRT teaches that while you cannot control others' words, you can choose your response. What have you chosen so far?

Mary: I have chosen to trust God's Word. The angel said, 'Thou art highly favored, the Lord is with thee' (Luke 1:28).

Therapist: That is truth. Lies must be replaced with truth. Romans 8:33 says, 'Who shall lay anything to the charge of God's elect?' How does that encourage you?

Mary: It reminds me that God has justified me, not people.

Therapist: Yes. Matthew 5:11 promises blessing when men revile you for righteousness. How can you keep your joy despite slander?

Mary: By remembering God's promises and magnifying Him, as I sang in my soul (Luke 1:46–55).

Therapist: Excellent. Accountability also sustains hope. Who supports you most?

Mary: Joseph stands by me, and Elizabeth encouraged me. I am not alone.

Therapist: Good. Isaiah 41:10 says, 'Fear thou not; for I am with thee.' God's presence and your covenant relationships keep you strong. Let's create a plan for peace and perseverance.

Intervention Plan (CCRT Plan of Success)

1) Repentance & Renewal: Reject lies of shame; renew trust in God's promises daily (Luke 1:28; Romans 8:33).

2) Accountability Structure: Strengthen support with Joseph, Elizabeth, and later the disciples (Ecclesiastes 4:9–10; Hebrews 10:24–25).

3) Replacement Behaviors: Replace fear of gossip with joy in God's calling (Luke 1:46–55). Replace bitterness with prayer for neighbors (Matthew 5:44).

4) Measurable Goals: Journal daily affirmations from God's Word; share gratitude reports with accountability partners weekly.

5) Long-term Maintenance: Celebrate faith milestones; guard against relapse into self-pity or bitterness; replace with rejoicing in God's favor.

CCRT Principles Applied

• Abnormal responses are chosen; responsibility is personal.

• Accountability is a Reality Key to normality; supportive fellowship sustains hope.

• Plans must be specific, measurable, and achievable.

• Directive, no-excuses stance: accountability and redirection without condemnation.

• Early intervention: replace misinformation with truth.

Key KJV Scriptures Used

Luke 1:26–28; Luke 1:46–55; Matthew 1:18–25; Matthew 5:11; Isaiah 41:10; Romans 8:33; John 8:41; Matthew 5:44; Ecclesiastes 4:9–10; Hebrews 10:24–25.

Expected Outcomes

Mary acknowledges the pain of false accusations without internalizing shame. By replacing lies with God's truth, relying on accountability through faithful relationships, and focusing on her calling, she sustains joy and peace despite community gossip, leaving a legacy of steadfast obedience and faith.

MOSES
ANGER, DISOBEDIENCE, & CONSEQUENCES

The story of Moses highlights the struggles of leadership, anger, and the painful consequences of disobedience. After leading Israel faithfully for forty years, Moses faced repeated complaints and rebellion from the people. In Numbers 20, when the congregation thirsted and quarreled, God instructed Moses to speak to the rock to bring forth water. Instead, Moses struck the rock twice in anger, saying, 'Hear now, ye rebels; must we fetch you water out of this rock?' (Numbers 20:10, KJV). Though water flowed, Moses' disobedience led God to declare that he would not bring the people into the Promised Land (Numbers 20:12). This moment shows how unchecked anger and frustration can derail even a faithful servant of God.

From a CCRT perspective, Moses' outburst reflects a breakdown in responsibility and accountability. Christ Centered Reality Therapy emphasizes that abnormal behavior is always chosen. Though provoked by the people's grumbling, Moses chose to act out of anger rather than obedience. His faulty thinking led him to believe that the burden of providing water rested on himself ('must we fetch you water'), rather than trusting God's power. CCRT stresses correcting such misinformation with truth. Counselors must help clients recognize that anger often flows from distorted beliefs about control, responsibility, or unmet needs.

Accountability is another key lesson from Moses' story. God held him accountable by declaring that his disobedience would prevent him from entering the Promised Land. CCRT identifies accountability as a Reality Key to restoring normal functioning. For counselees, consequences may take different forms, but the principle remains: disobedience carries costs. A counselor would emphasize that while forgiveness is available, certain outcomes of disobedience may remain. Scripture such as Galatians 6:7— 'Be not deceived; God is not mocked: for whatsoever a man soweth, that shall he also reap'—reinforces the principle of sowing and reaping.

In a counseling session, Moses might wrestle with grief, disappointment, and frustration over not entering the Promised Land despite decades of faithful service. A counselor using CCRT would acknowledge his sorrow but guide him to focus on God's mercy and continued presence. Though he would not enter Canaan, God allowed him to see the land (Deuteronomy 34:4), affirming His faithfulness. The counselor could help Moses reframe his perspective: instead of focusing solely on loss, he could find peace in God's sovereignty and grace. Scriptures such as Romans 8:18— 'For I reckon that the sufferings of this present time are not worthy to be compared with the glory which shall be revealed in us'—would provide hope and comfort.

For counselor training, Moses' example provides several key insights: (1) Leadership fatigue can fuel anger and poor choices; (2) Distorted beliefs about control must be corrected with truth; (3) Accountability means facing consequences, even when forgiveness is granted; (4) Counselors must help clients grieve losses while embracing God's sovereignty; (5) Hope must be anchored in God's promises, not in circumstances. New counselors must learn to balance compassion with firmness, reminding clients that while consequences may remain, God's grace sustains and restores.

The expected outcome for counseling someone like Moses would be acceptance of responsibility, peace with God's discipline, and renewed focus on God's mercy. Instead of being consumed by regret, the counselee would learn to trust God's faithfulness and embrace his role in preparing others, such as Joshua, for leadership. This case reassures counselors and counselees alike that even when anger and disobedience bring consequences, God's mercy provides hope, healing, and eternal reward.

Counseling Scenario: Moses

Anger, Disobedience, and Facing Consequences

Purpose: To demonstrate how Christ Centered Reality Therapy (CCRT) would address Moses' struggle with anger, disobedience, and grief over God's judgment that he would not enter the Promised Land after leading Israel for forty years. This scenario illustrates how responsibility, accountability, repentance, and perspective can restore peace and purpose.

Presenting Problem & Context

Client: Moses. Context: In Numbers 20:7–12, God commanded Moses to speak to the rock to bring forth water. Instead, Moses struck the rock in anger, misrepresenting God's holiness. As a result, God judged that Moses would not lead Israel into the Promised Land. After forty years of leadership, this consequence brought grief, loss, and the need to accept responsibility while preparing for transition (Deuteronomy 32:48–52).

CCRT Formulation

• Five Needs involved: Power/Self-worth (anger at people's rebellion), Love/Belonging (strain in relationship with Israel), Joy (loss of fulfillment in entering the land).

• Five Conflicts involved: Religion (misrepresenting God's holiness), Extended Family/Nation (anger toward Israel's complaints).

• Choice and Responsibility: Moses chose anger and disobedience in a moment of stress. CCRT stresses that abnormal behavior is a matter of choice and we control our responses.

• Accountability: God held Moses accountable as leader, showing that leadership carries greater responsibility.

• Directive, no-Excuses Stance: God did not excuse Moses' action despite stress, modeling accountability with no condemnation, but with consequences.

Session Goals

1) Help Moses acknowledge his responsibility for striking the rock in anger.

2) Support him in processing grief and disappointment without bitterness.

3) Encourage him to finish well by preparing Joshua and blessing Israel (Deuteronomy 31:7–8).

4) Restore peace by focusing on God's presence and eternal perspective (Psalm 90; Hebrews 11:26–27).

Counseling Dialogue (Role-Play)

Therapist: Moses, after years of faithful service, what happened at the rock?

Moses: The people complained again. I was angry. I struck the rock instead of speaking to it (Numbers 20:10–11).

Therapist: That was a choice. CCRT teaches, 'We control all of our choices'. God said, 'Ye believed me not, to sanctify me in the eyes of Israel' (Numbers 20:12). How do you see your responsibility?

Moses: I misrepresented God's holiness. My anger cost me entry into the land.

Therapist: Yes. Consequences are real, but God still values your legacy. Psalm 90:12 says, 'So teach us to number our days, that we may apply our hearts unto wisdom.' How can you use the days you have left?

Moses: I must prepare Joshua to lead and bless the people before I die (Deuteronomy 31:7–8).

Therapist: Good. Hebrews 12:6 reminds us, 'For whom the Lord loveth he chasteneth.' God's discipline is not rejection but love. How does this change your perspective?

Moses: I can see His correction as love. Though I won't enter, God remains faithful.

Therapist: Exactly. Your mission continues—mentoring Joshua, blessing Israel, and finishing well. Accountability now means focusing on legacy rather than regret.

Intervention Plan (CCRT Plan of Success)

1) Repentance & Renewal: Confess anger and disobedience to God; seek peace in His forgiveness (1 John 1:9; Psalm 51:10).

2) Accountability Structure: Work closely with Joshua and elders to ensure a smooth transition (Deuteronomy 31:7–8; Proverbs 27:17).

3) Replacement Behaviors: Replace anger with patience (Proverbs 16:32). Replace resentment with legacy-building (Psalm 71:18).

4) Measurable Goals: Weekly mentoring sessions with Joshua; public blessing of Israel before death (Deuteronomy 33).

5) Long-term Maintenance: Focus daily on God's presence rather than unfulfilled dreams (Deuteronomy 34:10; Hebrews 11:26–27).

CCRT Principles Applied

• Abnormal responses are chosen; responsibility is personal.

• Accountability is a Reality Key to normality; leaders are held accountable at higher standards.

• Plans must be specific, realistic, and achievable.

• Directive, no-excuses stance: accountability and redirection without condemnation.

• Early tracking: name the problem, recognize recurrence, guard against relapse into anger.

Key KJV Scriptures Used

Numbers 20:7–12; Deuteronomy 31:7–8; Deuteronomy 32:48–52; Deuteronomy 33; Deuteronomy 34:10; Psalm 90:12; Psalm 51:10; Psalm 71:18; Proverbs 16:32; Hebrews 11:26–27; Hebrews 12:6; 1 John 1:9.

Expected Outcomes

Moses accepts responsibility for his disobedience, processes grief without bitterness, and focuses on leaving a legacy of faith. Through accountability with Joshua and the elders, he prepares the next generation while drawing peace from God's presence and eternal promises.

PAUL
RIGID EXPECTATIONS & RECONCILIATION

The apostle Paul provides an example of how even strong leaders can struggle with anger, rigid expectations, and the challenge of reconciliation. After John Mark abandoned the first missionary journey (Acts 13:13), Paul strongly opposed giving him a second chance. When Barnabas wanted to bring Mark again, Paul refused, leading to a sharp disagreement that separated Paul and Barnabas (Acts 15:36–40). At this point, Paul's expectations for ministry partners were uncompromising. His anger and disappointment toward Mark illustrate the challenges counselors face when dealing with clients who hold rigid standards or unresolved frustration.

From a CCRT perspective, Paul's reaction demonstrates the principle that behavior is chosen and responsibility must be accepted. While Mark bore responsibility for his earlier desertion, Paul bore responsibility for how he responded to that failure. His rigid refusal to forgive revealed a choice to let anger dominate his response. CCRT teaches that counselors must help clients recognize that anger is not uncontrollable but is directed by choices and beliefs. By confronting Paul's harsh reaction, a counselor would seek to guide him toward balancing accountability with grace.

Paul's thinking also illustrates how misinformation can distort judgment. He may have believed the lie that granting Mark another chance would compromise the mission. The truth was that restoration could strengthen both Mark and the team in the long term. CCRT emphasizes correcting misinformation with truth. Counselors working with clients like Paul must uncover the lies behind rigid expectations and redirect them toward biblical truth about grace and restoration. Passages such as Colossians 3:13— 'Forbearing one another, and forgiving one another… even as Christ forgave you, so also do ye'—speak directly to this issue.

Accountability also plays a key role in Paul's story. Initially, Paul held Mark accountable in a punitive way by rejecting him, but later he balanced accountability with grace. By the end of his ministry, Paul wrote to Timothy, 'Take Mark, and bring him with thee: for he is profitable to me for the ministry' (2 Timothy 4:11, KJV). This transformation reflects a growth in Paul's maturity and an embrace of CCRT's principle that accountability is not about punishment but about restoration. For counselors, Paul's journey shows that clients can learn to temper justice with mercy, holding others accountable while also extending forgiveness.

In a counseling session, a client like Paul might express frustration over betrayal, disappointment, or unmet expectations. A counselor could acknowledge the pain while asking, 'What would happen if you balanced accountability with grace?' Scriptures such as Proverbs 14:29— 'He that is slow to wrath is of great understanding'—and Ephesians 4:32—'Be ye kind one to another… forgiving one another, even as God for Christ's sake hath forgiven you'—would be introduced to redirect thinking. A plan of success could include journaling frustrations, practicing intentional forgiveness, and seeking reconciliation where possible. CCRT emphasizes that such steps must be specific and measurable.

For counselor training, Paul's example offers several lessons: (1) Leaders can struggle with anger and rigid expectations; (2) Accountability must not become punitive; (3) Misinformation about grace must be corrected with biblical truth; (4) Forgiveness and restoration are as important as responsibility and discipline; (5) Counselors must help clients balance high standards with Christ like compassion. Paul's eventual reconciliation with Mark shows that even rigid or angry responses can be transformed by God's grace.

The expected outcome for counseling someone like Paul would be greater emotional balance, a willingness to forgive, and an embrace of accountability that builds rather than destroys relationships. Paul's story reminds both counselors and counselees that grace and truth together bring restoration. For Christian counselors, this example reinforces the importance of guiding clients from anger and rigidity toward forgiveness, grace, and reconciliation.

Counseling Scenario: Paul

Anger, Disappointment, and Reconciliation with John Mark

Purpose: To demonstrate how Christ Centered Reality Therapy (CCRT) would address Paul's emotions of anger and disappointment at John Mark's departure, while exploring the eventual change that led him to call Mark 'profitable' (2 Timothy 4:11).

Presenting Problem & Context

Client: Paul. Context: After John Mark deserted the mission field (Acts 13:13), Paul was unwilling to take him again, causing sharp contention with Barnabas (Acts 15:36–40). Paul's anger and disappointment reflected his passion for the mission but also strained relationships. Later, Paul matured in his perspective, acknowledging Mark's growth and usefulness (2 Timothy 4:11). Counseling focuses on processing anger, balancing high expectations with grace, and embracing reconciliation.

CCRT Formulation

• Five Needs involved: Power/Self-worth (protecting mission integrity), Love/Belonging (strained by conflict with Barnabas and Mark), Joy (robbed by disappointment).

• Five Conflicts involved: Extended Family/Community (conflict with Barnabas), Mission (anger over Mark's unreliability).

• Choice and Responsibility: Paul chose anger and rejection. CCRT stresses that even justified frustration must be managed responsibly.

• Accountability: Barnabas provided a balancing accountability perspective, emphasizing grace and mentoring. CCRT highlights that accountability prevents leaders from becoming overly harsh or rigid.

Session Goals

1) Help Paul process his anger and disappointment without rejecting future reconciliation.

2) Encourage him to balance mission urgency with patience for growth in others.

3) Rebuild accountability by valuing Barnabas' mentoring approach.

4) Embrace reconciliation and affirm restored usefulness in Mark.

Counseling Dialogue (Role-Play)

Therapist: Paul, how did you feel when Mark deserted the mission (Acts 13:13)?

Paul: I was angry and disappointed. The mission is too important for unreliability.

Therapist: Yes, but CCRT teaches that responsibility includes managing anger constructively. How did you handle your anger?

Paul: I refused to take him again. It caused sharp contention with Barnabas (Acts 15:39).

Therapist: That was a choice. Proverbs 14:29 says, 'He that is slow to wrath is of great understanding.' How could you have managed it differently?

Paul: Perhaps with more patience, trusting Barnabas' mentoring approach.

Therapist: Yes. Later you called Mark 'profitable' (2 Timothy 4:11). What changed?

Paul: I saw his growth. I matured too, realizing grace is vital for building leaders.

Therapist: Excellent. Ephesians 4:32 says, 'Be ye kind one to another, tenderhearted, forgiving one another.' How will you continue applying grace as a leader?

Paul: By holding people accountable, but also by encouraging and forgiving. Mission requires both truth and grace.

Intervention Plan (CCRT Plan of Success)

1) Repentance & Renewal: Confess harshness; embrace grace alongside accountability (Ephesians 4:32).

2) Accountability Structure: Maintain balance by working with leaders like Barnabas who emphasize encouragement (Proverbs 27:17).

3) Replacement Behaviors: Replace anger with patience; replace rejection with reconciliation (Colossians 3:13).

4) Measurable Goals: Journal responses to conflict; evaluate balance of truth and grace.

5) Long-term Maintenance: Celebrate growth in others; avoid relapse into rigidity by remembering God's grace toward himself.

CCRT Principles Applied

• Abnormal responses are chosen; responsibility is personal.

• Accountability is a Reality Key to normality; Barnabas modeled grace alongside accountability.

- Plans must be specific, measurable, and achievable.
- Directive, no-excuses stance: accountability with redirection, not condemnation.
- Early tracking: name the problem (anger), recognize recurrence, act quickly to prevent harshness.

Key KJV Scriptures Used

Acts 13:13; Acts 15:36–40; 2 Timothy 4:11; Proverbs 14:29; Colossians 3:13; Ephesians 4:32; Proverbs 27:17.

Expected Outcomes

Paul processes his anger and disappointment, learns to balance accountability with grace, and embraces reconciliation. Through maturity, he affirms Mark's usefulness, demonstrating that growth and restoration are essential in leadership.

PAUL IN PRISON
SUFFERING, LEGACY, AND FINISHING WELL

Near the end of his life, the apostle Paul faced imprisonment in Rome with the knowledge that his execution was imminent. In 2 Timothy 4:6–7, he wrote, 'For I am now ready to be offered, and the time of my departure is at hand. I have fought a good fight, I have finished my course, I have kept the faith' (KJV). Paul's reflections reveal the culmination of a life marked by suffering, perseverance, and hope in Christ. His journey had begun with a dramatic encounter on the Damascus road (Acts 9:3–6), where Ananias told him that he would suffer many things for the name of Christ (Acts 9:15–16). Now, years later, Paul sat in a Roman prison awaiting death, reflecting on both the cost and the reward of discipleship.

From a CCRT perspective, Paul's situation illustrates how responsibility and accountability remain central even in suffering. Christ Centered Reality Therapy emphasizes that choices, not circumstances, define responses. Paul chose to persevere despite hardship, declaring in Philippians 1:21, 'For to me to live is Christ, and to die is gain.' Even as he grieved that 'all men forsook me' (2 Timothy 4:16), he corrected misinformation by affirming the truth: 'Notwithstanding the Lord stood with me, and strengthened me' (2 Timothy 4:17). CCRT teaches that counselors must help clients replace lies of abandonment or despair with God's truth.

Another dimension of Paul's reflection is his acknowledgment of past sin. In 1 Timothy 1:15, he described himself as the 'chief of sinners,' yet affirmed that God had shown him mercy so that Christ's long-suffering might be displayed as an example. For counselors, this demonstrates how guilt and past failures must be reframed in light of grace. Paul's life reminds counselees that even the deepest failures can become testimonies of God's mercy when responsibility and repentance are embraced. CCRT's emphasis on responsibility aligns with this perspective—acknowledging wrong choices but refusing to let them define one's future.

Accountability also shaped Paul's final reflections. He maintained accountability to Christ as Judge and to Timothy as a spiritual son, passing on encouragement and instruction even as his life drew to a close. CCRT identifies accountability as a Reality Key that sustains direction and hope. Counselors should help clients in similar circumstances establish accountability structures that provide encouragement and remind them of their ongoing influence, even in suffering.

In practical counseling, a client like Paul might wrestle with grief, loneliness, or fear of death. The counselor could validate these struggles while redirecting focus to the legacy of faith and the eternal reward awaiting them. Scriptures such as Galatians 6:9— 'And let us not be weary in well doing: for in due season we shall reap, if we faint not'—and Romans 8:18—'For I reckon that the sufferings of this present time are not worthy to be compared with the glory which shall be revealed in us'—anchor hope in God's promises. A plan of success might include daily thanksgiving, letter writing to encourage others, and prayer for the churches. CCRT insists that such plans be specific and measurable.

For counselor training, Paul's final days provide key lessons: (1) Suffering can tempt believers toward despair, but truth restores perspective; (2) Past sins, when confessed, can serve as testimonies of grace; (3) Accountability sustains faithfulness until the end; (4) Hope must be anchored in eternal promises rather than temporary circumstances; (5) Counselors must help clients face death with peace and assurance in Christ. Paul's testimony illustrates the reality of sowing and reaping, but also the surpassing grace of finishing well in Christ.

The expected outcome for counseling someone like Paul in prison would be peace with God's sovereignty, assurance of eternal reward, and a sense of fulfillment in a life lived faithfully. Rather than being consumed by fear or regret, the counselee would embrace gratitude, legacy, and anticipation of glory. For Christian counselors, Paul's final reflections provide a model for guiding clients toward finishing well: with responsibility accepted, accountability maintained, and hope fully fixed on Christ.

Counseling Scenario: Paul

Imprisoned, Awaiting Execution, and Finishing Well

Purpose: To demonstrate how Christ Centered Reality Therapy (CCRT) would address Paul's reflections in prison as he awaited execution, helping him process suffering, abandonment, and closure with accountability, responsibility, and hope in God's mercy (KJV).

Presenting Problem & Context

Client: Paul (formerly Saul). Context: Once a persecutor of the church, Paul encountered Jesus on the Damascus road (Acts 9:3–6) and was told by Ananias that he would suffer greatly for Christ (Acts 9:15–16). He acknowledged himself as the 'chief among sinners,' yet was saved to demonstrate the depths of God's forgiveness and mercy (1 Timothy 1:15–16). Now, near the end of his life, Paul writes from prison knowing his execution is imminent (2 Timothy 4:6–8). He reflects on years of hardship, abandonment by some companions, and the law of sowing and reaping (Galatians 6:7–9). He struggles with grief, loneliness, and anticipation of death, while affirming his faith and legacy as an Apostle.

CCRT Formulation

• Five Needs involved: Love/Belonging (loss of companions), Power/Self-worth (redeemed identity as Apostle), Freedom (restricted in prison), Joy (anticipating eternal reward).

• Five Conflicts involved: Internal conflict (abandonment vs. hope), External conflict (persecution and imprisonment), Religion (faithfulness to Christ despite suffering).

• Choice and Responsibility: Paul owned his past as a persecutor, calling himself 'chief among sinners,' but chose obedience and perseverance after his conversion. CCRT stresses that we control our choices, and Paul consistently chose faithfulness.

• Accountability: Paul remained accountable to Timothy, the churches, and ultimately Christ as Judge. Accountability provided hope and courage even in suffering.

• Correcting Faulty Thinking: Though tempted to despair because 'all men forsook me' (2 Timothy 4:16), Paul replaced this with the truth that 'the Lord stood with me' (2 Timothy 4:17). CCRT emphasizes replacing lies with truth.

Session Goals

1) Help Paul process grief from abandonment without falling into despair.

2) Affirm the meaning of his suffering as sowing faithfully for eternal reward (Galatians 6:7–9).

3) Encourage him to focus on God's mercy in saving the 'chief among sinners' as his legacy of hope (1 Timothy 1:15–16).

4) Prepare him to face death with peace, joy, and anticipation of reward (2 Timothy 4:8).

Counseling Dialogue (Role-Play)

Counselor: Paul, as you await your execution, what weighs most on your heart?

Paul: At my first answer no man stood with me… notwithstanding the Lord stood with me (2 Timothy 4:16–17). I feel abandonment, but also Christ's presence.

Counselor: That reflects CCRT's truth: accountability is to Christ above all. When you look back, how do you see your life?

Paul: I was the chief among sinners, but Christ saved me to show His perfect mercy (1 Timothy 1:15–16). Since Damascus, I have fought a good fight, I have finished my course, I have kept the faith (2 Timothy 4:7).

Counselor: That is victory. Galatians 6:9 says, 'In due season we shall reap, if we faint not.' How does that promise comfort you?

Paul: It assures me that my suffering is not wasted. A crown of righteousness awaits me (2 Timothy 4:8).

Counselor: Yes. Philippians 1:21 says, 'For to me to live is Christ, and to die is gain.' How does this truth shape your final days?

Paul: It helps me face death with peace. Christ has forgiven my past and used me despite my sins. Now I rejoice in His mercy and look forward to His reward.

Intervention Plan (CCRT Plan of Success)

1) Repentance & Renewal: Continue confessing reliance on Christ's mercy, rejoicing that even the 'chief of sinners' is forgiven (1 Timothy 1:15–16; Romans 8:1).

2) Accountability Structure: Write final letters to Timothy and churches to strengthen faith and model perseverance (2 Timothy 4:6–8).

3) Replacement Behaviors: Replace grief with thanksgiving; replace fear with anticipation of eternal reward (Philippians 1:21; Romans 8:18).

4) Measurable Goals: Daily prayer and encouragement letters while awaiting execution.

5) Long-term Maintenance: Focus on Christ's presence and eternal crown, not on earthly suffering (2 Timothy 4:8; Galatians 6:9).

CCRT Principles Applied

• Abnormal responses are chosen; responsibility is personal.

• Accountability is a Reality Key to normality; Paul remained accountable to Timothy and Christ.

• Plans must be specific, measurable, and achievable.

• Directive, no-excuses stance: responsibility and redirection without condemnation.

• Correcting misinformation: replace despair ('all men forsook me') with truth ('the Lord stood with me').

Key KJV Scriptures Used

Acts 9:3–6; Acts 9:15–16; 1 Timothy 1:15–16; 2 Timothy 4:6–8, 16–17; Galatians 6:7–9; Philippians 1:21; Romans 8:1; Romans 8:18.

Expected Outcomes

Paul acknowledges both his sinful past and God's mercy in saving him as an example of grace. He processes grief and abandonment, but replaces despair with truth. Through responsibility and accountability, Paul affirms that his suffering fulfilled God's call, and he faces death with peace, joy, and anticipation of his eternal reward.

PETER
FEAR, FAILURE, AND RESTORATION

The apostle Peter provides one of the most relatable examples of fear and failure followed by forgiveness and restoration. Though Peter boldly declared that he would never deny Christ, Jesus foretold that before the rooster crowed, Peter would deny Him three times (Matthew 26:34). When the pressure of fear came upon him in the high priest's courtyard, Peter swore that he did not know Jesus (Matthew 26:74). After the third denial, the rooster crowed, and Peter remembered Jesus' words. Scripture says, 'he went out, and wept bitterly' (Matthew 26:75, KJV). This moment of brokenness reveals the deep pain of failure that many counselees experience after acting contrary to their convictions.

From a CCRT perspective, Peter's denial was a chosen behavior, rooted in fear. Fear of rejection, suffering, or death can push individuals to act against their values. Yet responsibility still rests with the person's choice. CCRT emphasizes that counselors must help clients recognize that fear does not excuse sinful behavior, though it may explain the context. Peter's case illustrates how counselees must face responsibility without excuses, confess their failure, and seek restoration in Christ.

Peter's restoration came through accountability and truth. After His resurrection, Jesus confronted Peter in love by asking three times, 'Lovest thou me?' (John 21:15–17). This mirrored Peter's three denials, offering him the chance to reaffirm his devotion. CCRT teaches that accountability is essential for redirecting behavior and rebuilding integrity. For new counselors, Peter's story demonstrates how accountability conversations can be both challenging and healing. Rather than condemning Peter, Jesus redirected him: 'Feed my sheep.' Counselors should likewise provide correction with a goal of restoration, not rejection.

Peter's thinking also shows the importance of correcting misinformation. In the moment of denial, he likely believed the lie that self-preservation was more important than loyalty. Afterward, guilt and shame may have tempted him to believe that he was disqualified from serving Christ. But the truth was that Christ's forgiveness restored him to leadership. In counseling, it is critical to expose lies of disqualification or despair and replace them with truth: 'If we confess our sins, he is faithful and just to forgive us our sins, and to cleanse us from all unrighteousness' (1 John 1:9).

In practical counseling, someone like Peter would need both confrontation and reassurance. The counselor could ask, 'What fears drove your choices?' and 'What lies are you believing about your failure?' By integrating Scripture such as Proverbs 24:16— 'For a just man falleth seven times, and riseth up again'—the counselor would emphasize hope after failure. The plan of success should include steps such as confession in prayer, accountability relationships, and opportunities to serve again. CCRT insists that plans must be specific, measurable, and achievable.

For counselor training, Peter's example teaches several lessons: (1) Even strong believers can fall into fear-driven failure; (2) Failure must be owned without excuses; (3)

Accountability and truth restore identity; (4) Lies of disqualification must be replaced with biblical truth; (5) Restoration includes re-engagement in meaningful service. New counselors should learn to balance confrontation with compassion, just as Jesus did with Peter.

The expected outcome for counseling someone like Peter would be the release of guilt and shame, acceptance of forgiveness, and renewed confidence in Christ's call. Rather than remaining paralyzed by failure, the counselee would move forward in faithful service. Peter's story assures both counselors and counselees that failure is not final when responsibility is accepted, accountability is embraced, and Christ's mercy is received.

Counseling Scenario: Peter

Fear, Denial, and Restoration

Purpose: To demonstrate how Christ Centered Reality Therapy (CCRT) addresses Peter's fear and denial of Christ, guiding him toward responsibility, accountability, repentance, and obedience to God's Word (KJV).

Presenting Problem & Context

Client: Peter. Context: On the night of Jesus' arrest, Peter denied knowing Him three times out of fear of association and possible punishment (Luke 22:54–62). Despite earlier bold claims of loyalty, fear overtook Peter. Afterward, he wept bitterly, demonstrating remorse but needing restoration and accountability.

CCRT Formulation

• Five Needs involved: Love/Belonging (fear of rejection), Power/Self-worth (desire to protect himself), Freedom (avoiding restraint/punishment), Joy (lost through fear and shame).

• Five Conflicts involved: Religion (denial of Christ), Extended Family/Community (fear of social rejection).

• Choice and Responsibility: Peter's denial was a chosen act under fear. CCRT stresses that abnormal responses, though pressured, remain personal choices.

• Accountability: Peter needed accountability and restoration. CCRT emphasizes accountability as encouragement, not condemnation. Christ Himself restored Peter, modeling accountability with love (John 21:15–19).

Session Goals

1) Help Peter recognize fear as the root of his denial and accept personal responsibility.

2) Guide him to repentance and restoration in obedience to Christ's calling.

3) Establish accountability supports to encourage faithfulness under pressure.

4) Replace fear with courage, rooted in God's presence and promises.

Counseling Dialogue (Role-Play)

Therapist: Peter, what happened in the courtyard that night?

Peter: I was afraid. I denied Jesus three times to save myself (Luke 22:57–60).

Therapist: Fear is powerful, but it does not remove responsibility. CCRT teaches, 'We control all of our choices'. What choice did you make under fear?

Peter: I chose to deny Him. I thought I was protecting myself.

Therapist: Yes. Jesus had warned you: 'Before the cock crow, thou shalt deny me thrice' (Matthew 26:34). What do you feel now?

Peter: Shame. I wept bitterly (Luke 22:62).

Therapist: That sorrow can lead to repentance. 2 Corinthians 7:10 says, 'For godly sorrow worketh repentance to salvation…' What does repentance mean for you now?

Peter: To confess my failure and turn back to Christ.

Therapist: Good. After His resurrection, Jesus restored you with accountability: 'Lovest thou me? Feed my sheep' (John 21:15–17). Accountability involves both love and responsibility. Who could help you remain faithful?

Peter: My fellow apostles, and the Holy Spirit's power.

Therapist: Exactly. Fear is replaced by boldness through God's Spirit (Acts 1:8). Accountability ensures encouragement and faithfulness (Hebrews 10:24–25). Let's create a plan for courage and obedience.

Intervention Plan (CCRT Plan of Success)

1) Repentance & Renewal: Confess fear and denial to God; receive forgiveness (1 John 1:9; Psalm 51:10).

2) Accountability Structure: Walk closely with fellow apostles; submit to mutual encouragement and correction (James 5:16; Proverbs 27:17).

3) Replacement Behaviors: Replace fear with courage through prayer and reliance on the Spirit (Acts 4:31). Recall Scriptures of courage (Joshua 1:9; Psalm 27:1).

4) Measurable Goals: Document instances of witnessing boldly; share with accountability group weekly.

5) Long-term Maintenance: Celebrate faithfulness and growth. Watch for relapse indicators: avoidance, silence under pressure, or isolation.

CCRT Principles Applied

- Abnormal responses are chosen; responsibility is personal.
- Accountability is a Reality Key to normality; supportive accountability fosters restoration.
- Plans must be specific, measurable, and realistic.
- Directive, no-excuses stance: accountability and redirection without condemnation.
- Early tracking: name the problem, recognize recurrence, know what to watch.

Key KJV Scriptures Used

Luke 22:54–62; Matthew 26:34; John 21:15–19; 2 Corinthians 7:10; 1 John 1:9; Psalm 51:10; Acts 1:8; Acts 4:31; Hebrews 10:24–25; James 5:16; Proverbs 27:17; Joshua 1:9; Psalm 27:1.

Expected Outcomes

Peter acknowledges fear as the root of denial, repents sincerely, and embraces restoration. Through accountability and the Spirit's empowerment, he grows in courage, boldness, and faithfulness, eventually becoming a fearless witness for Christ.

SAMSON
IMPULSES AND CONSEQUENCES

Samson's life, recorded in Judges 13–16, illustrates the dangers of unchecked impulses, compromise, and failure to live up to God's calling. Though set apart from birth as a Nazirite to deliver Israel from the Philistines, Samson repeatedly acted on impulse and desire rather than obedience. His attraction to Philistine women, disregard for his vows, and eventual entanglement with Delilah revealed a pattern of poor choices. Judges 16:20 records the tragic turning point: 'And he wist not that the LORD was departed from him.' Samson's downfall underscores how repeated compromise can erode spiritual strength and lead to devastating consequences.

From a CCRT perspective, Samson's failures demonstrate that abnormal behavior is always chosen. Though blessed with supernatural strength, Samson chose to indulge his impulses rather than exercise responsibility. His distorted thinking led him to believe that his strength was inherent to himself rather than a gift dependent on obedience to God. CCRT stresses the need to correct misinformation with truth. For counselors, this highlights the danger of entitlement thinking, where clients presume that blessings or abilities will remain regardless of choices. Counselors must redirect such thinking toward accountability and dependence on God.

Accountability played little role in Samson's life until his final moments. His parents warned him about marrying outside Israel, yet he ignored their counsel. Later, Delilah manipulated him into revealing the secret of his strength, exposing his lack of accountability to his covenant with God. CCRT identifies accountability as a Reality Key necessary for sustaining healthy functioning. In counseling, Samson's case teaches the necessity of helping clients establish accountability relationships to resist destructive impulses and maintain integrity.

In practical counseling, a client like Samson would need to confront patterns of impulsive behavior and compromise. The counselor could ask questions such as: 'What desires or impulses tend to control your decisions?' and 'How have your compromises weakened your integrity?' Scripture provides guidance in passages such as Proverbs 25:28— 'He that hath no rule over his own spirit is like a city that is broken down, and without walls.' A plan of success for someone like Samson would include identifying triggers for impulsive behavior, establishing accountability with trusted believers, and practicing spiritual disciplines such as prayer and fasting to strengthen self-control. CCRT emphasizes that such plans must be specific and measurable.

For counselor training, Samson's life offers several key lessons: (1) Impulsive desires can undermine spiritual calling; (2) Entitlement thinking must be replaced with truth about dependence on God; (3) Lack of accountability leaves individuals vulnerable; (4) Compromise, when repeated, leads to devastating consequences; (5) Counselors must help clients establish structures of accountability and truth-based thinking. Even in failure, Samson's final prayer— 'O Lord GOD, remember me, I pray thee, and strengthen me' (Judges 16:28)—shows that repentance can lead to renewed usefulness.

The expected outcome for counseling someone like Samson would be recognition of destructive patterns, acceptance of responsibility for choices, and reliance on accountability and God's strength. Though consequences may remain, as they did for Samson, repentance opens the door to redemption.

This case reassures counselors that even clients who have squandered opportunities can be restored to fruitfulness when responsibility and accountability are embraced.

Counseling Scenario: Samson

Compromise, Lack of Self-Control, and Redemption

Purpose: To demonstrate how Christ Centered Reality Therapy (CCRT) would address Samson's repeated compromise, lack of self-control, and eventual downfall, guiding him toward responsibility, accountability, repentance, and redemption according to God's Word (KJV).

Presenting Problem & Context

Client: Samson. Context: Samson, a judge of Israel, was set apart as a Nazirite from birth (Judges 13). Despite his calling, he repeatedly compromised with Philistine women, indulged his desires, and lacked self-control. His relationship with Delilah led to betrayal, loss of strength, and captivity (Judges 16:15–21). Samson's failure was rooted in unchecked impulses, pride, and disregard for boundaries, but his final act showed repentance and faith (Judges 16:28–30).

CCRT Formulation

• Five Needs involved: Sex (lustful desires), Power/Self-worth (pride in strength), Freedom (refusal to submit to God's boundaries), Joy (seeking pleasure over obedience).

• Five Conflicts involved: Sex (Philistine women), Religion (violation of Nazirite vows), Extended Family/Nation (failure in leadership calling).

• Choice and Responsibility: Samson repeatedly chose compromise. CCRT emphasizes that abnormal behavior is always a matter of choice and that self-destructive choices must be owned.

• Accountability: Samson resisted accountability and secrecy allowed his compromises to continue. CCRT teaches that accountability is a Reality Key, necessary for maintaining integrity.

Session Goals

1) Help Samson acknowledge lust, pride, and compromise as personal responsibility.

2) Lead him to repentance, confession, and renewed dependence on God's strength.

3) Establish accountability safeguards to prevent relapse into self-destructive patterns.

4) Replace self-indulgence with obedience, purity, and faithful stewardship of his calling.

Counseling Dialogue (Role-Play)

Therapist: Samson, tell me about your choices with Delilah and the Philistines.

Samson: I loved her. I thought I could control the situation, but I was betrayed (Judges 16:15–21).

Therapist: You chose compromise. CCRT teaches, 'We control all of our choices'. How do you see your responsibility?

Samson: I gave away my secret. I broke my vow. I failed my calling.

Therapist: Yes. Proverbs 25:28 says, 'He that hath no rule over his own spirit is like a city that is broken down, and without walls.' What walls did you let down?

Samson: I let my desires rule me. I put trust in the wrong person.

Therapist: Exactly. Lust and pride blinded you. James 1:14–15 says that lust leads to sin and sin to death. What do you need to do now?

Samson: I must repent and depend on God again. My strength was always from Him.

Therapist: Yes. Judges 16:28 records your prayer: 'O Lord GOD, remember me, I pray thee, and strengthen me…' Accountability now means living within God's boundaries. Who could help you remain faithful?

Samson: Faithful elders or judges in Israel to hold me accountable.

Therapist: Good. Accountability structures ensure progress. Obedience, not compromise, will define your legacy (Hebrews 11:32–34).

Intervention Plan (CCRT Plan of Success)

1) Repentance & Renewal: Confess lust and compromise; pray for renewal of calling (Judges 16:28; 1 John 1:9).

2) Accountability Structure: Commit to spiritual mentors and elders for oversight (Proverbs 27:17; James 5:16).

3) Replacement Behaviors: Replace lust with purity (Job 31:1; Matthew 5:8). Replace pride with humility (James 4:6–7).

4) Measurable Goals: Document temptations and responses; share weekly with accountability partner.

5) Long-term Maintenance: Celebrate milestones of purity and obedience; watch for relapse indicators such as secrecy, arrogance, or rationalization.

CCRT Principles Applied

• Abnormal behaviors are chosen; responsibility is personal.

• Accountability is a Reality Key to normality; external support is necessary.

• Plans must be specific, measurable, and achievable.

• Directive, no-excuses stance: accountability and redirection without condemnation.

• Early tracking: name the problem, recognize recurrence, act quickly to prevent relapse.

Key KJV Scriptures Used

Judges 16:15–21; Judges 16:28–30; Proverbs 25:28; James 1:14–15; Job 31:1; Matthew 5:8; James 4:6–7; Proverbs 27:17; James 5:16; Hebrews 11:32–34; 1 John 1:9.

Expected Outcomes

Samson accepts responsibility for compromise and lack of self-control, repents, and embraces God's strength. Through accountability, purity, and humility, he reorients his life toward faithful obedience, leaving a legacy of faith despite past failure.

SUMMARY AND CONCLUSION

This section presents a series of counseling examples using well-known biblical characters as case studies. These examples do not seek to rewrite biblical history but to illustrate how timeless struggles such as deceit, anger, despair, rebellion, failure, and restoration can be addressed through a Christ-centered counseling model. Each biblical figure serves as a mirror to modern struggles, showing how principles of responsibility, accountability, repentance, forgiveness, and obedience to God remain essential for spiritual and emotional healing. The narratives demonstrate how CCRT moves clients away from excuses and blame-shifting and toward personal ownership of choices, correction of distorted thinking, and alignment with God's truth.

This section provides an in-depth exploration of how biblical narratives can be used as powerful teaching tools for modern counseling. The section is structured around counseling examples drawn from the lives of various biblical characters, each of whom faced unique struggles that mirror the kinds of issues counselees experience today. While the scriptural accounts stand as historical truth, the counseling illustrations are constructed to help modern readers and practitioners see how these same struggles—whether deceit, anger, despair, rebellion, fear, failure, or compromise—can be meaningfully addressed through a Christ-centered counseling model. The goal is not to alter or retell the biblical accounts but to draw out principles and applications that reveal how God's truth, when applied through CCRT, can bring healing, accountability, and transformation.

The section emphasizes that all abnormal behaviors are chosen and that individuals must accept responsibility for their actions. Whether dealing with Ananias and Sapphira's deceit, Cain's anger, David's moral failure, or Elijah's despair, CCRT insists that counselors confront sin with clarity and compassion while guiding counselees toward repentance and restoration. Accountability emerges as a consistent Reality Key—counselees must face truth, commit to transparency, and engage in measurable steps of change. Scripture is woven throughout the examples, reminding both counselor and counselee that the Word of God is the foundation for correction, healing, and transformation. For trainees, these scenarios highlight the practical application of CCRT in real-life counseling contexts, stressing prevention, redirection, and the replacement of lies with biblical truth.

By grounding counseling practices in biblical truth, the counselor confronts deception, blame-shifting, excuses, and denial head-on, not with condemnation, but with consistent redirection toward honesty, responsibility, and repentance. For instance, Ananias and Sapphira serve as an example of how deception and image management can destroy integrity, while Cain reveals how unchecked anger and jealousy can lead to devastating outcomes when accountability is rejected. David illustrates how even those close to God can fall grievously into sin, yet his restoration demonstrates the power of repentance and confession. Each case study reinforces the idea that individuals must recognize their freedom to choose, acknowledge their missteps, and embrace God's corrective truth as the only path forward.

The examples also highlight the corrective role of accountability. Within CCRT, accountability is treated as a Reality Key—an essential element of normal functioning and growth. Without accountability, deception flourishes, anger festers, despair deepens, and rebellion hardens into destructive patterns. Counselors are therefore called to confront clients with firm but compassionate truth, offering no space for rationalization, but every opportunity for renewal. As Nathan confronted

David, and as God confronted Cain, so too must Christian counselors provide direct challenges that bring sin into the light. In doing so, they act not as judges but as guides, redirecting individuals toward the freedom that comes through obedience to Christ. This emphasis on accountability distinguishes CCRT from many secular counseling models, which often focus on self-esteem or symptom management without addressing the moral and spiritual dimensions of behavior.

Another profound insight from Section 5 is the emphasis on misinformation and the necessity of replacing lies with truth. Many of the biblical figures, like Cain and Jonah, believed false narratives that fueled destructive choices. CCRT insists that counselors help clients identify and challenge these distortions. The process involves anchoring conversations in Scripture, using God's Word as the standard of reality and the measure of truth. In this way, clients are led to see that God's commands are not arbitrary restrictions but life-giving principles designed for their good. The use of biblical passages throughout the counseling examples ensures that the work of counseling is not divorced from the authority of Scripture but is immersed in it, providing both conviction and comfort.

Section 5 also underscores the importance of practical application. CCRT is not merely a theoretical framework but a directive counseling model that insists on measurable goals, plans of success, and consistent follow-through. Whether addressing dishonesty, anger, lust, despair, or rebellion, each example includes clear steps that a counselee could take—steps such as confession, the establishment of accountability partners, the practice of daily truth-telling, or the memorization of key passages of Scripture. These practices remind counselors-in-training that change is not an abstract ideal but a process of intentional actions guided by biblical truth. This focus on specificity, prevention, and redirection demonstrates that CCRT is deeply practical, equipping counselors with strategies that produce lasting transformation rather than temporary relief.

For new counselors, the lessons of Section 5 are manifold. First, they must learn to distinguish between feelings and choices, recognizing that while emotions are real, they do not dictate behavior. Second, they must understand that denial, excuse-making, and blame-shifting are barriers to growth that must be confronted quickly and compassionately. Third, they must appreciate the role of confrontation and accountability as loving expressions of God's desire for holiness. Finally, they must realize that repentance is not merely sorrow but a deliberate turning from sin toward God, accompanied by specific, measurable changes. These insights not only strengthen the counselor's skillset but also provide a deeply biblical lens through which to interpret the struggles of their clients.

In conclusion, Section 5 offers more than a series of case studies; it provides a vision for how Christ-centered counseling can transform lives by grounding every step of the process in Scripture. The examples remind us that the struggles faced by biblical figures remain strikingly relevant today, and the solutions offered by God's Word remain fully sufficient. It is the hope of this material that counselors and students alike will find these outlines, scenarios, and insights to be both practical and spiritually enriching. By applying these principles, counselors can guide clients toward honesty, integrity, accountability, repentance, and restoration. May the truths gleaned from Section 5 not only inform your understanding but also inspire your counseling practice, equipping you to help others experience the freedom, healing, and joy that are found in Christ alone.

STUDY GUIDE QUESTIONS – SECTION V

Directions: These questions are designed to help you understand and apply the material presented in this section. Answer each question completely, writing one to two paragraphs.

1. How does the example of Ananias and Sapphira highlight the importance of honesty and accountability in counseling?
2. In counseling someone like Cain, how should a counselor address the difference between emotions and choices?
3. What lessons can counselors learn from David's repentance and restoration after his fall into sin?
4. How does CCRT interpret abnormal behavior as a choice, and how is this principle demonstrated in the story of Cain?
5. What role does accountability play in helping clients move beyond deception or denial?
6. Why is it important for counselors to use Scripture when correcting misinformation in a counseling session?
7. How might the despair of Elijah provide insight for counseling individuals who feel hopeless or misinformed?
8. In what ways does the failure and later restoration of John Mark illustrate the importance of mentorship in counseling?
9. How does the example of Jonah emphasize the need for surrendering to God's will in counseling contexts?
10. How can counselors apply the principle of 'no excuses, no condemnation, only redirection' when addressing dishonesty?
11. What steps could be included in a CCRT 'plan of success' for someone struggling with anger, as seen in Cain's story?
12. How does the jealousy of King Saul demonstrate the destructive power of insecurity, and how should counselors address this issue?
13. What is the significance of using accountability partners or community supports in helping clients make lasting change?
14. How does the example of Paul's endurance in prison illustrate the importance of focusing on legacy and finishing well?

15. What overall lessons can be drawn from these biblical counseling examples for applying CCRT in modern contexts?

16. How do the counseling examples in Section V demonstrate that human struggles remain consistent across biblical history and modern counseling situations?

17. Select two individuals from Section V and explain how their belief systems influenced their choices and resulting consequences.

18. How do the counseling examples in Section V illustrate the role of confrontation and accountability in the process of restoration?

19. In what ways does Section V distinguish between emotional symptoms and underlying spiritual causes within the counseling process?

20. How can the biblical counseling examples in Section V be used as practical models for applying CCRT principles in contemporary counseling sessions?

SECTION VI
INTERVENTION STATEGIES

SECTION VI – TABLE OF CONTENTS

INTRODUCTION TO SECTION VI

Understanding Intervention Strategies in Scripture and CCRT

Intervention Strategies (IS) are purposeful, biblically grounded actions employed to bring about emotional, spiritual, and behavioral transformation in the life of a counselee. Throughout Scripture, God uses a vast array of methods—direct rebuke, gentle comfort, structured lament, covenant reminders, narrative confrontation, accountability, discipline, encouragement, and more—to correct His people, strengthen their faith, guide their decisions, and restore their relationship with Him. These strategies are not incidental; they reflect God's character, His wisdom, and His therapeutic approach to human brokenness. In counseling, an Intervention Strategy is not merely a technique. It is a truth-centered action that addresses beliefs, emotions, and behaviors in a way that leads counselees toward growth, stability, and Christlikeness.

When examined closely, the Bible reveals well over one hundred distinct intervention strategies used by God, Christ, the prophets, apostles, and wise spiritual leaders. Scripture is far more than a book of doctrine; it is also a record of divine-human interaction. God consistently intervenes in human lives using diverse methods that match the needs, personalities, situations, and spiritual conditions of His people. Jesus Himself employed a remarkable range of interventions—sometimes asking probing questions, other times teaching, correcting, comforting, confronting, reframing truth, restoring the fallen, guiding lament, exposing false beliefs, or calling for action. Because the Bible is filled with divine interventions, the Christian counselor who studies Scripture finds a rich treasury of methods for guiding people toward healing and wholeness.

In Christ Centered Reality Therapy (CCRT), Intervention Strategies serve a critical role. They form the bridge between insight and transformation. While understanding a counselee's needs, conflicts, and distorted beliefs is essential, insight alone does not produce change. Transformation occurs when truth is applied through intentional, structured intervention. A well-chosen IS targets the specific beliefs fueling emotional distress or unhealthy behavior. It redirects the counselee's interpretation, stabilizes their emotional system, and empowers them to move toward healthier, Christ-centered patterns of thought and action. In this sense, Intervention Strategies are the practical expression of biblical wisdom in the counseling process.

Because Scripture contains more than one hundred ISs, this chapter does not attempt to list or analyze them all. Instead, we have selected twenty representative strategies that illustrate the breadth, depth, and diversity of God's counseling methods. These twenty interventions are not exhaustive—they are a meaningful sample chosen to acquaint students with the profound wisdom embedded in biblical counseling. Each IS presented here demonstrates a different dimension of God's approach to human transformation: restoration after failure, teaching dependence on God, challenging fear, guiding lament, exposing idols, calling for responsibility, and many others. Together, they reveal that the Bible is a living counseling manual, rich with principles capable of addressing the full spectrum of human struggles.

Students should understand that effective use of Intervention Strategies requires more than memorizing definitions. It requires discernment—knowing which intervention best fits the counselee's emotional state, spiritual maturity, personality, and presenting problem. Not every strategy fits every situation. Jesus did not confront every person the same way; He approached Nicodemus differently from the Samaritan woman, Peter differently from Judas, and the rich young ruler differently from the Syrophoenician woman. Likewise, the wise counselor learns to apply the right biblical method at the right moment, guided by the Spirit of God and grounded in truth.

This chapter is therefore designed as both an introduction and a foundation. It introduces students to the concept of biblical Intervention Strategies, and it establishes a framework for integrating these methods within the CCRT model. As students study the scenarios that follow, they will observe how each IS addresses core beliefs, stabilizes emotions, corrects distortions, redirects behavior, and restores spiritual clarity. These examples will deepen the student's understanding of biblical counseling and equip them to employ Scripture-based interventions with wisdom, compassion, and effectiveness.

The twenty-nine Intervention Strategies in this chapter provide a strong beginning, but they should inspire students to explore Scripture more deeply. The Word of God is filled with countless examples of divine interventions—moments where God speaks, confronts, comforts, redefines, restores, reframes, and renews. As students grow in their skill and spiritual maturity, they will learn to identify even more strategies within the biblical narrative and apply them with skill in real counseling contexts. In this way, counselors not only learn from Scripture—they participate in its ongoing work of healing and transformation in the lives of God's people.

INTERVENTION 1: DIRECT CONFRONTATION OF SIN

Direct confrontation is one of the most recognizable and frequently used intervention patterns in Scripture. From Nathan confronting David, to Jesus addressing the Pharisees, to Paul correcting Peter in Antioch, confrontation—when practiced biblically—is purposeful, redemptive, and designed to reveal truth that leads to repentance, restoration, and personal transformation. In CCRT, direct confrontation is not harsh or adversarial. Instead, it is a structured appeal to truth grounded in love, clarity, and responsibility. The goal is always the same: to move the counselee from denial or avoidance into honest evaluation, truth alignment, and a commitment to appropriate action. The following scenario demonstrates how a CCRT counselor may employ this biblical intervention using the full methodology of the model, integrating the Five Needs, the Five Conflicts, Reality Keys, and the belief–emotion–behavior cycle.

Case Presentation

Michael, a 34-year-old married father of two, seeks counseling after several weeks of escalating marital conflict. His wife, Sarah, insists that his anger, defensiveness, and withdrawal are destroying their home. Michael believes the problem is exaggerated. He claims Sarah is overly emotional and frequently misinterprets his intentions. During the intake session, his tone is sarcastic, dismissive, and slightly combative. Michael expresses no ownership for his role in the conflict and implies that counseling is unnecessary. His primary belief is: 'I wouldn't get angry if people stopped provoking me.' This externalized belief prevents him from recognizing the internal roots of his behavior.

Counseling Objective

The counselor's objective is to confront Michael's distorted belief system directly and lovingly, bringing attention to his anger, denial, and failure to take responsibility. The confrontation is not about humiliating him, arguing, or proving him wrong. Instead, the CCRT therapist seeks to illuminate truth, help him evaluate his own behavior accurately, and guide him toward the internal transformation Scripture requires.

CCRT Analysis

Primary Needs Involved:

• Power – Michael feels disrespected and reacts through control and anger.
• Love & Belonging – His marriage bond is strained, and he fears rejection.

Primary Conflicts:

• Emotional Conflict – Anger masking insecurity.
• Behavioral Conflict – Destructive verbal interactions and withdrawal.
• Insight Conflict – Believes others cause' his anger, preventing self-awareness.

Distorted Beliefs Identified:

• "My anger is justified because others provoke me."
• "I have the right to respond however I want when I feel disrespected." \
• "If my wife changed, we wouldn't have any problems."

CCRT Reality Keys Used:

• RK1 – Belief Determines Experience. • RK6 – Truth Heals.
• RK8 – Personal Responsibility Leads to Freedom.

• RK11 – Discipline Produces Emotional and Spiritual Growth.

Biblical Foundation:
James 1:20 – 'For the anger of man does not produce the righteousness of God.'
Proverbs 12:1 – 'Whoever loves discipline loves knowledge, but he who hates correction is stupid.'
Ephesians 4:26–27 – 'Be angry and do not sin… give no opportunity to the devil.'

Counseling Conversation
Counselor: "Michael, I'm hearing that your anger shows up often in your home. Would that be accurate?"
Michael: "If people stopped attacking me, I wouldn't be angry. Anyone would react the same way."
Counselor: "I want to confront something directly, but only because I'm committed to helping you grow. Your belief that others cause' your anger is preventing you from taking responsibility. Anger doesn't come from outside you—it comes from beliefs, expectations, and reactions inside you. Until you take ownership for your responses, nothing in your marriage will improve."
Michael: "So you're saying this is my fault?"
Counselor: "I'm saying your reactions are your responsibility. And taking responsibility isn't blame—it's power. You can't change your wife, but you can change your beliefs and behaviors. CCRT teaches that when you change what you believe, you change what you feel and what you do. That's where real freedom begins."
Michael: (quiet for a moment) "I never thought about it like that."
Counselor: "Direct confrontation is about truth. And the truth is this: your anger is damaging your home, and it's coming from inside you. But that is good news, because it means you have the power, through Christ, to change it."

Counselor's Strategy Explanation

The counselor confronted Michael's distorted belief directly and immediately, naming the issue without shaming the counselee. In CCRT, confrontation requires three components:
1.Clarity – Clearly identifying the destructive behavior or belief.
2.Compassion – Communicating value, worth, and partnership.
3.Direction – Guiding the counselee toward responsibility and truth-based action.
The counselor did not argue, justify, or intellectualize. Instead, he used concise truth statements that exposed the belief-emotion-behavior sequence and repositioned responsibility onto Michael. This breaks denial, interrupts the cycle of blame, and sets the stage for growth.

Action Plan

Michael's first assignment is to complete a written evaluation using the CCRT Behavioral Evaluation Sheet:
• What did I WANT in each conflict with my wife?
• What was I DOING (specifically) when I did not get it?
• What was I SAYING to myself (beliefs) that fueled the anger?
• When I evaluate this behavior honestly, is it helping or harming my relationship?
• What is ONE responsibility I can take before our next session?
Additionally, Michael will memorize Ephesians 4:26–27 and journal the triggers that activate his anger. The counselor will review these writings next session, beginning to retrain Michael's belief system using Reality Keys and Scripture-based cognitive reframing.

Expected Outcome

Within several sessions, Michael is expected to gain insight into the internal nature of anger, accept responsibility for his reactions, and understand that he must change his beliefs before he can change his behavior. By confronting him lovingly and directly, the counselor has opened the path toward a more honest, teachable posture. This intervention lays the groundwork for repentance, improved communication, and long-term relational restoration.

INTERVENTION 2: QUESTION-BASED SELF-REFLECTION

One of the most powerful and frequently used intervention strategies in Scripture is God's use of purposeful questions. From Genesis to the Gospels, the Lord uses questions not because He lacks information, but because people lack insight. Questions uncover hidden beliefs, expose motives, confront self-deception, and invite honest evaluation. In CCRT, question-based self-reflection is essential because the model is built on the principle that change begins with accurate self-evaluation. A well-crafted question bypasses defensiveness, opens cognitive awareness, and allows the counselee to see what the counselor could never simply tell them. This scenario demonstrates how a CCRT counselor uses probing, targeted, and biblically grounded questions to help a counselee gain insight into their internal conflicts.

Case Presentation

Rebecca is a 28-year-old single woman who reports chronic anxiety related to perfectionism at work and in church ministry. She describes constant fear of disappointing others, making mistakes, or being seen as incompetent. Rebecca is friendly, polite, and articulate, but her emotional life is dominated by a relentless internal pressure to perform flawlessly. She prays often but confesses that she rarely feels peace. Her primary belief is: "If I am not perfect, I am unworthy." This distorted belief fuels anxiety, inhibits rest, and undermines her ability to establish healthy boundaries.

Counseling Objective

The counselor's objective is to help Rebecca identify the beliefs driving her anxiety by using precise, reflective questions. She does not yet understand the internal nature of her fear, nor does she see how her beliefs contradict Scripture. Through guided questioning, the CCRT counselor aims to illuminate her inner dialogue, reveal the source of her emotional disturbance, and help her reinterpret her identity through a biblical framework.

CCRT Analysis

Primary Needs Involved:

• Love & Belonging – Desire for approval, fear of rejection.

• Power – Desire to feel competent and valued.

Primary Conflicts:

• Emotional Conflict – Anxiety rooted in unrealistic expectations.

• Insight Conflict – Belief that worth depends on flawless performance.

• Belief Conflict – Confusion between biblical identity and self-imposed standards.

Distorted Beliefs Identified:

• "My value is based on what I do, not who I am in Christ."

• "If I make mistakes, people will reject me."

• "God is disappointed when I fall short."

CCRT Reality Keys Used:

• RK1 – Belief Determines Experience.

• RK4 – Identity Determines Relationship.

• RK6 – Truth Heals.

• RK7 – Identity in Christ.

Biblical Foundation:

Genesis 3:9 – God's first question reveals the condition of the heart.

Mark 8:29 – Jesus uses questions to reveal personal belief.

Psalm 139:23 – 'Search me, O God… and know my heart.'

Counseling Conversation

Counselor: "Rebecca, you've said several times that you're afraid of disappointing people. Can I ask—what do you believe would happen if you did?"

Rebecca: "I don't know… I guess they would think less of me."

Counselor: "And if someone thought less of you, what would that mean about you as a person?"

Rebecca: (pauses) "Maybe… that I'm not good enough."

Counselor: "Not good enough for what? Or for whom?"

Rebecca: "For anyone. For God. For myself."

Counselor: "That's an important belief to look at. Who told you that your worth depends on perfection?"

Rebecca: "No one said it. I've just always felt it."

Counselor: "Feelings often come from beliefs we've never examined. Let me ask another question: Does Scripture teach that your worth comes from what you do—or from who God declares you to be?"

Rebecca: (quietly) "From who God says I am."

Counselor: "So if your belief contradicts God's truth, which one is creating your anxiety?"

Counselor's Strategy Explanation

The counselor uses layered, progressive questioning—not to interrogate Rebecca, but to guide her toward insight. Each question is targeted:

1.Clarifying questions uncover assumptions she has never verbalized.

2.Identity-based questions connect emotional fear to core beliefs.

3.Contrast questions place her beliefs next to Scripture for evaluation.

4.Responsibility questions invite awareness of internal ownership.

CCRT emphasizes that a person cannot change what they cannot see. Questions create visibility. They slow down emotional reactivity and pull hidden beliefs to the surface so they can be evaluated in the light of Scripture and Reality Keys.

Action Plan

Rebecca's assignment is a structured self-reflection exercise using the CCRT Insight Evaluation Worksheet:

• Identify three situations this week where anxiety appeared.

• Write what you were THINKING in those moments.

• Identify the belief beneath the thought.

• Compare that belief to a specific Scripture.

• Write a truth-based replacement belief.

She will also memorize Psalm 139:23–24 and journal one reflective question each day: "What belief created my emotion today?"

Expected Outcome

As Rebecca practices self-reflection, she will begin noticing patterns she previously overlooked. The goal is that she recognizes the origin of her anxiety within her belief system, understands how perfectionism contradicts her identity in Christ, and develops the ability to challenge distorted beliefs with biblical truth. Over time, her emotional distress will decrease as truth replaces fear and responsibility replaces self-imposed pressure.

INTERVENTION 3: CALLING FOR REPENTANCE

Repentance is one of the central intervention strategies in Scripture. It is not merely an emotional expression of regret, but a decisive turning of the mind, heart, and will toward God and truth. Biblical repentance involves confession, change, responsibility, and restoration. CCRT aligns naturally with this intervention, because repentance requires accurate belief, honest evaluation, and deliberate behavioral change—three pillars of the CCRT model. In counseling, calling for repentance is not accusatory or condemning; it is an invitation to transformation. This scenario demonstrates how a CCRT counselor guides a counselee toward repentance by integrating theological truth, clinical insight, and the structured methodology of the model.

Case Presentation

Daniel, a 42-year-old church deacon, seeks counseling after his wife discovers inappropriate text messages exchanged with a female coworker. Although there was no physical contact, the emotional and romantic tone of the conversations has deeply wounded his wife and jeopardized their marriage. Daniel admits the messages were "unwise," but he downplays their significance. He insists that because no physical affair occurred, his actions are not serious. His primary belief is: "Since I didn't cross physical lines, it's not a sin that requires repentance." This belief allows him to minimize the betrayal and avoid responsibility.

Counseling Objective

The counselor's objective is to help Daniel recognize the seriousness of his actions, understand the biblical definition of sin, and acknowledge the need for repentance. The goal is not shame or punishment, but genuine transformation through truth, responsibility, and restoration. The CCRT counselor must challenge Daniel's minimization, confront the distorted beliefs enabling the behavior, and guide him toward a biblically grounded understanding of repentance.

CCRT Analysis

Primary Needs Involved:

• Love & Belonging – Searching for emotional affirmation outside marriage.

• Power – Desire for validation, admiration, and control in relational dynamics.

Primary Conflicts:

• Belief Conflict – Believing emotional infidelity is harmless.

• Insight Conflict – Blindness to his wife's emotional injury.

• Moral Conflict – Rationalizing sin to avoid responsibility.

Distorted Beliefs Identified:

• "It's not really adultery unless it becomes physical."

• “Intentions matter more than the impact of my actions.”

• “If my wife wasn’t as distant, I wouldn’t have drifted emotionally.”

CCRT Reality Keys Used:

• RK1 – Belief Determines Experience.

• RK2 – We Move Toward What We Focus On.

• RK6 – Truth Heals.

• RK8 – Personal Responsibility Leads to Freedom.

Biblical Foundation:

Psalm 51:4 – 'Against You, you only, have I sinned.'

Matthew 5:28 – Jesus equates lustful intent with adultery of the heart.

1 John 1:9 – Confession is required for cleansing and restoration.

Counseling Conversation

Counselor: “Daniel, you’ve acknowledged the texting was unwise. Let me ask—what made it unwise?”

Daniel: “Well… my wife didn’t like it. It upset her.”

Counselor: “Why do you think it upset her?”

Daniel: “She thought I crossed a boundary, I guess.”

Counselor: “Let me ask a more direct question. Do you believe you crossed a boundary?”

Daniel: (hesitates) “I mean… maybe emotionally. But nothing physical happened.”

Counselor: “Daniel, I want to confront this gently but truthfully. In God’s eyes, sin begins in the heart. Jesus taught that even the intent of adultery is sin. So let me ask you: Did your heart cross a boundary?”

Daniel: (quiet) “…Yes.”

Counselor: “When you pursued emotional intimacy outside your marriage, who were you sinning against first—your wife or God?”

Daniel: “…God.”

Counselor: “And what is the biblical response when we sin against God?”

Daniel: “Repentance.”

Counselor: "Exactly. Repentance is not punishment—it's the pathway to freedom, restoration, and healing. If you avoid repentance, you avoid healing. But if you repent, God begins rebuilding what you damaged."

Counselor's Strategy Explanation

The counselor uses progressive confrontation combined with reflective questioning. Daniel is invited to evaluate his actions in light of Scripture rather than emotion or rationalization. The counselor is careful to:

1.Identify minimization ("Just texting")

2.Expose distorted beliefs (Sin is only physical)

3.Present biblical truth (Sin begins in the heart)

4.Lead the counselee to self-acknowledged responsibility

5.Invite repentance as a redemptive act

This is consistent with CCRT, which requires that the counselee recognize internal causes, not external excuses, for their behavior. Repentance is the fruit of corrected belief, honest evaluation, and accepted responsibility.

Action Plan

Daniel is assigned the following repentance framework based on CCRT principles:

•Confession – Write a prayer of confession acknowledging sin before God.

•Responsibility Statement – Identify specifically what he did, without excuses.

•Impact Analysis – Write how his actions affected his wife emotionally and spiritually.

•Truth Alignment – List three Scriptures correcting his distorted beliefs.

•Boundary Reconstruction – Identify the emotional boundaries he must rebuild.

•Restoration Plan – Prepare a humble, accountable conversation with his wife.

Additionally, Daniel must cease all non-essential communication with the coworker and share his plan with the counselor for accountability.

Expected Outcome

If Daniel embraces repentance, he will begin experiencing conviction, humility, and clarity. The minimization of sin will fade as truth replaces rationalization. Over time, genuine repentance will lead to restored intimacy with his wife, healthier boundaries, and a renewed walk with God. This intervention lays the foundation for rebuilding trust, healing marital wounds, and establishing long-term behavioral change.

INTERVENTION 4: ENCOURAGEMENT TOWARD FAITHFULNESS

Encouragement is a core biblical intervention that strengthens weary believers, restores hope, and reorients a person toward faithful obedience. Unlike flattery or emotional soothing, biblical encouragement is rooted in truth, identity, and calling. In Scripture, encouragement is often given when someone is discouraged, afraid, overwhelmed, or tempted to abandon their responsibilities. Jonathan strengthened David's hand in God; Paul strengthened the early churches; and Jesus repeatedly spoke words of courage to His disciples. In CCRT, encouragement is an intentional intervention designed to stabilize emotion, reinforce truth, and help the counselee re-engage with responsibility. It addresses discouragement at the belief level and calls the counselee toward renewed faithfulness.

Case Presentation

Lydia, a 31-year-old children's ministry volunteer, enters counseling due to exhaustion and a growing desire to quit all ministry responsibilities. She has been serving faithfully for nine years but recently feels invisible, unsupported, and unappreciated. Lydia reports, "No one notices how much I do. I feel like God isn't using me anymore." She cries frequently, struggles to pray, and feels guilty about wanting to give up. Her primary belief is: "If people don't affirm my service, God must not value me either." This belief produces shame, hopelessness, and spiritual fatigue.

Counseling Objective

The counselor's objective is to encourage Lydia toward renewed faithfulness by addressing the distorted beliefs fueling her discouragement. The goal is not to pressure her into continuing ministry, but to restore her confidence in God's calling, identity, and pleasure in her service. Encouragement, when done correctly, strengthens both emotional resilience and spiritual motivation. The counselor must guide her to see her worth in Christ rather than in human affirmation.

CCRT Analysis

Primary Needs Involved:

• Love & Belonging – Desire for recognition and connection.

• Power – Desire to feel meaningful and effective.

Primary Conflicts:

• Emotional Conflict – Discouragement leading to hopelessness.

• Belief Conflict – Equating God's approval with human praise.

• Insight Conflict – Misinterpreting ministry challenges as divine disapproval.

Distorted Beliefs Identified:

• "If people don't affirm me, God doesn't value me."

• “My worth is measured by visible results.”

• “Faithfulness only matters if others notice.”

CCRT Reality Keys Used:

• RK4 – Identity Determines Relationship.

• RK6 – Truth Heals.

• RK9 – Faithfulness is Success.

• RK11 – Discipline Produces Spiritual Growth.

Biblical Foundation:

1 Corinthians 15:58 – 'Your labor in the Lord is not in vain.'

Galatians 6:9 – 'Let us not grow weary in well-doing.'

Matthew 25:21 – 'Well done, good and faithful servant.'

Counseling Conversation

Counselor: “Lydia, you’ve been faithful for years. What makes you feel like God isn’t using you now?”

Lydia: “No one ever says thank you. It feels like no one sees what I do.”

Counselor: “Let me ask an important question: Who are you ultimately serving—your church or your Lord?”

Lydia: “Well… the Lord, I guess.”

Counselor: “Does God’s pleasure in your service depend on people noticing?”

Lydia: “No… but it’s hard when no one does.”

Counselor: “Of course it’s hard. Discouragement is real. But let me speak truth into that discouragement: God sees every act of your service—even the ones no one else sees. Scripture says your labor in the Lord is never in vain. So let me ask: Is it possible you’ve allowed human recognition to define your worth rather than your identity in Christ?”

Lydia: (tears) “Yes… I think so.”

Counselor: “Then let me encourage you. God has not forgotten you. Faithfulness is success in His eyes. Your identity is not ‘unnoticed volunteer’ but ‘beloved daughter who is pleasing to God.’ I want to help you rediscover that truth so you can serve from strength rather than exhaustion.”

Counselor's Strategy Explanation

Biblical encouragement strengthens identity, reorients belief, and restores hope. The counselor intentionally:

1.Validated her emotional experience without fostering self-pity.

2.Spoke truth-based encouragement rooted in Scripture.

3.Exposed the distorted belief connecting human approval to divine acceptance.

4.Reinforced her identity as a beloved, valued servant of God.

5.Redirected her focus from outcomes and recognition to faithfulness.

This mirrors the way Jonathan strengthened David: not with empty comfort, but by reminding him of God's calling and faithfulness. CCRT uses encouragement as a corrective intervention—replacing emotional fatigue with Truth-anchored hope.

Action Plan

Lydia's assignments are designed to strengthen her identity and restore joy in service:

•Identity Reflection – Write five Scriptures affirming her worth in Christ.

•Gratitude Journal – Record three ways God has used her each week.

•Service Reframing Exercise – Write what faithfulness means from God's perspective.

•Boundary Evaluation – Identify ministries she should continue and any she should release.

•Prayer of Realignment – Ask God to restore her motivation and align her heart with His pleasure.

These tasks reinforce truth, reduce emotional overwhelm, and prepare her for sustainable ministry.

Expected Outcome

With consistent encouragement and truth realignment, Lydia is expected to experience renewed purpose, emotional strength, and a healthier understanding of ministry. She will learn to serve from identity rather than insecurity and to measure success by faithfulness rather than recognition. Over time, her joy in serving will increase, and her relationship with God will deepen as she internalizes truth and releases distorted expectations.

INTERVENTION 5: TEACHING AND INSTRUCTION

Teaching and instruction are central to biblical intervention. From Moses teaching Israel, to Ezra reading the Law, to Jesus unfolding the Scriptures, to Paul grounding churches in doctrine, biblical change is built on truth taught clearly and applied practically. In CCRT, instruction is more than giving information. Teaching restructures the counselee's belief system, renews the mind, and equips them to act in a manner consistent with truth. Instruction targets distorted thinking, replaces confusion with clarity, and provides the cognitive framework necessary for emotional and behavioral transformation. This scenario demonstrates how a CCRT counselor uses teaching to correct misunderstanding, strengthen belief, and guide a counselee toward responsible action.

Case Presentation

Aaron, a 25-year-old new Christian, seeks counseling due to confusion about spiritual growth. He feels spiritually inadequate, believes God is constantly disappointed in him, and interprets every hardship as punishment. Aaron says, "I must be doing something wrong. God is probably upset with me." He reads Scripture inconsistently, misunderstands passages, and constructs beliefs based on fear rather than truth. His primary belief is: "If anything goes wrong in my life, it means God is angry at me." This belief produces anxiety, guilt, and spiritual instability. Aaron needs structured instruction to correct his understanding of God, grace, sanctification, and spiritual growth.

Counseling Objective

The CCRT counselor's objective is to provide biblical teaching that dismantles Aaron's distorted beliefs and replaces them with truth. This requires instruction about God's character, the nature of discipline, the process of sanctification, and the difference between consequences and condemnation. The goal is not merely to give Aaron information but to reform his internal belief system so his experiences and emotions begin aligning with biblical truth.

CCRT Analysis

Primary Needs Involved:

• Love & Belonging – Desire to feel accepted by God.

• Security – Need for stability and assurance.

Primary Conflicts:

• Belief Conflict – Misinterpreting hardship as divine anger.

• Insight Conflict – Lack of understanding regarding spiritual growth.

• Emotional Conflict – Anxiety fueled by false doctrine.

Distorted Beliefs Identified:

• "Hardship means God is angry with me."

• “God’s love depends on my performance.”

• “If I fail, God withdraws from me.”

CCRT Reality Keys Used:

• RK1 – Belief Determines Experience.

• RK3 – Truth Defines Reality.

• RK4 – Identity Determines Relationship.

• RK6 – Truth Heals.

Biblical Foundation:

Hebrews 12:6 – Discipline is a sign of God’s love, not His wrath.

Romans 8:1 – No condemnation for those who are in Christ.

John 17:17 – Sanctification occurs through truth.

Counseling Conversation

Counselor: “Aaron, you mentioned that when something goes wrong, you assume God is angry. Where did that belief come from?”

Aaron: “I don’t know… I’ve always thought God blesses you when you’re good and punishes you when you’re bad.”

Counselor: “That’s a common misunderstanding. Can I show you what the Bible actually teaches about God’s discipline?”

Aaron: “Yes, please.”

Counselor: “Hebrews 12 teaches that discipline is proof of God’s love, not His rejection. Discipline shapes us, but it doesn’t condemn us. Let me ask: If God disciplines because He loves, then can hardship mean God is abandoning you?”

Aaron: “…No. I guess not.”

Counselor: “Right. Now look at Romans 8:1— ‘There is therefore now no condemnation for those in Christ.’ If that is true, is your belief that God is constantly disappointed accurate?”

Aaron: “Not if I believe the verse… I guess I’ve been assuming a lot.”

Counselor: “That’s why teaching matters. When your beliefs change, your fears will change too. God isn’t punishing you—He’s growing you. Instruction helps you interpret your life the way Scripture does.”

Counselor's Strategy Explanation

Teaching in CCRT is targeted, not general. The counselor:

1.Identified the distorted belief creating emotional instability.

2.Provided biblical instruction that corrected the misunderstanding.

3.Used Scripture to reframe hardship as love-driven growth.

4.Tied truth to Aaron's identity to stabilize his relationship with God.

5.Invited evaluation by comparing Aaron's belief to Scripture.

This instructional approach restructures the belief system so emotional experience can shift. Teaching is transformative when it clarifies truth, connects identity, and assigns responsibility.

Action Plan

Aaron's homework includes a structured teaching-based exercise:

•Doctrine Review – Read Hebrews 12:1–11 and list what discipline is and what it is not.

•Belief Correction Chart – Identify three fears and replace each with a Scripture.

•Identity in Christ Study – Journal five truths about who he is in Christ.

•Sanctification Reflection – Write one paragraph explaining how God uses hardship for growth.

•Prayer of Alignment – Ask God to renew his mind and anchor him in truth.

These tasks ensure that instruction translates into internalized belief.

Expected Outcome

With consistent teaching, Aaron will begin interpreting life through a biblical lens. As false beliefs collapse and are replaced with truth, his emotions will stabilize. Anxiety will decrease, confidence in God's character will grow, and his spiritual foundation will strengthen. Over time, Aaron will develop resilience, healthier doctrine, and a deeper relationship with God built on truth rather than fear.

INTERVENTION 6: REFRAMING CIRCUMSTANCES WITH GOD'S SOVEREIGNTY

Reframing circumstances through the lens of God's sovereignty is a deeply biblical intervention used repeatedly by prophets, apostles, and Christ Himself. Joseph reframed betrayal through God's redemptive plan; Paul reframed suffering as purposeful; Jesus reframed the disciples' fears with reminders of the Father's control. Reframing is not denial—it is reinterpretation. It challenges the counselee's perception and invites them to see their circumstances as God sees them. In CCRT, reframing is a corrective intervention that targets the belief level, reshaping emotional experience and behavioral response. It replaces fear, confusion, and hopelessness with theological clarity, stabilizing the counselee in truth and redirecting them toward responsibility and spiritual growth.

Case Presentation

Tamara, a 46-year-old woman, seeks counseling after losing her job unexpectedly. She interprets the loss as a sign that God has abandoned her or is punishing her. Tamara says, "Everything in my life is falling apart. God must be done with me." She feels ashamed, anxious about finances, and fearful of disappointing her adult children. Although she has been faithful in her walk with Christ, Tamara views hardship primarily through a negative, punitive lens. Her core belief is: "Hardship means God has withdrawn His goodness from me." This distorted interpretation fuels emotional overwhelm, spiritual confusion, and paralysis in decision-making.

Counseling Objective

The counselor's objective is to help Tamara reinterpret her circumstances biblically by reframing hardship through God's sovereignty and love. The counselor must address her distorted beliefs, challenge the assumption that suffering equals divine rejection, and guide her toward truth-based evaluation. Reframing will help Tamara anchor herself in God's character, regain emotional stability, and respond to her situation with courage and responsibility rather than fear and despair.

CCRT Analysis

Primary Needs Involved:

• Security – Fear of instability and uncertainty.

• Love & Belonging – Feeling unseen and abandoned

Primary Conflicts:

• Belief Conflict – Misinterpreting hardship as divine punishment.

• Emotional Conflict – Anxiety, fear, and discouragement.

• Insight Conflict – Viewing circumstances only through immediate emotion

Distorted Beliefs Identified:

• "If something bad happens, God must be angry."

• "Hardship means God has abandoned me."

• "My worth and security rise and fall with circumstances."

CCRT Reality Keys Used:

• RK1 – Belief Determines Experience.

• RK3 – Truth Defines Reality.

• RK5 – God Uses Circumstances to Shape Us.

• RK6 – Truth Heals.

Biblical Foundation:

Genesis 50:20 – God uses what others meant for evil for His purposes.

Romans 8:28 – God works all things together for good.

James 1:2–4 – Trials produce maturity and endurance.

Counseling Conversation

Counselor: "Tamara, you said losing your job means God has abandoned you. Let me ask—what makes you believe that?"

Tamara: "Because everything went wrong so suddenly. God wouldn't let this happen if He were still with me."

Counselor: "So your belief is that hardship equals rejection. Can I ask an important question? Is that what Scripture teaching?"

Tamara: (pauses) "Not really… but it feels that way."

Counselor: "Feelings are powerful, but they're not always truthful. Scripture repeatedly shows God using hardship to shape, position, and refine His people. Joseph said what others meant for evil, God meant for good. So let me ask you: Is it possible that God is working in your situation even if you can't see it yet?"

Tamara: (tearful) "I want to believe that."

Counselor: "Then let's reframe what's happening. Instead of 'God has abandoned me,' what if the truth is 'God is guiding me into a new season, and He is with me through the entire process'? Does that change how you feel?"

Tamara: "It feels… lighter. Like maybe this isn't the end."

Counselor: "Exactly. Reframing is about seeing your life the way God sees it. Hardship isn't rejection—it's preparation. And God is not done with you. He is shaping you."

Counselor's Strategy Explanation

Reframing is not about positive thinking—it is about truth-based reinterpretation. The counselor intentionally:

1.Identified the distorted interpretation ("God abandoned me").

2.Contrasted emotion with Scripture, clarifying truth.

3.Reframed the circumstance through God's sovereignty and goodness.

4.Connected the new frame to Tamara's identity as a loved daughter of God.

5.Invited belief evaluation to help her internalize the theological reframe.

This shifts Tamara from emotional instinct to biblical understanding. CCRT leverages reframing to stabilize emotion, restore clarity, and empower the counselee to respond responsibly rather than react fearfully.

Action Plan

Tamara will complete a structured reframing exercise using the Truth Alignment Worksheet:

• Write the circumstance that triggered fear.

• Identify the belief she attached to it.

• Compare that belief to Scripture.

• Rewrite the belief in truth-based language.

• Identify one action of responsibility she can take in faith.

She will also memorize Romans 8:28 and journal daily how she sees God's presence in small ways during her transition.

Expected Outcome

As Tamara reframes her situation with biblical truth, her emotional distress will lessen, her sense of security will stabilize, and her confidence in God's presence will deepen. Her new belief—rooted in sovereignty rather than fear—will produce healthier responses, renewed motivation, and greater spiritual resilience. Over time, she will interpret life less through emotion and more through truth, experiencing peace that aligns with God's character.

INTERVENTION 7: ACCOUNTABILITY

Accountability is a deeply biblical intervention in which believers support, correct, and strengthen one another through honest companionship and shared responsibility. Moses had Aaron and Hur, David had Nathan, Paul had Barnabas, and the early church formed communities that confronted sin, encouraged righteousness, and upheld one another in truth. Accountability is not surveillance or punishment; it is relational strengthening. In CCRT, accountability reinforces responsibility, challenges avoidance, and provides structure for change. It activates community support, reduces isolation, and helps the counselee remain aligned with biblical truth and disciplined practice. This scenario demonstrates how a CCRT counselor uses accountability to guide a counselee toward lasting transformation.

Case Presentation

Marcus, a 38-year-old husband and father, seeks counseling for a recurring struggle with pornography. He has experienced seasons of victory but falls back into the behavior during periods of stress or conflict. Marcus says, "I want to stop, but I always end up isolated, ashamed, and keeping secrets." His wife is devastated, trust is fragile, and Marcus feels stuck in a cycle of guilt and temporary reform. His primary belief is: "I have to fight this alone because no one would understand." This belief keeps him isolated, vulnerable, and spiritually discouraged.

Counseling Objective

The counselor's objective is to help Marcus embrace biblical accountability as a tool for strength and transformation. The goal is to break secrecy, address distorted beliefs about isolation, and provide a structured support system. Accountability partners, check-ins, and confession are introduced not as punishment, but as pathways to freedom, responsibility, and spiritual growth. Marcus must learn that secrecy is the soil in which sin grows, but accountability is the structure in which healing thrives.

CCRT Analysis

Primary Needs Involved:

• Security – Desire for safety and stability.

• Love & Belonging – Need for connection and acceptance.

• Power – Need for self-mastery and spiritual victory.

Primary Conflicts:

• Behavioral Conflict – Repeated relapse patterns.

• Belief Conflict – Belief that isolation equals strength.

• Emotional Conflict – Shame and self-condemnation.

Distorted Beliefs Identified:

• “No one would understand my struggle.”

• “Asking for help means weakness.”

• “Accountability is punishment or humiliation.”

CCRT Reality Keys Used:

• RK1 – Belief Determines Experience.

• RK8 – Personal Responsibility Leads to Freedom.

• RK10 – Community Strengthens Transformation.

• RK11 – Discipline Produces Growth

Biblical Foundation:

Proverbs 27:17 – 'Iron sharpens iron.'

James 5:16 – 'Confess your faults… that you may be healed.'

Ecclesiastes 4:9–10 – 'Two are better than one.'

Counseling Conversation

Counselor: “Marcus, you’ve tried to fight this alone for years. How has that worked for you?”

Marcus: (sighs) “Not very well.”

Counselor: “What’s the belief behind not asking anyone for help?”

Marcus: “Honestly… I’m afraid people will judge me.”

Counselor: “Let me ask a direct question: Does Scripture teach that transformation happens in isolation or in community?”

Marcus: “…Community.”

Counselor: “Exactly. Accountability isn’t humiliation—it’s protection. Iron sharpens iron. You cannot sharpen yourself in secret. What if accountability is actually the path God wants to use to strengthen you?”

Marcus: “I’ve never thought about it that way.”

Counselor: “This struggle grows in secrecy. But healing grows in confession, partnership, and discipline. I want to help you build a support structure—not to punish you, but to strengthen you.”

Marcus: “I think… I think I need that.”

Counselor's Strategy Explanation

The counselor dismantles Marcus's distorted belief that isolation equals strength. Through questioning and teaching, the counselor reframes accountability as a biblical, protective, and strengthening intervention. The strategy includes:

1.Normalizing struggle to reduce shame.

2.Introducing biblical examples of accountability.

3.Explaining the purpose of accountability as support, not surveillance.

4.Connecting accountability to identity and the need for community.

5.Structuring specific accountability practices that produce consistency.

In CCRT, accountability reinforces responsibility and creates an environment where truth-based change is maintained through external support and internal discipline.

Action Plan

Marcus is given a multi-step accountability plan:

•Accountability Partner – Choose a spiritually mature man for weekly check-ins.

•Daily Status Report – Send a brief message confirming victory or struggle.

•Belief Identification – Journal the lies that precede temptation.

•Trigger Analysis – Identify emotional states associated with relapse. Replacement Strategy – Create truth-based responses for triggers.

•Confession Practice – Meet biweekly with his pastor or mentor.

The plan emphasizes responsibility, community support, and structured habits that foster long-term change.

Expected Outcome

As Marcus embraces accountability, secrecy will diminish, shame will weaken, and responsibility will increase. Over time, Marcus will develop stronger self-mastery, healthier beliefs, and greater relational support. Accountability will provide the structure necessary for consistent victory, rebuilding trust with his wife and strengthening his walk with God.

INTERVENTION 8: SCRIPTURE-BASED CORRECTION & TRAINING

Scripture-based correction and training is one of the most foundational biblical interventions. Paul instructed Timothy that all Scripture is profitable for doctrine, reproof, correction, and instruction in righteousness. Throughout the Bible, God uses His Word to confront error, realign beliefs, and train His people in holiness. This intervention is not merely about quoting verses; it involves applying Scripture accurately to distorted thinking, harmful behaviors, and emotional confusion. In CCRT, Scripture-based correction replaces false beliefs with truth, stabilizes emotional experience, and provides the framework for responsible action. Correction is transformative when delivered with clarity, compassion, and a commitment to truth-based renewal.

Case Presentation

Sophia, a 29-year-old woman, seeks counseling after months of emotional instability following a breakup. She reports intense feelings of rejection, unworthiness, and hopelessness. Sophia frequently says, "God must be punishing me for my past." She views the breakup not as a relational incompatibility but as divine retribution. Though she reads Scripture occasionally, she interprets it through the lens of shame. Sophia's primary belief is: "My past failures make me unlovable to God." This false belief drives anxiety, emotional withdrawal, and self-condemnation.

Counseling Objective

The counselor's objective is to apply Scripture in a corrective manner, dismantling Sophia's shame-based beliefs and guiding her toward truth-based identity. The goal is not to overwhelm her with verses, but to help her interpret Scripture correctly, understand grace, and differentiate conviction from condemnation. The counselor must help her replace distorted beliefs with biblical truth so her emotions and behaviors can realign with reality.

CCRT Analysis

Primary Needs Involved:

• Love & Belonging – Fear of rejection and abandonment.

• Security – Need for emotional stability.

Primary Conflicts:

• Belief Conflict – Interpreting life through shame rather than grace.

• Emotional Conflict – Anxiety and despair rooted in false interpretation.

• Insight Conflict – Misunderstanding the nature of God's love and forgiveness.

Distorted Beliefs Identified:

• "My past failures make me unlovable to God."

• "Hardship is God's punishment."

• "God withdraws from me when I fail."

CCRT Reality Keys Used:

• RK1 – Belief Determines Experience.

• RK3 – Truth Defines Reality.

• RK4 – Identity Determines Relationship.

• RK6 – Truth Heals.

• RK7 – Identity in Christ.

Biblical Foundation:

Romans 8:1 – 'There is therefore now no condemnation for those who are in Christ.'

Psalm 103:12 – God removes sin as far as east from west.

Isaiah 43:25 – God remembers sin no more.

Counseling Conversation

Counselor: "Sophia, you've said several times that God must be punishing you. What evidence are you using to support that?"

Sophia: "Just how everything feels. I feel guilty all the time."

Counselor: "Feelings can be powerful, but feelings are not the standard for truth. Can we look at what Scripture says about your relationship with God?"

Sophia: "Okay."

Counselor: "Read Romans 8:1 aloud: 'There is therefore now no condemnation for those who are in Christ Jesus.' What does that say about God's posture toward you?"

Sophia: "…That He's not condemning me."

Counselor: "Correct. So is the belief 'God is punishing me for my past' consistent or inconsistent with this verse?"

Sophia: “Inconsistent.”

Counselor: “Right. This is what Scripture-based correction does—it shows us truth so our beliefs can change. Now look at Psalm 103:12. How far has God removed your sin?”

Sophia: “As far as the east is from the west.”

Counselor: “So if God removed your sin, are your feelings of shame telling you the truth?”

Sophia: (tearful) “I guess not… I’ve believed lies for so long.”

Counselor’s Strategy Explanation

The counselor uses Scripture as a corrective tool, not a weapon. The strategy includes:

1.Identifying distorted beliefs rooted in shame.

2.Introducing Scripture that directly contradicts those beliefs.

3.Helping the counselee interpret the Scripture accurately.

4.Guiding the counselee to compare belief vs. biblical truth.

5.Inviting emotional realignment through acceptance of truth.

Scripture-based correction in CCRT clarifies identity, dismantles lies, and stabilizes emotional experience. It grounds the counselee in objective truth rather than fluctuating emotion.

Action Plan

Sophia is assigned a structured correction exercise:

•Truth Replacement Chart – List three shame-based beliefs and find Scriptures that refute them.

•Identity Study – Read Ephesians 1 and write ten identity statements.

•Truth Meditation – Spend 10 minutes daily meditating on Romans 8:1.

•Prayer of Acceptance – Thank God daily for His forgiveness and ask Him to align her emotions with truth.

These assignments translate correction into personal transformation.

Expected Outcome

As Sophia internalizes Scripture, her belief system will shift from shame to identity in Christ. Emotional stability will increase as condemnation is replaced by confidence in God's love and forgiveness. Her sense of worth will deepen, her anxiety will decrease, and she will learn to interpret hardships through the lens of grace rather than punishment.

INTERVENTION 9: VALIDATION OF EMOTION + TRUTH ALIGNMENT

Validation is a powerful biblical intervention that acknowledges human emotion without surrendering to it. Throughout Scripture, God validates the emotional experiences of His people—Hannah's anguish, David's lament, Elijah's exhaustion, and Mary's grief—before speaking truth that reorients their hearts. Validation provides safety, reduces emotional tension, and softens defensiveness. Truth alignment then follows, helping the counselee interpret their emotions correctly through Scripture. In CCRT, this two-part intervention stabilizes emotion and restructures belief so the counselee can act responsibly and faithfully.

Case Presentation

Elena, a 40-year-old wife and mother, seeks counseling after months of feeling overwhelmed. Her husband travels frequently for work, leaving her to manage the household and children alone. She reports crying often, feeling abandoned, and wrestling with resentment. Elena says, "I feel like I'm carrying everything myself, and I hate that I feel this way." She believes her emotions indicate spiritual weakness. Her core distorted belief is: "If I were spiritually stronger, I wouldn't feel overwhelmed." This belief leads to shame, emotional suppression, and self-criticism.

Counseling Objective

The counselor aims to validate Elena's emotional experience—affirming its legitimacy—while guiding her toward truth-based interpretation. The goal is not to eliminate emotion but to anchor it in truth. Validation reduces shame and opens the door for truth alignment, where Scripture reframes her beliefs about weakness, identity, and emotional struggle.

CCRT Analysis

PRIMARY NEEDS:

• Love & Belonging – Desire for support and connection.

• Security – Need for emotional grounding.

Primary Conflicts:

• Emotional Conflict – Overwhelm mixed with guilt.

• Belief Conflict – Misinterpreting emotion as spiritual weakness.

• Insight Conflict – Not recognizing normal human emotion.

Distorted Beliefs:

• "Emotion = spiritual failure."

• "Strength means never feeling overwhelmed."

• "Needing help makes me weak."

CCRT Reality Keys Used:

• RK1 – Belief Determines Experience.

• RK4 – Identity Determines Relationship.

• RK6 – Truth Heals.

• RK7 – Identity in Christ.

• RK11 – Discipline Produces Growth.

Biblical Foundation:

Psalm 34:18 – God is near to the brokenhearted.

1 Kings 19 – God validates Elijah's exhaustion before addressing his thinking.

John 11 – Jesus validates the grief of Mary before revealing deeper truth.

Counseling Conversation

Counselor: "Elena, you're carrying a heavy load. Anyone in your situation would feel overwhelmed. Your feelings make sense."

Elena: (crying) "I feel guilty for feeling this way."

Counselor: "Feeling overwhelmed isn't sin—it's human. Even Elijah felt this way, and God met him with compassion, not rebuke."

Elena: "I never thought of it like that."

Counselor: "Let me ask—what belief makes you think that experiencing emotion makes you spiritually weak?"

Elena: "Probably the idea that strong Christians always stay calm."

Counselor: "Is that what Scripture actually shows us? Or do we see faithful people experiencing deep emotion?"

Elena: "…Scripture shows emotion."

Counselor: "Exactly. Your emotions are real, but they don't define your identity. Now let's align your emotions with truth. What does God say about His presence when you feel weak?"

Elena: "That He is near… and that He strengthens me."

Counselor: "Right. So your emotions are valid, but they must be guided by truth—not guilt."

Counselor's Strategy Explanation

The counselor uses a two-stage CCRT approach:

1. **VALIDATION:** Normalizing Elena's emotional experience reduces shame, defensiveness, and emotional shutdown.

Validation provides safety and acknowledges the emotional reality without endorsing distorted beliefs.

2. **TRUTH ALIGNMENT**: Once stable, the counselor gently challenges the belief that emotion equals weakness.

Truth from Scripture reframes Elena's identity and interpretation of her experience.

This integrated method allows Elena to feel understood while her belief system is corrected, creating a pathway to healthier emotional and spiritual functioning.

Action Plan

Elena is given a structured two-part assignment:

• Emotion Log – Record three moments of overwhelm with the statement: "My emotion is valid."

• Truth Alignment Worksheet – For each emotional moment, pair it with a specific biblical truth.

• Belief Replacement Exercise – Identify one guilt-producing belief per day and replace it with Scripture.

• Support Step – Reach out to a trusted Christian friend twice this week for encouragement.

These exercises help Elena internalize validation and truth alignment in daily life.

Expected Outcome

As Elena practices validation and truth alignment, her shame will diminish, emotional stability will increase, and her beliefs will shift toward a biblical understanding of human emotion. Over time, she will interpret her experience through truth rather than guilt, resulting in greater resilience, healthier self-perception, and deeper dependence on God.

INTERVENTION 10: COMFORT IN AFFLICTION

Comfort in affliction is one of the most compassionate interventions seen throughout Scripture. God is repeatedly described as the Father of mercies and the God of all comfort. Jesus comforted the grieving, upheld the fearful, and restored the broken. Comfort does not deny pain; it acknowledges suffering while anchoring the counselee in divine truth. In CCRT, comfort stabilizes the emotional system, restores hope, and provides the relational safety needed for healing. This intervention validates pain while guiding the counselee toward a truth-based interpretation of suffering.

Case Presentation

Jared, a 52-year-old widower, seeks counseling nine months after the unexpected death of his wife. He describes feeling numb, spiritually disconnected, and emotionally isolated. He attends church but avoids interaction, often leaving immediately. Jared says, "I feel like God abandoned me. If He cared, He wouldn't have taken her." His grief is deep and unresolved, and he feels guilty for still struggling. His primary distorted belief is: "If God loved me, He wouldn't have allowed this loss." This interpretation turns his sorrow into despair.

Counseling Objective

The counselor seeks to provide biblical comfort—validating Jared's grief while gently guiding him toward truth. Comfort calms emotional distress and provides a foundation for truth-based reframing. The goal is not the removal of pain but anchoring Jared in God's compassion, presence, and faithfulness.

CCRT Analysis

PRIMARY NEEDS:

• Security – Need for stability following traumatic loss.

• Love & Belonging – Desire for relational and spiritual connection.

Primary Conflicts:

• Emotional Conflict – Deep grief and emotional exhaustion.

• Belief Conflict – Interpreting loss as divine rejection.

• Insight Conflict – Difficulty separating emotion from theology.

Distorted Beliefs:

• "God abandoned me."

• "If God loved me, this wouldn't have happened."

• "Grief means weak faith."

CCRT Reality Keys Used:

• RK1 – Belief Determines Experience.

• RK3 – Truth Defines Reality.

• RK5 – God Uses Circumstances to Shape Us.

• RK6 – Truth Heals.

• RK12 – God Is Present in Suffering.

Biblical Foundation:

2 Corinthians 1:3–4 – God comforts us in all affliction.

Psalm 34:18 – God is near to the brokenhearted.

John 14:18 – Jesus will not leave His people as orphans.

Counseling Conversation

Counselor: "Jared, your grief is real, and your pain is real. Anyone who loved deeply would grieve deeply."

Jared: (teary) "But it feels like God abandoned me."

Counselor: "Feeling abandoned is part of grief, but it does not mean God has left you. Scripture says the Lord is near to the brokenhearted. Your feelings matter—but they are not the whole truth."

Jared: "It's hard to believe God is near when everything feels empty."

Counselor: "David felt the same way at times, yet he discovered God was closest in those moments. What if, instead of seeing your loss as God leaving you, we consider the possibility—based on Scripture—that God is carrying you through it?"

Jared: (quiet) "I want to believe that…"

Counselor: "That desire is evidence of faith, even in sorrow. God's comfort isn't the absence of pain—it's His presence in the pain."

Counselor's Strategy Explanation

The counselor uses comfort as a stabilizing intervention:

1.Validation – Affirming Jared's emotional reality.

2.Reducing guilt – Helping him see grief as a natural human response.

3.Biblical reassurance – Reminding him of God's nearness and compassion.

4.Correcting distorted beliefs – Challenging his interpretation that loss equals abandonment.

5.Identity reinforcement – Rooting him in God's faithful presence.

This reflects CCRT's integrated approach: validating emotion while grounding belief in truth.

Action Plan

Jared receives a structured comfort plan:

•Grief Journal – Write daily about moments of pain and where he sensed God's presence.

•Comfort Verses – Meditate on Psalm 34:18 and 2 Corinthians 1:3–4.

•Connection Step – Meet weekly with a trusted Christian friend.

•Faithfulness Memory List – Identify three ways God has been faithful since the loss.

•Lament Prayer – Write a Psalm-like lament expressing sorrow honestly to God.

These steps help Jared grieve while staying anchored in truth.

Expected Outcome

As Jared internalizes comfort and truth, his despair will lessen. Emotional pain will remain, but hopelessness will diminish as he experiences God's presence through Scripture, community, and reflection. Over time, he will move from isolated grief to grieving with hope, grounded in the truth of God's faithful character.

INTERVENTION 11: NARRATIVE CONFRONTATION / PARABLES

Narrative confrontation—using story, metaphor, or parable to expose hidden beliefs—is a deeply biblical intervention. God used narrative confrontation when Nathan confronted David with the parable of the stolen lamb. Jesus used parables to reveal the heart, challenge assumptions, expose sin, and invite repentance. Narratives bypass defensiveness, allowing counselees to see themselves objectively before recognizing the personal application. In CCRT, narrative confrontation helps the counselee identify distorted beliefs, self-deception, and harmful patterns by seeing them presented in another context. This intervention creates emotional safety while delivering profound insight.

Case Presentation

Samuel, a 47-year-old business owner, seeks counseling for escalating anger and strained family relationships. He frequently interrupts loved ones, dismisses opinions, and becomes defensive when confronted. His teenage daughter no longer speaks to him, and his wife describes him as 'impossible to talk to.' Samuel insists he is merely 'strong-willed' and denies having an anger issue. His primary belief is: "People need to respect my authority; if they disagree, they are being disrespectful." This belief fuels control, defensiveness, and emotional intimidation.

Counseling Objective

The counselor's objective is to help Samuel gain insight into how his behavior affects others and how his beliefs distort his interpretation of family dynamics. Because direct confrontation triggers defensiveness, narrative confrontation provides a safer method. The counselor will use a story to mirror Samuel's behavior, allowing him to evaluate it without self-protection, then guide him toward recognition and responsibility.

CCRT Analysis

PRIMARY NEEDS:

• Power – Desire for control, influence, and authority.

• Love & Belonging – Fear of relational disconnection.

Primary Conflicts:

• Insight Conflict – Inability to see personal contribution to conflict.

• Behavioral Conflict – Patterns of anger, interruption, and dominance.

• Belief Conflict – Equating disagreement with disrespect.

Distorted Beliefs:

• "Respect means compliance."

• "Disagreement is a threat to my authority."

• "People must yield for relationships to work."

CCRT Reality Keys Used:

• RK1 – Belief Determines Experience.

• RK4 – Identity Determines Relationship.

• RK6 – Truth Heals.

• RK8 – Personal Responsibility Leads to Freedom.

Biblical Foundation:

2 Samuel 12 – Nathan exposes David's sin with a story.

Luke 10 – Jesus uses narrative to confront prejudice and self-justification.

Matthew 21 – Parables reveal motives and challenge resistance.

Counseling Conversation

Counselor: "Samuel, can I tell you a short story? I'd like your honest reaction."

Samuel: "Sure."

Counselor: "Imagine a ship captain who loves his crew. He works hard, leads strongly, and wants the ship to run well. But whenever a crew member offers feedback, he cuts them off. Whenever someone suggests a different course, he sees it as a threat. The crew stops speaking up. They avoid the captain unless they must. The captain believes he is commanding respect, but in reality, he is feared—not trusted. The ship still moves, but the crew moves silently, carefully, and without connection."

Samuel: (frowns) "That sounds like a bad leader."

Counselor: "What makes him a bad leader?"

Samuel: "He doesn't listen. He thinks disagreement is disrespect."

Counselor: (pauses gently) "Do you see any similarities between the captain's belief and your home?"

Samuel: (quiet, eyes down) "…Yes."

Counselor: "What similarities do you see?"

Samuel: "I guess… I shut people down. I don't listen. I make them walk on eggshells. I thought I was being strong."

Counselor: "Strength isn't intimidation. Strength is influence. And influence grows when people feel heard. Your family doesn't need a captain—they need a father who listens."

Counselor's Strategy Explanation

Narrative confrontation bypasses Samuel's defensiveness by placing his behavior in a non-threatening story. The counselor:

1.Created a parallel narrative that mirrors Samuel's relational patterns.

2.Asked evaluative questions that allow Samuel to critique the story objectively.

3.Invited connection between the fictional captain and Samuel's real behavior.

4.Affirmed insight as Samuel recognized the impact of his beliefs.

5.Shifted focus to responsibility, encouraging Samuel to adopt healthier relational patterns.

This technique leads the counselee to self-awareness without triggering defensiveness, facilitating deeper transformation.

Action Plan

Samuel receives a structured responsibility plan:

•Listening Exercise – In three conversations this week, Samuel must allow the other person to finish without interruption.

•Belief Identification – Write moments where disagreement triggered defensiveness and the belief behind it.

•Truth Alignment – Replace the belief "Disagreement = disrespect" with biblical truth about humility and patience.

•Family Check-In – Ask his wife and daughter one question: "How can I listen better this week?"

•Prayer of Humility – Daily prayer from Psalm 139 asking God to reveal blind spots.

These steps transform insight into relational change.

Expected Outcome

As Samuel recognizes and replaces distorted beliefs, his defensiveness will decrease, communication will improve, and relational tension will ease. The narrative confrontation opens the door to humility, emotional connection, and responsibility, leading to healthier family dynamics and deeper spiritual growth.

INTERVENTION 12: RESTORATION AFTER FAILURE

Restoration after failure is one of the most compassion-filled interventions in Scripture. Throughout the Bible, God restores those who fall—David after moral failure, Peter after denial, Jonah after rebellion, and Israel after repeated wandering. Restoration does not erase consequences, but it renews fellowship, reestablishes identity, and redirects purpose. In CCRT, restoration after failure involves guiding the counselee to confront truth, process shame, receive God's grace, and rebuild forward movement rooted in responsibility, repentance, and hope.

Case Presentation

Daniel, a 38-year-old youth leader, comes to counseling devastated after a moral failure that forced him to step down from ministry. He feels ashamed, defeated, and spiritually disqualified. Daniel says, "God can't use me anymore. I've ruined everything." His marriage is strained, his prayer life feels frozen, and he avoids church out of embarrassment. His primary distorted belief is: "A single failure permanently disqualifies me."

Counseling Objective

The counselor's objective is to help Daniel process his failure truthfully, break the belief that failure cancels identity, and understand God's restorative nature. Restoration will require responsibility, repentance, and rebuilding trust, but its foundation rests in God's grace rather than Daniel's perfection.

CCRT Analysis

PRIMARY NEEDS:

• Identity – Reestablishing worth grounded in Christ.

• Security – Emotional stability after crisis.

Primary Conflicts:

• Belief Conflict – Interpreting failure as permanent identity.

• Emotional Conflict – Shame, fear, and self-condemnation.

• Responsibility Conflict – Confusing repentance with disqualification.

Distorted Beliefs:

• "God cannot restore me after failure."

• "My usefulness to God is based on perfection."

• "People will never trust me again."

CCRT Reality Keys Used:

• RK1 – Belief Determines Experience.

• RK4 – Identity Determines Relationship.

• RK6 – Truth Heals.

• RK10 – Grace Restores.

• RK12 – God Meets Us in Brokenness.

Biblical Foundation:

Psalm 51 – David restored after sin.

John 21 – Jesus restores Peter.

Micah 7:8 – Though I fall, I will rise.

Counseling Conversation

Counselor: "Daniel, you've described heavy shame. What belief drives the idea that God can't use you anymore?"

Daniel: "I failed. Leaders aren't supposed to fail like this."

Counselor: "That's true—leaders are called to integrity. But does failure erase God's ability to restore?"

Daniel: (quiet) "Maybe not… but it feels that way."

Counselor: "Peter denied Jesus three times. Was he restored?"

Daniel: "…Yes."

Counselor: "David fell and repented. Was he restored?"

Daniel: "Yes."

Counselor: "Your failure requires responsibility, repentance, and rebuilding trust—but it does not erase your identity. Shame tells you the story is over. God says restoration is possible. Which voice aligns with Scripture?"

Daniel: (tears) “God’s… I just don’t feel worthy.”

Counselor: “Worthiness never qualified you in the first place. Grace did.”

Counselor’s Strategy Explanation

The counselor leads Daniel through restoration using:

1.Truth Alignment – Distinguishing responsibility from condemnation.

2.Grace Integration – Reconnecting identity to Christ rather than performance.

3.Emotional Processing – Allowing space for grief, confession, and lament.

4.Repentance and Repair – Identifying steps to rebuild trust and integrity.

5.Future Reframing – Helping Daniel see restoration as a process, not a moment.

This mirrors the biblical pattern of fall → confession → restoration → renewed purpose.

Action Plan

Daniel receives a structured restoration plan:

•Confession & Clarity – Meet with church leadership to express repentance and accept guidance.

•Accountability Structure – Weekly check-ins with a mature mentor.

•Identity Statements – “I am forgiven,” “I am being restored,” “God is not finished with me.”

•Scripture Meditation – John 21 (Peter’s restoration) for 7 days.

•Repair Steps – Develop a plan to rebuild trust with spouse and ministry leaders.

These steps help Daniel move from shame to restoration.

Expected Outcome

As Daniel processes failure biblically, shame will lose its hold, emotional stability will return, and identity will be restored. Over time, he will regain confidence, rebuild damaged relationships, and experience renewed purpose grounded in grace rather than perfection.

INTERVENTION 13: TEACHING DEPENDENCE ON GOD

Teaching dependence on God is one of the most foundational interventions in Scripture and appears repeatedly throughout the ministry of Jesus and the experience of God's people. Human independence—rooted in self-reliance, self-protection, and self-exaltation—is a primary source of emotional instability and spiritual drift. In contrast, dependence on God grounds the counselee in humility, trust, obedience, and stability. In CCRT, teaching dependence on God involves revealing the limits of self-strength, reframing struggles through God's sufficiency, and helping the counselee adopt patterns of trust, surrender, and reliance upon God's character rather than personal capacity.

Case Presentation

Amanda, a 44-year-old accountant, comes to counseling overwhelmed by anxiety, insomnia, and chronic exhaustion. She explains, "I have to keep everything together. If I don't do it, everything will fall apart." Amanda manages household finances, cares for aging parents, supervises staff at work, and volunteers at church. Her relentless drive reflects a deeper belief: that she must hold life together by her own strength. Her primary distorted belief is: "If I stop controlling everything, disaster will follow."

Counseling Objective

The counselor's objective is to help Amanda recognize the emotional and spiritual burden of self-reliance, understand the biblical call to trust God, and shift from control-based functioning to dependence-based living. The goal is to restructure her beliefs so that stability comes from God's sovereignty rather than her own efforts.

CCRT Analysis

PRIMARY NEEDS:

• Security – Emotional stability that comes from trust.

• Identity – Understanding worth independent of performance.

Primary Conflicts:

• Belief Conflict – Confusing responsibility with control.

• Emotional Conflict – Anxiety produced by self-reliance.

• Insight Conflict – Measuring life by personal capacity rather than divine sufficiency.

Distorted Beliefs:

• "Everything depends on me."

• "If I don't control outcomes, everything will fall apart."

• "God helps others, but He won't come through for me."

CCRT Reality Keys Used:

• RK1 – Belief Determines Experience.

• RK3 – Truth Defines Reality.

• RK5 – God Uses Circumstances to Shape Us.

• RK7 – Identity in Christ.

• RK12 – God Is Present in All Circumstances.

Biblical Foundation:

Psalm 46:1 – God is our refuge and strength.

2 Corinthians 12:9 – His strength is made perfect in weakness.

Proverbs 3:5–6 – Trust in the Lord with all your heart.

Counseling Conversation

Counselor: "Amanda, you've described exhaustion. What belief keeps you driving yourself at this level?"

Amanda: "If I don't, everything will fall apart."

Counselor: "That's a heavy burden. Who told you everything depends on you?"

Amanda: (quiet) "No one… I just feel like it."

Counselor: "Feelings can be powerful, but they don't always reflect truth. Scripture says God is the One who sustains, protects, and upholds. When we try to take God's job, we collapse under the weight. What might change if you allowed God to carry what you were never meant to hold?"

Amanda: "I… don't know how to do that."

Counselor: "Dependence begins where your strength ends. It's choosing to trust God's sufficiency. Your role is obedience, not control. God carries outcomes. Which role have you been living?"

Amanda: “Control… everything is control.”

Counselor: “And how has that worked?”

Amanda: (tearful) “It’s killing me.”

Counselor’s Strategy Explanation

To teach dependence, the counselor helps Amanda:

1.Identify the burden created by self-reliance.

2.Contrast human limitation with God’s sufficiency.

3.Reframe responsibility as obedience rather than control.

4.Integrate truth through meditation and prayer.

5.Practice release—choosing to surrender outcomes to God.

This mirrors the biblical pattern of weakness → surrender → divine strength.

Action Plan

Amanda receives a dependence-building plan:

•Daily Surrender Prayer – Release specific burdens to God each morning.

•Responsibility Chart – Distinguish between what is hers to do and what belongs to God.

•Scripture Meditation – Reflect on 2 Corinthians 12:9 for 14 days.

•Weekly Rest Practice – One intentional period of Sabbath rest.

•Accountability Partner – Share weekly progress with a mature believer.

These steps help shift her emotional posture from control toward trust.

Expected Outcome

As Amanda learns to depend on God, anxiety will decrease, emotional stability will increase, and her identity will shift from self-reliance to Christ-reliance. Over time, she will experience deeper spiritual peace, healthier boundaries, and renewed confidence in God’s sustaining power.

INTERVENTION 14: CHALLENGING FEAR AND STRENGTHENING COURAGE

Challenging fear and strengthening courage is a major biblical intervention found throughout both the Old and New Testaments. God repeatedly commands His people, "Fear not," not because danger never exists, but because fear distorts truth, weakens faith, and undermines obedience. Courage is not the absence of fear—it is obedience in the presence of fear. In CCRT, this intervention helps the counselee identify fear-based beliefs, confront distortions, and replace them with truth-based courage rooted in God's presence, promises, and sovereignty.

Case Presentation

Michelle, a 31-year-old elementary school teacher, seeks counseling because fear dominates her daily life. She fears failure, criticism, conflict, and disappointing others. These fears cause her to avoid leadership roles, overthink decisions, and retreat emotionally in relationships. Michelle admits, "I know God says not to fear, but the fear feels more real than the promise." Her primary distorted belief is: "Fear protects me from danger."

Counseling Objective

The counselor's objective is to help Michelle challenge fear-based interpretations, identify the beliefs that sustain her fears, and strengthen courage through scriptural truth. The goal is not to eliminate all risk but to reframe fear through God's presence and empower Michelle to move forward in obedience despite emotional discomfort.

CCRT Analysis

PRIMARY NEEDS:

• Security – Need for emotional and spiritual stability.

• Identity – Confidence rooted in Christ.

Primary Conflicts:

• Belief Conflict – Fear as truth rather than interpretation.

• Emotional Conflict – Avoidance and anxiety controlling behavior.

• Responsibility Conflict – Fear preventing obedience.

Distorted Beliefs:

• "Fear keeps me safe."

• "If I step out, I will fail."

• "I am alone when I face fear."

CCRT Reality Keys Used:

• RK1 – Belief Determines Experience.

• RK3 – Truth Defines Reality.

• RK4 – Identity Determines Relationship.

• RK5 – God Uses Circumstances to Shape Us.

• RK12 – God Is Present in Every Situation.

Biblical Foundation:

Isaiah 41:10 – "Fear not, for I am with you."

Joshua 1:9 – "Be strong and courageous."

2 Timothy 1:7 – God has given us a spirit of power, love, and sound mind.

Counseling Conversation

Counselor: "Michelle, you've described fear as a constant presence. What belief gives fear so much power?"

Michelle: "It feels like fear warns me and keeps me from making mistakes."

Counselor: "Does fear actually protect you, or does it limit you?"

Michelle: (pauses) "Honestly… it limits me."

Counselor: "Exactly. Fear pretends to be safety, but it becomes a prison. Scripture says God—not fear—is your protector. What would change if you believed God's presence was more real than the fear?"

Michelle: "I guess I'd try things instead of avoiding them."

Counselor: "Courage isn't the absence of fear. It's choosing obedience while trusting God's presence. The more truth you hold; the less space fear has to control you."

Counselor's Strategy Explanation

The counselor helps Michelle challenge fear and strengthen courage by:

1.Identifying fear-based beliefs and tracing their emotional influence.

2.Evaluating fear through the lens of biblical truth.

3.Teaching presence-based courage—courage rooted in God's nearness.

4.Gradual exposure to feared situations paired with truth repetition.

5.Replacing fear statements with Scripture-based courage statements.

This process replaces fear-based interpretation with God-centered courage.

Action Plan

Michelle receives a courage-building plan:

•Fear Inventory – Identify top 3 fears and the beliefs behind them.

•Courage Statements – "God is with me," "Fear is not my guide," "Obedience brings strength."

•Small Risk Practice – Weekly action confronting a mild fear.

•Scripture Meditation – Isaiah 41:10 and Joshua 1:9 for 14 days.

•Accountability Partner – Share fear-challenging steps with a trusted believer.

These steps strengthen courage and weaken fear's emotional influence.

Expected Outcome

As Michelle practices truth-centered courage, fear will lose its power, and obedience will increase. Emotional stability will grow as she learns to trust God's presence more than her fear. Over time, she will develop confidence, resilience, and a renewed willingness to face challenges with faith rather than avoidance.

INTERVENTION 15: GUIDING LAMENT AND EMOTIONAL HONESTY

Guiding lament and emotional honesty is a deeply biblical intervention grounded in the Psalms, Lamentations, the prophets, and even the life of Jesus Himself. Scripture does not silence human pain—it gives it language. Biblical lament creates a space for grief, disappointment, confusion, and emotional struggle to be expressed before God without shame. In CCRT, guiding lament helps counselees acknowledge difficult emotions, identify the beliefs shaping those emotions, and bring their pain honestly to God so that healing, clarity, and truth can replace despair and emotional suppression. Lament is not complaining; it is structured honesty before God that leads the heart toward hope.

Case Presentation

Caroline, a 47-year-old mother of three, seeks counseling after the sudden death of her younger sister. Though months have passed, Caroline feels numb, spiritually disconnected, and emotionally overwhelmed. She says, "I know I'm supposed to be strong. I shouldn't question God. But inside, I feel abandoned." Caroline avoids prayer because she fears expressing her feelings would be irreverent. Her primary distorted belief is: "Strong Christians don't express sorrow to God."

Counseling Objective

The counselor's objective is to help Caroline understand the biblical role of lament, give her permission to express her grief honestly before God, identify beliefs that restrict emotional expression, and guide her toward healing through structured lament. The goal is not to eliminate grief but to redirect it in a healthy, faith-strengthening direction.

CCRT Analysis

PRIMARY NEEDS:

• Security – Emotional grounding and spiritual reassurance.

• Love & Belonging – Connection with God in the midst of sorrow.

Primary Conflicts:

• Emotional Conflict – Suppression of grief and overwhelming sorrow.

• Belief Conflict – Misinterpreting emotional honesty as spiritual weakness.

• Insight Conflict – Difficulty recognizing lament as biblical worship.

Distorted Beliefs:

• "Strong Christians should not cry out to God."

• "Expressing grief is unspiritual."

• "If I express pain, I'm dishonoring God."

CCRT Reality Keys Used:

• RK1 – Belief Determines Experience.

• RK6 – Truth Heals.

• RK12 – God Meets Us in Suffering.

• RK14 – Grace Welcomes Honesty.

• RK16 – Emotional Awareness Produces Clarity.

Biblical Foundation:

Psalm 13 – David asks, "How long, O Lord?"

Lamentations – Honest grief expressed in faith.

Matthew 26:38 – Jesus: "My soul is overwhelmed with sorrow."

Counseling Conversation

Counselor: "Caroline, you've carried deep grief alone. What keeps you from bringing it to God?"

Caroline: "I don't want to dishonor Him. I should trust Him without questioning."

Counselor: "Is lament the same as questioning God's goodness, or is it bringing your pain to Him?"

Caroline: (pauses) "I guess… it's bringing pain to Him."

Counselor: "Exactly. Over a third of the Psalms are laments. God included them to teach us how to process grief. Lament is worship—it is trust in the middle of pain. What if God is inviting you to bring your sorrow to Him instead of hiding it?"

Caroline: (tearful) "I never thought of lament as worship."

Counselor: "Lament is faith expressing hurt while still reaching for God. It is the cry of someone who trusts God enough to be honest."

Counselor's Strategy Explanation

The counselor guides Caroline through lament by:

1.Teaching the biblical structure of lament—complaint, request, remembrance, trust.

2.Creating safe space for emotional expression without judgment.

3.Identifying suppressed emotions and the beliefs behind them.

4.Helping her write a personal lament modeled after Psalm 13.

5.Integrating truth and hope while acknowledging ongoing grief.

This process helps her move from suppression → expression → truth → trust.

Action Plan

Caroline receives a grief-processing plan:

•Lament Writing Exercise – Write her own Psalm-style lament each week.

•Emotion Naming Practice – Identify and name emotions daily.

•Scripture Meditation – Read Psalm 13 and Lamentations 3 for 14 days.

•Support Conversation – Share her lament with a trusted friend or mentor.

•Prayer of Honesty – Daily prayer expressing real emotions to God.

These practices validate emotions and guide them toward spiritual healing.

Expected Outcome

As Caroline practices biblical lament, emotional suppression will lessen, grief will become manageable, and her connection with God will deepen. Over time, she will experience healing, clarity, and renewed trust as she learns that God welcomes honest sorrow and meets His people in their pain.

INTERVENTION 16: EXPOSURE OF FALSE BELIEFS AND IDOLS

Exposing false beliefs and idols is a core biblical intervention because human suffering often flows from misplaced trust, distorted beliefs, or elevating something—approval, control, success, comfort—to a position only God should hold. Throughout Scripture, God confronts His people's idols not to condemn them, but to free them. In CCRT, exposing false beliefs and idols invites the counselee to examine the internal structures shaping fear, shame, anger, or unhealthy patterns. This intervention helps the counselee replace the old belief system with truth, grounding identity, meaning, and purpose in God rather than in false sources of security.

Case Presentation

Ethan, a 42-year-old sales manager, seeks counseling after months of tension, irritability, and emotional volatility at home. He explains that most of his stress comes from work because he fears losing his performance ranking. Ethan admits, "I have to be the best. If I'm not number one, I'm nothing." His worth rises and falls with his productivity, and his anger erupts whenever his performance drops. Ethan's wife says he is emotionally unavailable, chronically anxious, and increasingly perfectionistic. His primary distorted belief is: "My success determines my value."

Counseling Objective

The counselor's objective is to help Ethan uncover the false belief functioning as an idol—the belief that success defines his identity. This requires exposing the root fear beneath the idol, challenging the belief with truth, and guiding Ethan to replace performance-based identity with Christ-centered identity.

CCRT Analysis

PRIMARY NEEDS:

• Identity – Deep desire for worth and significance.

• Security – Emotional stability threatened by performance.

Primary Conflicts:

• Belief Conflict – Success equals worth.

• Emotional Conflict – Anxiety and anger linked to performance.

• Identity Conflict – Basing identity on achievement rather than Christ.

Distorted Beliefs:

• "Failure makes me worthless."

• "If others outperform me, I lose value."

• "Success is the source of identity and security."

CCRT Reality Keys Used:

• RK1 – Belief Determines Experience.

• RK4 – Identity Determines Relationship.

• RK6 – Truth Heals.

• RK7 – Identity in Christ.

• RK13 – Reflection Exposes Hidden Beliefs.

Biblical Foundation:

Exodus 20 – Idols distort worship and identity.

Matthew 6:24 – No one can serve two masters.

Philippians 3:7–9 – Paul redefines worth through Christ alone.

Counseling Conversation

Counselor: "Ethan, what happens emotionally when you slip from first place at work?"

Ethan: "I panic… I get angry. I feel like I'm losing something important."

Counselor: "What do you believe you're losing?"

Ethan: (quiet) "Worth. Respect. Identity."

Counselor: "Those are powerful words. Let me ask: Who gave you your identity—your job or your Creator?"

Ethan: "…God, I guess."

Counselor: "If God gives identity, can performance erase it?"

Ethan: "No… but it feels like it."

Counselor: "That feeling comes from a false belief—a functional idol. Not a carved statue, but an internal belief that says, 'My worth is found here.' Scripture shows that idols demand everything and give nothing. What has your success idol cost you?"

Ethan: (tears) "My peace… my family… my joy."

Counselor's Strategy Explanation

To expose false beliefs and idols, the counselor guides Ethan through:

1.Identifying the functional idol—beliefs elevating success to the role of savior.

2.Tracing emotional patterns—fear, anger, shame linked to performance.

3.Confronting the idol with Scripture—truth about identity, worth, and God's sovereignty.

4.Replacing the idol—rooting identity in Christ.

5.Establishing new practices that reinforce truth over performance.

This intervention dismantles the inner belief structure driving emotional dysfunction.

Action Plan

Ethan receives a truth-replacement plan:

•Belief Inventory – Write out the top three performance-based beliefs.

•Truth Replacement – Match each belief with Scripture (Phil. 3:7–9, Eph. 1:3–7).

•Identity Confession – Daily statements: "Christ defines my worth," "Success is not my savior."

•Performance Detachment – Intentionally choose one task to complete without overworking.

•Accountability Partner – Weekly identity-focused check-in.

These steps help shift Ethan from performance-driven identity to Christ-centered identity.

Expected Outcome

As Ethan exposes the false beliefs shaping his identity, fear and anger will diminish, emotional stability will increase, and relationships will strengthen. Over time, he will experience peace, purpose, and security grounded in Christ—not performance.

INTERVENTION 17: CALLING FOR RESPONSIBILITY AND ACTION

Calling for responsibility and action is a core biblical intervention because spiritual and emotional growth requires not only insight, but obedient follow-through. Throughout Scripture, God invites His people to respond actively to truth— 'Arise,' 'Go,' 'Repent,' 'Strengthen,' 'Put off,' 'Put on.' Insight without action leads to stagnation; action rooted in truth leads to transformation. In CCRT, this intervention helps the counselee move from passive awareness to active obedience, connecting belief, behavior, and responsibility in a way that produces measurable growth and breaks cycles of avoidance or immobility.

Case Presentation

Tanya, a 36-year-old nursing assistant, seeks counseling because she feels stuck in life. She continually talks about goals—going back to school, improving her marriage, strengthening her walk with God—but never takes concrete steps. Tanya admits, "I know what I should do… I just never do it. I freeze." Her inaction leads to frustration, disappointment, and growing hopelessness. Her primary distorted belief is: "Thinking about change is the same as taking responsibility."

Counseling Objective

The counselor's objective is to help Tanya recognize the gap between intention and action, confront passive patterns, and take ownership of concrete steps toward change. The goal is to move her from reflective awareness to responsible follow-through, empowered by biblical truth and guided by CCRT's integration of belief, behavior, and responsibility.

CCRT Analysis

PRIMARY NEEDS:

• Competence – Building confidence through action.

• Security – Stability through responsible choices.

Primary Conflicts:

• Responsibility Conflict – Mistaking intention for obedience.

• Belief Conflict – Believing change will "just happen someday."

• Emotional Conflict – Fear, anxiety, and overwhelm blocking action.

Distorted Beliefs:

• "I'll change when I feel ready."

• "Thinking about change is enough."

• "Taking responsibility is risky."

CCRT Reality Keys Used:

• RK1 – Belief Determines Experience.

• RK2 – Choices Shape Direction.

• RK3 – Truth Defines Reality.

• RK9 – Responsibility Produces Freedom.

• RK11 – Discipline Produces Growth.

Biblical Foundation:

James 1:22 – Be doers of the Word.

Philippians 2:12–13 – Work out your salvation with reverence.

Luke 6:46–49 – Obedience builds a strong foundation.

Counseling Conversation

Counselor: "Tanya, you've described wanting change for years. What has kept you from taking the first step?"

Tanya: "I don't know… fear, I guess. I overthink everything."

Counselor: "Let me ask: What do you believe will happen if you take responsibility and move forward?"

Tanya: "What if I fail? What if I can't do it?"

Counselor: "Avoidance feels safe, but it keeps you stuck. Scripture shows that obedience begins with a step—not a feeling. James says to be doers of the Word. What if responsibility is the path to the confidence you're waiting for?"

Tanya: "I never thought of action as something that builds confidence."

Counselor: "Confidence grows from responsibility. You don't wait until you feel ready—you grow as you obey. What is one small, specific step toward your goal that you could take this week?"

Tanya: "I could look up the nursing program at the community college."

Counselor's Strategy Explanation

The counselor strengthens responsibility and action by:

1.Identifying passive beliefs that keep Tanya stuck.

2.Teaching responsibility as obedience, not emotion-based motivation.

3.Breaking goals into actionable steps to reduce overwhelm.

4.Establishing accountability structures for consistent follow-through.

5.Reinforcing progress to strengthen confidence and motivation.

This intervention shifts the counselee from passive dreaming to active commitment.

Action Plan

Tanya receives an action-oriented responsibility plan:

•Define One Goal – Enroll in the nursing program.

•Weekly Step List – Complete one small action toward the goal each week.

•Responsibility Statements – "Action produces change," "Avoidance keeps me stuck," "Obedience precedes confidence."

•Scripture Meditation – James 1:22 for 14 days.

•Accountability Partner – Report her weekly steps to a trusted mentor.

These steps transform intention into consistent action.

Expected Outcome

As Tanya embraces responsibility and action, she will break cycles of stagnation, overcome fear-based avoidance, and develop confidence rooted in obedience rather than emotion. Over time, she will gain momentum, stability, and clarity as she moves forward in her goals with God's guidance.

INTERVENTION 18: MEDIATION AND RECONCILIATION

Mediation and reconciliation are central biblical interventions because God Himself is a God of reconciliation. From Genesis to Revelation, Scripture presents God as restoring broken relationships—between Himself and humanity, and among His people. Mediation helps counselees move toward understanding, responsibility, confession, forgiveness, and relational repair. In CCRT, mediation aims to reduce emotional reactivity, expose distorted beliefs fueling conflict, clarify responsibility, and lead both parties toward peace rooted in truth rather than avoidance or superficial agreement.

Case Presentation

Anthony (45) and Melissa (43), married for 19 years, come to counseling after several months of escalating conflict. Arguments center around finances, parenting styles, and unspoken resentments. Anthony withdraws emotionally when tension rises, while Melissa becomes increasingly critical and anxious. Both feel unheard and misunderstood. Their primary distorted beliefs are:

• Anthony: 'Conflict means I'm failing as a husband; withdrawal keeps the peace.'

• Melissa: 'If I don't push for change, nothing will get better.'

Counseling Objective

The counselor's objective is to mediate communication, help each spouse identify and express underlying beliefs and emotions, reduce reactivity, and guide them toward reconciliation through truth, responsibility, and compassion. The goal is not a quick fix, but renewed understanding and relational healing.

CCRT Analysis

Primary Needs:

• Anthony – Security, competence, emotional safety.

• Melissa – Love/belonging, reassurance, emotional connection.

Primary Conflicts:

• Belief Conflict – Conflicting interpretations of conflict.

• Emotional Conflict – Withdrawal vs. intensity.

• Communication Conflict – Reactivity blocking understanding.

Distorted Beliefs:

• 'Avoidance prevents conflict.'

• 'Intensity equals communication.'

• 'If my spouse disagrees, I am rejected.'

CCRT Reality Keys Used:

• RK1 – Belief Determines Experience.

• RK2 – Choices Shape Direction.

• RK4 – Identity Determines Relationship.

• RK6 – Truth Heals.

• RK12 – God Is Present in Conflict.

Biblical Foundation:

Matthew 18:15–17 – Addressing conflict with truth and grace.

2 Corinthians 5:18 – God has given us the ministry of reconciliation.

Romans 12:18 – As much as possible, live at peace with all.

Counseling Conversation

Counselor: "Anthony, when conflict rises, what do you feel internally?"

Anthony: "Like I'm failing. I shut down to avoid making things worse."

Counselor: "And Melissa, what do you feel when he withdraws?"

Melissa: "Alone. Like he doesn't care."

Counselor: "So his withdrawal feels like rejection to you, and her intensity feels like danger to you. Yet both of you are reacting from fear, not intention. Let's slow this down so each of you can hear the other's heart."

Counselor guides them to restate emotions, clarify beliefs, and validate each other without defensiveness.

Counselor's Strategy Explanation

The counselor facilitates reconciliation using:

1.Slowing the Interaction – Helping each spouse pause before reacting.

2.Reflective Listening – Each repeats the other's words until understanding is achieved.

3.Belief Identification – Exposing the internal fears and assumptions.

4.Responsibility Clarification – Each takes ownership of their contribution.

5.Forgiveness and Repair – Guiding them toward confession, grace, and cooperative solutions.

This process restores truth, reduces reactivity, and supports emotional safety.

Action Plan

Anthony and Melissa receive a reconciliation plan:

•Daily Check-In – 10-minute conversation using reflective listening.

•Conflict Pause Rule – When emotions rise, pause for 5 minutes, then return calmly.

•Belief Journaling – Each identifies distorted beliefs that trigger reactions.

•Forgiveness Practice – Weekly discussion acknowledging hurts and offering grace.

•Prayer Together – Asking God for unity and understanding.

These steps build relational safety and support long-term peace.

Expected Outcome

As Anthony and Melissa practice reconciliation, emotional safety will rise, misunderstandings will decrease, and patterns of withdrawal and intensity will weaken. Over time, they will develop healthier communication, deeper trust, and a more stable, Christ-centered union.

INTERVENTION 19: USE OF CONSEQUENCES TO TEACH

The use of consequences as a teaching tool is deeply biblical and appears repeatedly throughout Dr. Barnette's work. In Scripture, consequences are not punishments for the sake of pain but instruments for correction, awakening, discipline, and redirection. God consistently employs consequences to reveal the implications of choices, illuminate distorted beliefs, and guide His people toward wiser, healthier, and more righteous behavior. In CCRT, consequences function as a therapeutic mirror, helping the counselee connect choices with outcomes so they may internalize truth, develop responsibility, and adopt patterns aligned with God's wisdom. Dr. Barnette emphasizes consequences as God's pedagogical system—cause and effect—that teaches reality and fosters growth.

Case Presentation

Marcus, a 29-year-old delivery driver, seeks counseling after nearly losing his job due to repeated tardiness and careless mistakes. He explains that he "never means to mess up," but circumstances, lack of planning, and emotional distractions consistently set him back. When disciplined at work, Marcus responds with frustration: "They're too strict. Everyone makes mistakes." However, the true problem is that he fails to connect his choices with their consequences. He sees consequences as personal attacks rather than predictable outcomes. His primary distorted belief is: "If my intentions are good, the consequences shouldn't matter."

Counseling Objective

The counselor's objective is to help Marcus understand that consequences are not arbitrary punishments but predictable results. The goal is to teach Marcus to view consequences as information—signals pointing to the real issues in his choices, habits, and beliefs. Through CCRT, the counselor will help Marcus replace emotional reasoning with truthful evaluation and responsibility.

CCRT Analysis

Primary Needs:

- Security – Stability that comes from responsible behavior.

- Competence – The ability to make wise and effective choices.

Primary Conflicts:

- Belief Conflict – Minimizing the relationship between choices and outcomes.

- Emotional Conflict – Interpreting consequences as attacks rather than learning tools.

- Responsibility Conflict – Believing intentions outweigh actions.

Distorted Beliefs:

• "If I didn't mean to do wrong, the consequence is unfair."

• "Rules are too strict when they inconvenience me."

• "Outcomes should adjust to my intentions."

CCRT Reality Keys Used:

• RK1 – Belief Determines Experience.

• RK2 – Choices Shape Direction.

• RK3 – Truth Defines Reality.

• RK9 – Responsibility Produces Freedom.

• RK11 – Discipline Produces Growth.

Biblical Foundation:

Proverbs 1:29–31 – Those who reject wisdom eat the fruit of their choices.

Galatians 6:7 – A man reaps what he sows.

Hebrews 12:5–11 – God uses discipline to train His children in righteousness.

Counseling Conversation

Counselor: "Marcus, tell me what you think caused the warning you received at work."

Marcus: "Honestly, they're overreacting. I was only late a few minutes."

Counselor: "Were you late only once?"

Marcus: (sighs) "No… several times."

Counselor: "What do you think your employer expects from you?"

Marcus: "Consistency… I guess."

Counselor: "In Scripture, consequences are often God's way of teaching us the seriousness of repeated choices. They are not attacks—they are information. What information do these consequences give you about your patterns?"

Marcus: "That I need to take this more seriously."

Counselor: "Exactly. You're not being punished—you're being taught. The consequence reveals the truth: your habits are not working. What would change if you began viewing consequences as lessons rather than criticisms?"

Marcus: "I might stop blaming everything else and take responsibility."

Counselor's Strategy Explanation

The counselor uses consequences-to-teach by:

1.Reframing consequences from punishment to instruction.

2.Helping Marcus see patterns between choices and outcomes.

3.Moving him from intention-based reasoning to responsibility-based reasoning.

4.Identifying the beliefs that justify or excuse dysfunctional behavior.

5.Teaching him to anticipate outcomes before making decisions.

This aligns with Dr. Barnette's emphasis on God's use of consequences as a training mechanism for wisdom.

Action Plan

Marcus receives a consequence-awareness plan:

•Choice-Outcome Chart – Track specific actions and their outcomes for 14 days.

•Morning Planning Routine – Set alarms, prepare work items, plan drive time.

•Responsibility Statements – "My choices have predictable outcomes," "I own my actions," "I cannot change outcomes without changing habits."

•Scripture Meditation – Reflect on Galatians 6:7 daily.

•Accountability Partner – Weekly check-in with a mature believer.

These practices strengthen responsibility and reduce impulsive habits.

Expected Outcome

As Marcus learns to connect choices with consequences, responsibility will replace defensiveness, stability will replace chaos, and wisdom will replace impulsivity. Over time, he will adopt healthier habits, become dependable at work, and experience greater emotional and spiritual growth.

INTERVENTION 20: CULTIVATING GRATITUDE

Cultivating gratitude is a biblically grounded intervention that reorients the counselee's emotional and spiritual posture toward truth, provision, and God's faithfulness. Gratitude is not denial of hardship—it is the intentional practice of seeing God's goodness within hardship. Scripture repeatedly commands gratitude because it redirects the heart away from fear, discouragement, and resentment toward worship, trust, and emotional stability. In CCRT, cultivating gratitude challenges distorted beliefs, broadens emotional perspective, and anchors the counselee in truth rather than circumstance.

Case Presentation

Tyrone, a 50-year-old warehouse supervisor, comes to counseling experiencing chronic irritability and frustration. He feels overworked, underappreciated, and burdened by financial pressures. Tyrone says, "Nothing ever goes right for me. Everyone else gets ahead, and I'm stuck." His negativity affects his marriage, work relationships, and spiritual life. He admits neglecting prayer and Bible reading because "there's nothing to be thankful for lately." Tyrone's primary distorted belief is: "My circumstances determine my joy."

Counseling Objective

The counselor's objective is to help Tyrone identify the beliefs fueling negativity, redirect his focus toward God's gifts and grace, and cultivate gratitude as a daily discipline. The goal is to break the cycle of resentment, restore emotional balance, and strengthen Tyrone's spiritual resilience.

CCRT Analysis

Primary Needs:

• Security – Emotional grounding and stability.

• Meaning & Hope – Confidence in God's work within his life.

Primary Conflicts:

• Emotional Conflict – Persistent frustration and negativity.

• Belief Conflict – Circumstantial definition of joy.

• Insight Conflict – Inability to recognize blessings.

Distorted Beliefs:

• "I have nothing to be thankful for."

• "My joy depends on my circumstances."

• "God is not doing anything for me."

CCRT Reality Keys Used:

• RK1 – Belief Determines Experience.

• RK3 – Truth Defines Reality.

• RK5 – God Uses Circumstances to Shape Us.

• RK6 – Truth Heals.

• RK15 – Gratitude Reorients the Heart.

Biblical Foundation:

1 Thessalonians 5:18 – Give thanks in all circumstances.

Philippians 4:6 – Bring requests to God with thanksgiving.

Psalm 103 – Bless the Lord and remember His benefits.

Counseling Conversation

Counselor: "Tyrone, you've described constant frustration. What do you believe fuels that emotion?"

Tyrone: "Everything feels unfair. Nothing good ever happens."

Counselor: "When you say 'nothing good,' does that mean literally nothing? Or does it feel that way emotionally?"

Tyrone: (pauses) "It feels that way."

Counselor: "Feelings are real, but they don't always tell the truth. Gratitude helps us see what emotions blur. Tell me—what has God provided even in this difficult season?"

Tyrone: (hesitates) "I mean… I still have my job… my health… my family."

Counselor: "Those are significant gifts. Gratitude doesn't ignore hardship—it balances perspective. When circumstances dominate your focus, frustration grows. When God's faithfulness enters your focus, hope grows."

Tyrone: "I never thought about it like that."

Counselor: "Let's begin shifting your focus—not by pretending everything is perfect, but by acknowledging the good that is real."

Counselor's Strategy Explanation

The counselor uses gratitude cultivation by:

1.Identifying distorted beliefs that magnify negativity.

2.Validating emotion while expanding perspective beyond circumstance.

3.Using Scripture to anchor gratitude in truth.

4.Helping Tyrone practice daily gratitude as spiritual discipline.

5.Reframing difficulties in light of God's faithfulness.

Gratitude redirects attention from scarcity to provision, from frustration to faith.

Action Plan

Tyrone receives a gratitude-based plan:

•Daily Gratitude List – Write 5 blessings each morning.

•Blessing Prayer – Thank God for one specific gift each night.

•Truth Replacement – Replace the statement "Nothing ever goes right" with "God is working, even when I don't see it."

•Weekly Reflection – Identify one-way God showed provision.

•Gratitude Conversation – Share one blessing each week with his spouse.

These steps strengthen Tyrone's emotional stability and reorient his beliefs.

Expected Outcome

As Tyrone practices gratitude, frustration and negativity will decrease. He will gain emotional clarity, spiritual renewal, and greater joy as his focus shifts from circumstances to God's provision. Over time, gratitude will reshape his beliefs, mood, and relationships, grounding him in truth and strengthening his resilience.

INTERVENTION 21: TEACHING WISDOM AND DISCERNMENT

Wisdom and discernment are essential biblical interventions that shape how a counselee interprets life, makes decisions, and responds to emotional or relational pressure. Scripture describes wisdom as the skill of living rightly (Proverbs 1:2–7), and discernment as the ability to distinguish truth from error, good from harmful, and God's direction from one's own impulses. In CCRT, cultivating wisdom and discernment helps the counselee pause, reflect, evaluate beliefs, and align decisions with biblical truth rather than emotion, fear, or habit. This intervention strengthens judgment, stabilizes emotional reactivity, and produces long-term maturity.

Case Presentation

Lisa, a 32-year-old office administrator, seeks counseling after repeatedly making impulsive decisions in relationships and finances. She admits, "I know the right thing after the fact, but in the moment I get swept up in feelings or pressure. I want to be wiser." Lisa's decisions often create emotional regret, relational strain, and instability. Her primary distorted belief is: "My feelings in the moment are the best guide for my decisions."

Counseling Objective

The counselor's objective is to help Lisa slow down her decision-making process, evaluate beliefs driving her impulses, and develop a biblically grounded framework for discernment. The goal is to strengthen reflective thinking, reduce impulsivity, and teach her to filter decisions through Scripture and truth rather than emotion.

CCRT Analysis

Primary Needs:

• Security – Emotional stability through wise choices.

• Meaning – Desire for maturity and spiritual growth.

Primary Conflicts:

• Belief Conflict – Following emotion instead of wisdom.

• Emotional Conflict – Impulse overriding discernment.

• Insight Conflict – Difficulty recognizing harmful patterns in the moment.

Distorted Beliefs:

• "If I feel it strongly, it must be right."

• "Slowing down means missing an opportunity."

• "Thinking it through is overreacting."

CCRT Reality Keys Used:

• RK1 – Belief Determines Experience.

• RK2 – Choices Shape Direction.

• RK3 – Truth Defines Reality.

• RK8 – Wisdom Guards the Heart.

• RK13 – Reflection Precedes Understanding.

Biblical Foundation:

Proverbs 2 – Seek wisdom as treasure.

Philippians 1:9–10 – Grow in discernment.

James 1:5 – God gives wisdom generously.

Counseling Conversation

Counselor: "Lisa, you've said you regret decisions afterward. What typically drives the choices you make in the moment?"

Lisa: "Usually whatever I'm feeling strongest—fear, excitement, pressure."

Counselor: "Let me ask: Do strong feelings always equal truth?"

Lisa: (shakes head) "Not really."

Counselor: "Biblical wisdom teaches us to pause before choosing. Proverbs says wisdom protects us from impulsive mistakes. Discernment isn't hesitation—it's evaluation. What would change if you paused before reacting?"

Lisa: "I'd probably avoid a lot of trouble."

Counselor: "Discernment means filtering feelings, options, and outcomes through truth. Instead of 'What do I feel?' ask 'What is wise? What honors God? What leads to peace?' These questions create space for wisdom to speak."

Counselor's Strategy Explanation

The counselor teaches wisdom and discernment using the following steps:

1.Emotion Identification – Recognizing when feelings are overtaking judgment.

2.Pause-and-Reflect Method – A required gap between feeling and decision.

3.Wisdom Questions – Scriptural filters such as: "Is this true?" "Is this wise?" "Is this honoring to God?"

4.Outcome Evaluation – Considering the trajectory of each choice.

5.Scriptural Anchoring – Using Proverbs and James as the framework for sound judgment.

This strengthens reflective thinking and aligns decisions with Scripture rather than impulses.

Action Plan

Lisa receives a structured wisdom-building plan:

•Discernment Journal – Record decisions, emotions involved, and outcomes.

•Wisdom Questions Card – Keep a list of 4–5 questions to pause and ask before making decisions.

•Scripture Study – Read Proverbs 2–4 daily for one week.

•Counsel Check – Contact a mature believer for guidance regarding one major decision per week.

•Prayer for Wisdom – Daily prayer based on James 1:5.

These steps build cognitive, emotional, and spiritual maturity over time.

Expected Outcome

As Lisa practices wisdom and discernment, impulsive decisions will decrease, emotional stability will increase, and she will grow in confidence, maturity, and spiritual clarity. Over time, her choices will reflect truth rather than emotion, producing peace, stability, and healthier relationships.

INTERVENTION 22: FORGIVENESS & RELEASE

Forgiveness is one of the most transformational and theologically rich interventions in Scripture. Jesus repeatedly commanded believers to forgive as they have been forgiven. Forgiveness does not minimize pain or excuse wrongdoing; rather, it releases the counselee from bitterness, resentment, and emotional bondage. In CCRT, forgiveness is a dual-layer intervention: it involves emotional release (letting go of the internal power of the offense) and belief realignment (accepting God's justice, sovereignty, and command to forgive). Forgiveness restores spiritual clarity, reframes emotional experience, and opens the door to relational healing.

Case Presentation

Alonzo, a 55-year-old contractor, seeks counseling due to long-standing anger toward his brother, with whom he has not spoken in eight years. The conflict began over a financial disagreement, but Alonzo explains the deeper issue: betrayal, disrespect, and the feeling that he was taken advantage of. He admits, "I know I should forgive, but I can't. I replay what he did over and over." His anger has led to emotional exhaustion, strained family relationships, and a diminished spiritual life. His primary distorted belief is: "Holding on to anger protects me from being hurt again."

Counseling Objective

The counselor's objective is to help Alonzo understand the emotional and spiritual cost of forgiveness, identify distorted beliefs about justice and self-protection, and guide him toward biblical forgiveness. The goal is not forced reconciliation but heart-level release, freeing Alonzo from emotional captivity and restoring fellowship with God.

CCRT Analysis

Primary Needs:

• Security – Fear of future harm.

• Love & Belonging – Desire for relational restoration.

Primary Conflicts:

• Emotional Conflict – Bitterness and unresolved anger.

• Belief Conflict – Misunderstanding forgiveness as weakness.

• Insight Conflict – Unaware of how bitterness shapes choices.

Distorted Beliefs:

• "Forgiving means letting him off the hook."

• "If I forgive, he wins."

• "Bitterness protects me."

CCRT Reality Keys Used:

• RK1 – Belief Determines Experience.

• RK3 – Truth Defines Reality.

• RK6 – Truth Heals.

• RK10 – Forgiveness Frees the Heart.

• RK12 – God Is Present in Suffering.

Biblical Foundation:

Ephesians 4:31–32 – Forgive as God forgave you.

Matthew 18 – The parable of the unforgiving servant.

Romans 12:19 – God alone judges with righteousness.

Counseling Conversation

Counselor: "Alonzo, you've held on to this pain for eight years. How has it affected you?"

Alonzo: "It's worn me down. I'm angry all the time."

Counselor: "Bitterness is a heavy burden. What belief keeps you holding on to it?"

Alonzo: (pauses) "I guess… I feel like letting it go means he gets away with it."

Counselor: "Let's compare that to Scripture. Does forgiveness mean pretending nothing happened?"

Alonzo: "No… but it feels like it sometimes."

Counselor: "Forgiveness doesn't erase the offense—it releases *you* from bondage. Scripture teaches that God handles justice. Forgiveness hands the gavel back to Him."

Alonzo: "I never thought of it like that."

Counselor: “What if the very thing you believe protects you is actually hurting you? Forgiveness isn’t weakness—it’s freedom.”

Counselor’s Strategy Explanation

The counselor guides Alonzo through a structured forgiveness process:

1.Identifying beliefs that fuel bitterness.

2.Exploring emotional costs of forgiveness.

3.Teaching biblical truth about forgiveness and justice.

4.Guiding a forgiveness decision, not based on emotion but obedience.

5.Helping Alonzo release the offense to God's authority.

This approach integrates emotional processing with biblical truth to produce genuine freedom.

Action Plan

Alonzo’s forgiveness plan includes:

•Write the Offense Letter – Describe what happened and how it affected him (not to send).

•Release Statement – “I release my brother from my judgment; God is the righteous Judge.”

•Scripture Meditation – Ephesians 4:31–32 and Romans 12:19.

•Prayer of Release – Daily prayer acknowledging surrender of the offense.

•Boundary Clarification – Identify healthy relational boundaries for future interactions.

These steps reinforce emotional release and spiritual alignment.

Expected Outcome

As Alonzo practices forgiveness, his emotional tension will decrease, bitterness will lose its power, and relational healing will become possible. His identity and peace will be restored as he entrusts justice to God and releases the offense from his heart.

INTERVENTION 23: INTERCESSORY PRAYER & GUIDED PRAYER

Intercessory prayer is one of Scripture's most powerful relational and transformative interventions. Throughout both the Old and New Testaments, God invites His people to bring their burdens, sins, fears, and needs directly to Him. Jesus prayed for His disciples (John 17), Paul interceded continually for the churches, and the early church prayed for strength, healing, unity, and deliverance. In counseling, intercessory prayer becomes a sacred moment of alignment—where the counselee is invited into God's presence and the counselor models trust, surrender, and spiritual dependence. In CCRT, intercessory prayer helps re-center the counselee's beliefs, calm emotional reactivity, and reconnect identity to Christ's sufficiency through guided, truth-based petitions.

Case Presentation

Daphne, a 33-year-old wife and mother, seeks counseling for intense anxiety. She describes waking up with dread, experiencing constant tension, and struggling with intrusive thoughts of failure. Daphne fears disappointing her husband, failing as a parent, and being rejected by those close to her. Although she reads Scripture, she admits, "I feel like my mind is louder than God." Her primary distorted belief is: "If I can't control everything, everything will fall apart." This belief fuels fear, perfectionism, and emotional exhaustion. Despite a strong biblical foundation, she feels disconnected from God's peace.

Counseling Objective

The objective of this intervention is to help Daphne experience emotional grounding and spiritual alignment through intercessory prayer. The counselor models surrender, dependence, and trust while guiding Daphne into a prayer that reorients her beliefs toward Scripture and God's faithfulness. The goal is not merely emotional relief, but spiritual re-anchoring—helping Daphne interpret her fear through the truth of God's presence, sovereignty, and care.

CCRT Analysis

Primary Needs:

• Security – Need for emotional stability and assurance.

• Love & Belonging – Need for relational and spiritual connection.

Primary Conflicts:

• Emotional Conflict – Chronic fear and internal tension.

• Belief Conflict – Belief that control prevents catastrophe.

• Insight Conflict – Difficulty recognizing the role of distorted beliefs.

Distorted Beliefs:

• "If I lose control, everything will collapse."

• "God will let me fail unless I hold everything together."

• "My fear is more powerful than God's promises."

CCRT Reality Keys Used:

• RK1 – Belief Determines Experience.

• RK2 – God Designed Us for Relationship.

• RK3 – Truth Defines Reality.

• RK7 – Identity in Christ.

• RK12 – God Is Present in Suffering.

Biblical Foundation:

Philippians 4:6–7 – Prayer brings peace that surpasses understanding.

1 Peter 5:7 – Cast all your anxieties on Him, for He cares for you.

Romans 8:26–27 – The Spirit intercedes in our weakness.

Counseling Conversation

Counselor: "Daphne, before we go deeper into your fear, would you allow me to pray for you? Not as a formality, but as a way to bring this weight before God together?"

Daphne: (tearful) "Yes… I think I need that."

Counselor: "Let's start by naming the fear honestly before God. He invites us to bring our anxieties to Him."

Daphne: "I'm afraid of failing… of letting my family down."

Counselor: "Thank you for trusting me with that. Let's pray."

Counselor (praying): "Father, you see Daphne fully—her heart, her fear, her exhaustion. You tell us to cast our anxieties on You because You care for us. We bring her fear to You now. Remind her that Your strength sustains her, not her own effort. Surround her with Your peace and anchor her thoughts in Your truth."

Daphne: (quiet weeping) "I feel… calmer."

Counselor: "That calm is not from us—it is from the Spirit ministering to your heart. Now let me ask: what belief was driving the anxiety you brought before God?"

Daphne: "That I have to control everything."

Counselor: "And what does Scripture say about who holds all things together?"

Daphne: "…Christ does. Not me."

Counselor: "Exactly. Prayer isn't about escaping fear—it's about aligning your belief with truth while you're in it."

Counselor's Strategy Explanation

Intercessory prayer in CCRT functions as both emotional grounding and theological recalibration. The counselor:

1.Creates a sacred space where Daphne can bring fear honestly before God.

2.Models biblical surrender, demonstrating trust in God's character.

3.Verbally acknowledges emotion in the prayer, validating her experience.

4.Incorporates truth statements, correcting distorted beliefs with Scripture.

5.Invites Daphne into reflection, helping her identify belief patterns revealed during prayer.

Guided prayer becomes a therapeutic tool that unites emotional experience with biblical truth, satisfying both spiritual and psychological needs.

Action Plan

Daphne's prayer-based action plan includes:

•Morning Surrender Prayer – A 2-minute prayer releasing control to God.

•Scripture Meditation – Focus daily on Philippians 4:6–7.

•Fear Identification – Write down one fear daily and pair it with a truth statement.

•Prayer Partnership – Ask a trusted believer to pray with her once weekly.

•Breath Prayer Practice – Repeat: “God is near; I will trust Him”—especially during anxious moments.

These practices reinforce alignment between belief, emotion, and truth.

Expected Outcome

As Daphne continues guided prayer and truth alignment, anxiety will gradually diminish. She will experience increased emotional stability, a stronger sense of God’s presence, and reduced dependence on control. Over time, prayer will shift from a crisis response to a stabilizing rhythm that shapes her beliefs, strengthens her identity in Christ, and restores inner peace.

INTERVENTION 24: CONFESSION & RESTITUTION

Confession and restitution form one of the clearest biblical patterns of relational and spiritual restoration. From the Law of Moses to the teachings of Jesus, Scripture presents confession as a pathway to truth, cleansing, and reconciliation. Restitution, where appropriate, becomes the outward expression of inward repentance. In counseling, confession helps bring hidden guilt, shame, or sin into the light, while restitution addresses the relational or practical consequences of those actions. In CCRT, confession restores connection to truth (RK3), aligns identity with Christ (RK7), and removes the internal conflict caused by distorted beliefs, while restitution becomes a tangible step toward rebuilding trust, repairing relationships, and accepting responsibility.

Case Presentation

Anthony, a 29-year-old man, seeks counseling after months of relational instability and emotional turmoil. He explains that he has lost the trust of his girlfriend, his parents, and several coworkers. Through gentle questioning, the truth emerges: Anthony has been lying—sometimes to avoid conflict, sometimes to appear competent, and sometimes simply out of habit. He minimizes the severity of the behavior, saying, "It's not like I'm hurting anybody… I just don't want to disappoint people." Beneath the surface is deep insecurity, fear of rejection, and a belief that "If people knew the real me, they wouldn't accept me." Anthony feels increasingly isolated and ashamed but does not know how to heal the relational damage he has caused.

Counseling Objective

The counselor's objective is to help Anthony acknowledge his dishonesty, understand the underlying beliefs driving it, confess truthfully, and—where appropriate—take steps toward restitution. The intervention aims to address both the internal conflict causing guilt and the external relational damage created by deception. Through confession, Anthony confronts distorted beliefs about identity, acceptance, and rejection. Through restitution, he demonstrates responsibility and begins rebuilding trust.

CCRT Analysis

Primary Needs:

• Love & Belonging – Desire for acceptance and relational security.

• Power – Desire to manage how others perceive him.

Primary Conflicts:

• Identity Conflict – Belief that the truth about himself is unworthy.

• Behavioral Conflict – Habitual dishonesty.

• Belief Conflict – "People will reject me if they know the truth."

Distorted Beliefs:

• "I must hide my flaws to be accepted."

• "Deception protects relationships."

• "My worth depends on others' approval."

CCRT Reality Keys Used:

• RK1 – Belief Determines Experience.

• RK3 – Truth Defines Reality.

• RK6 – Truth Heals.

• RK7 – Identity in Christ.

• RK8 – Responsibility Restores Freedom.

Biblical Foundation:

1 John 1:9 – Confession leads to cleansing and restoration.

Proverbs 28:13 – Concealing sin leads to bondage; confession brings mercy.

Luke 19 – Zacchaeus makes restitution as evidence of repentance.

Counseling Conversation

Counselor: "Anthony, can I share something I've observed? You seem exhausted—not just emotionally, but spiritually."

Anthony: (sighs) "I feel like I'm living two different lives."

Counselor: "You've mentioned dishonesty several times. How does it feel to carry that alone?"

Anthony: (tears forming) "Like I'm constantly waiting to be found out."

Counselor: "That's a heavy burden. What belief makes you think people can't accept the real you?"

Anthony: "Because… the real me is disappointing."

Counselor: “Anthony, Scripture says your identity isn’t defined by failure but by Christ. Hiding doesn’t protect relationships—it strangles them. What do you believe confession might accomplish?”

Anthony: “…Maybe freedom?”

Counselor: “Exactly. Confession opens the door to healing. And sometimes restitution helps repair the damage caused. You don’t have to fix everything instantly, but you can take steps toward truth and restoration.”

Anthony: “I’m scared.”

Counselor: “Courage isn’t the absence of fear—it’s choosing truth while afraid. And you won’t walk this alone.”

Counselor’s Strategy Explanation

The counselor leads Anthony through a four-step process:

1.Internal Exposure – Helping Anthony see the emotional and spiritual cost of dishonesty.

2.Belief Identification – Revealing the distorted belief: “I must hide to be accepted.”

3.Biblical Reframing – Replacing the lie with truth about identity, acceptance, and worth.

4.Confession & Restitution Plan – Helping him confess appropriately and take steps to rebuild trust.

This intervention focuses on integrating emotional honesty, biblical truth, and responsible action. The counselor emphasizes that confession is not about punishment but freedom—and restitution is not about earning forgiveness but demonstrating change.

Action Plan

Anthony is given a structured 5-part plan:

•Written Confession – Identify the individuals he has repeatedly deceived (family, girlfriend, coworker).

•Truth Statement – Write one paragraph confessing dishonesty, without excuses.

•Restitution Step – If deception caused practical harm (lost time, misinformation, broken commitments), take concrete steps to repair it.

•Identity Reinforcement – Memorize Ephesians 1:6 and repeat: “I am accepted in the Beloved.”

•Accountability Partner – Meet weekly with a trusted believer to maintain honesty.

These steps move Anthony from hidden shame to visible transformation.

Expected Outcome

As Anthony practices confession and restitution, emotional tension will decrease and relational trust will begin to rebuild. His distorted belief—that honesty leads to rejection—will weaken as he experiences mercy, understanding, and restored relationships. Over time, his identity will shift from performance-based acceptance to Christ-centered acceptance, producing freedom, integrity, and relational healing.

INTERVENTION 25: REDIRECTION TOWARD GOD'S PURPOSE

Redirection toward God's purpose is a biblical intervention used whenever individuals drift into patterns, desires, or priorities that move them away from God's design. Throughout Scripture, God redirects His people: Moses is redirected from fear to leadership, Jonah from rebellion to obedience, Peter from shame to mission, and Paul from zeal without knowledge to gospel-centered calling. Redirection does not condemn the counselee; it reorients focus and purpose. In CCRT, redirection helps the counselee evaluate the path they are on, identify the beliefs shaping their choices, and redirect their energy toward a purpose aligned with God's truth, identity, and calling.

Case Presentation

Maria, a 38-year-old professional, seeks counseling due to feelings of aimlessness and spiritual dryness. She works long hours, rarely attends church, and admits she has not prayed regularly in months. Maria reports feeling disconnected from God and uncertain about her purpose. She says, "I feel like I'm just existing. I'm not doing anything meaningful." Beneath her discouragement is the belief that career success is the primary measure of her worth, and that spiritual life can be postponed until she 'has more time.' Her life direction is shaped by a subtle but powerful belief: "My value comes from accomplishment, not identity."

Counseling Objective

The counselor's objective is to help Maria recognize how misplaced priorities and beliefs have led to spiritual disconnection and emotional emptiness. Redirection will guide her toward a renewed alignment with God's priorities, clarify her sense of calling, and help her redirect her energy toward actions that nourish both her faith and personal stability. The goal is to shift Maria from performance-driven identity to purpose-driven obedience rooted in Christ's sufficiency.

CCRT Analysis

Primary Needs:

• Power – Desire for achievement, competence, and control.

• Meaning & Purpose – Core need for identity-driven direction.

Primary Conflicts:

• Identity Conflict – Equating worth with success.

• Belief Conflict – Viewing spiritual growth as optional or secondary.

• Behavioral Conflict – Neglecting spiritual rhythms.

Distorted Beliefs:

• "My worth depends on achievement."

• "I don't have time for spiritual growth."

• "Purpose is something I create, not something God reveals."

CCRT Reality Keys Used:

• RK1 – Belief Determines Experience.

• RK3 – Truth Defines Reality.

• RK7 – Identity in Christ.

• RK9 – Purpose Comes from God.

• RK11 – Growth Requires Discipline.

Biblical Foundation:

Jeremiah 29:11 – God's plans provide hope and purpose.

Matthew 6:33 – Seek first the kingdom of God.

Ephesians 2:10 – Believers are created for good works prepared in advance.

Counseling Conversation

Counselor: "Maria, you've described feeling empty even though you're achieving a lot. Why do you think that is?"

Maria: "Because none of it feels meaningful. It's just work."

Counselor: "Meaninglessness often shows us we're pursuing a path God did not design. Let me ask—what do you believe gives your life value?"

Maria: "Being successful… achieving something important."

Counselor: "And who taught you that your value rests in performance instead of identity?"

Maria: (quiet) "I don't know… I guess I've always believed it."

Counselor: "Scripture says your value is rooted in Christ, not accomplishment. When your purpose drifts from Him, your heart naturally loses its anchor. What if the emptiness you feel is not failure—but a divine invitation to redirect your life toward a purpose God has prepared?"

Maria: "…I want that. I just don't know where to start."

Counselor: "That's why we redirect—not by abandoning your responsibilities, but by making your relationship with God the center of your purpose again."

Counselor's Strategy Explanation

The counselor uses CCRT redirection to:

1.Identify the distorted belief that success equals worth.

2.Highlight emotional consequences—emptiness, fatigue, spiritual distance.

3.Introduce biblical truth about God's purpose and identity.

4.Reorient goals toward spiritual and relational priorities.

5.Establish new patterns of discipline that reinforce purpose alignment.

Redirection is not correction through pressure, but reorientation through truth.

Action Plan

Maria receives a practical redirection plan:

•Daily Spiritual Rhythm – 10 minutes of Scripture and prayer before work.

•Purpose Reflection Journal – Write one sentence daily answering: "What is God calling me toward today?"

•Weekly Worship Commitment – Attend Sunday service for spiritual grounding.

•Boundary Practice – Set one work boundary (no emails after 8 p.m., one night free of work).

•Service Step – Engage in a monthly church or community service opportunity.

These steps help redirect Maria's identity and purpose toward God's design.

Expected Outcome

As Maria aligns her beliefs with biblical truth and redirects her priorities, emotional stability and spiritual vitality will increase. Her worth will become anchored in Christ rather than performance, providing clarity, peace, and renewed purpose. Over time, she will experience greater satisfaction and connection as she walks in the identity and calling God designed for her.

INTERVENTION 26: ESTABLISHING BOUNDARIES

Establishing boundaries is a biblically grounded intervention that protects emotional, relational, and spiritual well-being. Throughout Scripture, God models boundaries—He defines moral limits, separates light from darkness, and instructs His people to guard their hearts. Jesus set personal boundaries as well: withdrawing to pray, choosing when to engage, and refusing to be manipulated by pressure from others. Healthy boundaries clarify responsibility, define relational space, and preserve identity. In CCRT, boundaries help counselees move from unhealthy compliance, people-pleasing, or relational enmeshment toward responsibility, truth, and emotional stability.

Case Presentation

Lauren, a 41-year-old mother and administrative assistant, seeks counseling for emotional burnout. She feels overwhelmed by constant demands from family, coworkers, and church members. Lauren says yes to everything—car rides, extra shifts, last-minute projects, babysitting, ministry tasks—because she fears disappointing others. She confesses, “If I say no, they’ll think I’m selfish or unspiritual.” Her exhaustion has produced resentment, anxiety, and physical fatigue. Her core belief is: “I am responsible for other people’s happiness.”

Counseling Objective

The counselor’s objective is to help Lauren evaluate the unhealthy beliefs driving her over commitment, clarify what she is and is not responsible for, and establish healthy boundaries rooted in biblical truth. The goal is to reduce burnout, restore emotional stability, and help Lauren practice responsibility without self-sacrifice driven by fear, guilt, or people-pleasing.

CCRT Analysis

Primary Needs:

• Love & Belonging – Fear of rejection drives over compliance.

• Security – Loss of stability due to burnout.

Primary Conflicts:

• Boundary Conflict – Inability to say no or limit demands.

• Belief Conflict – Equating boundaries with selfishness.

• Identity Conflict – Deriving value from approval.

Distorted Beliefs:

• "I must say yes to be accepted."

• "Others' needs are more important than my health."

• "God expects me to sacrifice constantly."

CCRT Reality Keys Used:

• RK1 – Belief Determines Experience.

• RK2 – God Designed Us for Relationship.

• RK7 – Identity in Christ.

• RK8 – Responsibility Restores Freedom.

• RK11 – Discipline Produces Growth.

Biblical Foundation:

Proverbs 4:23 – Guard your heart.

Mark 1:35–38 – Jesus withdraws and sets boundaries on demands.

Galatians 6:5 – Each must carry their own load.

Counseling Conversation

Counselor: "Lauren, you've described exhaustion and resentment. What do you think drives your inability to say no?"

Lauren: "If I say no, people will think I don't care."

Counselor: "What makes you responsible for everyone's expectations?"

Lauren: "I guess… I feel like it's my job to keep everyone happy."

Counselor: "That's a heavy burden. And Scripture never places that burden on you. Jesus met needs—but He didn't meet every need. Even the Son of God set boundaries. Why do you believe you cannot?"

Lauren: (tears) "Because I'm afraid people won't like me if I stop helping."

Counselor: "So your yes is driven by fear, not love. Fear is a cruel master. What if boundaries are not rejection—but an expression of wisdom and obedience?"

Lauren: "I've never thought of it that way."

Counselor: "Let's redefine boundaries—not as selfishness, but stewardship. Boundaries help you offer what you can without destroying yourself. They also allow others to carry their own responsibilities, as Scripture teaches."

Counselor's Strategy Explanation

The counselor guides Lauren through:

1.Identifying beliefs behind over commitment.

2.Connecting emotional exhaustion to distorted beliefs.

3.Introducing biblical truth about responsibility and stewardship.

4.Defining practical boundaries within work, family, and church.

5.Practicing assertive communication with compassion and clarity.

This intervention shifts Lauren from guilt-driven compliance to responsibility grounded in identity and purpose.

Action Plan

Lauren receives a boundary-building plan:

•Boundary Inventory – List all obligations and identify which drain energy.

•Three 'No' Statements – Prepare three polite, assertive responses for upcoming requests.

•Responsibility Chart – Separate what is her responsibility and what belongs to others.

•Weekly Sabbath Practice – One 2-hour block per week without service or obligations.

•Accountability Partner – Share boundary goals with a trusted friend.

These intentional steps help Lauren align responsibility with truth rather than fear.

Expected Outcome

As Lauren practices boundaries, emotional exhaustion will decrease and relational resentment will diminish. Her identity will become anchored in Christ instead of approval. Over time, she will experience healthier relationships, increased stability, and renewed spiritual vitality as she learns that boundaries are an expression of wisdom, stewardship, and freedom—not selfishness.

INTERVENTION 27: CLARIFYING IDENTITY IN CHRIST

Clarifying identity in Christ is one of the most transformative interventions in both Scripture and CCRT. Many counselees experience emotional instability, distorted beliefs, and harmful relational patterns because their sense of worth is rooted in performance, approval, failure, or past wounds rather than the finished work of Christ. Throughout Scripture, God repeatedly reminds His people who they are—chosen, redeemed, beloved, forgiven, empowered—because identity shapes interpretation, behavior, and emotional response. In CCRT, identity clarification helps the counselee reinterpret life through the truth of their position in Christ, breaking the power of shame, insecurity, and performance-driven living.

Case Presentation

Monique, a 35-year-old children's ministry volunteer, seeks counseling for deep insecurity and persistent feelings of inadequacy. Despite serving faithfully, she constantly compares herself to others and believes she is spiritually inferior. Monique says, "I feel like God tolerates me, but He's not pleased with me. I'm not good enough." Her insecurity affects her marriage, friendships, and ministry. She avoids leadership roles, fears criticism, and interprets minor mistakes as spiritual failure. Her primary distorted belief is: "My worth is determined by how well I perform spiritually."

Counseling Objective

The counselor's objective is to help Monique identify the beliefs shaping her insecurity, confront the lie that worth is performance-based, and replace those beliefs with biblical truths about identity in Christ. This intervention aims to stabilize her emotional system, reduce fear of failure, and strengthen her confidence in God's character and love.

CCRT Analysis

Primary Needs:

• Identity & Meaning – Desire for security, acceptance, and stability.

• Love & Belonging – Fear of rejection or divine disappointment.

Primary Conflicts:

• Identity Conflict – Misunderstanding her standing before God.

• Belief Conflict – Rooting worth in spiritual performance.

• Emotional Conflict – Chronic insecurity and self-doubt.

Distorted Beliefs:

• "God tolerates me, but does not delight in me."

• "If I fail, my worth decreases."

• "Others are more valuable because they are more spiritual."

CCRT Reality Keys Used:

• RK1 – Belief Determines Experience.

• RK4 – Identity Determines Relationship.

• RK6 – Truth Heals.

• RK7 – Identity in Christ.

• RK14 – Grace Establishes True Worth.

Biblical Foundation:

Ephesians 1 – Believers are chosen, accepted, redeemed, and sealed.

Romans 8 – Nothing can separate us from God's love.

1 Peter 2:9 – Believers are a royal priesthood and God's treasured possession.

Counseling Conversation

Counselor: "Monique, you've described feeling 'not good enough.' Who taught you that God sees you that way?"

Monique: (quiet) "I don't know… I guess I've always felt that way."

Counselor: "Let's examine that belief. What does Scripture say about your standing in Christ—earned or given?"

Monique: "Given… I know that in my head."

Counselor: "And what belief controls your emotions right now?"

Monique: "That I have to keep proving myself."

Counselor: "That belief contradicts the gospel. You are accepted because Christ is perfect—not because you are. What if the insecurity you feel comes from measuring yourself by a standard God never gave you?"

Monique: (tears) "I've never thought about it like that."

Counselor: "Let me show you something." (opens Bible) "Ephesians 1 says you are chosen, accepted, adopted, redeemed, sealed. Which of those depend on your performance?"

Monique: "…None of them."

Counselor: "Exactly. Your identity is stable because it rests in Christ. When you root worth in performance, insecurity grows. When you root worth in Christ, confidence grows."

Counselor's Strategy Explanation

The counselor uses identity clarification by:

1.Identifying the core belief driving insecurity.

2.Contrasting emotional interpretation with biblical truth.

3.Reframing worth around Christ's finished work instead of performance.

4.Introducing key identity passages (Ephesians 1, Romans 8, 1 Peter 2).

5.Helping Monique internalize identity statements that reshape her emotional experience.

Identity clarification is not mere encouragement; it is theological realignment.

Action Plan

Monique receives a structured identity-building plan:

•Identity Statements – Read aloud daily: "I am accepted in Christ," "I am chosen," "I am redeemed," "I am loved."

•Scripture Meditation – Focus on Ephesians 1:3–14 for the next 14 days.

•Belief Replacement Chart – Identify one insecure thought daily and replace it with Scripture.

•Affirmation Practice – Write one-way God has shown acceptance each day.

•Service Reframing Step – Serve once weekly without evaluating performance.

These practices reinforce identity at the belief and emotional level.

Expected Outcome

As Monique's identity becomes grounded in Christ, her insecurity will diminish, emotional stability will increase, and service will shift from performance-driven anxiety to gratitude-driven obedience. Over time, she will experience joy, confidence, and relational freedom as she embraces who she truly is in Christ.

INTERVENTION 28: RENEWING THE MIND

Renewing the mind is a core biblical intervention grounded in Romans 12:2, where believers are commanded to be transformed by the renewing of their minds. Scripture teaches that thoughts shape emotions, choices, and spiritual direction. When a counselee's thinking becomes distorted—shaped by fear, shame-based assumptions, or ungodly interpretations—renewing the mind reorients them toward truth. In CCRT, mind renewal functions as both cognitive and spiritual restructuring, integrating biblical principles with the counseling process to help the counselee interpret life through the lens of Scripture rather than emotion or circumstance.

Case Presentation

Jonathan, a 27-year-old graduate student, comes to counseling feeling defeated and discouraged. He describes ongoing anxiety about his academic performance, constant self-criticism, and intrusive thoughts of failure. Despite receiving good grades, he believes he is one mistake away from disaster. Jonathan says, “If I don’t excel, I’m worthless.” His identity is tied to achievement, and every disappointment triggers emotional collapse. Jonathan’s primary distorted belief is: “My value is based on how perfectly I perform.”

Counseling Objective

The counselor’s objective is to help Jonathan identify distorted thinking patterns, confront the false beliefs fueling his anxiety, and replace them with biblical truth. Renewing the mind will help him break the cycle of fear-based thinking, develop emotional resilience, and root his identity in Christ rather than performance.

CCRT Analysis

Primary Needs:

• Security – Need for emotional stability and assurance.

• Identity – Need for worth established in Christ, not achievement.

Primary Conflicts:

• Belief Conflict – Performance-based worth.

• Emotional Conflict – Anxiety following perfectionistic thoughts.

• Insight Conflict – Difficulty seeing thought patterns as distorted.

Distorted Beliefs:

• “If I fail, I am worthless.”

• "My future depends entirely on my performance."

• "God is disappointed when I fall short."

CCRT Reality Keys Used:

• RK1 – Belief Determines Experience.

• RK3 – Truth Defines Reality.

• RK4 – Identity Determines Relationship.

• RK6 – Truth Heals.

• RK11 – Discipline Produces Growth.

Biblical Foundation:

Romans 12:2 – Be transformed by the renewing of your mind.

2 Corinthians 10:5 – Take every thought captive.

Philippians 4:8 – Think on what is true, honorable, just, and pure.

Counseling Conversation

Counselor: "Jonathan, you mentioned that when a grade is not perfect, you feel worthless. What belief produces that emotion?"

Jonathan: "That failure means I'm not good enough."

Counselor: "And where did that belief come from? Scripture, or past expectations?"

Jonathan: (pauses) "Definitely expectations. Not Scripture."

Counselor: "Let's compare the belief to truth. What does Romans 12:2 say about how transformation happens?"

Jonathan: "By renewing the mind."

Counselor: "Right. And Philippians 4:8 tells us to think on what is true and honorable. So let's ask: Is the belief 'I am worthless if I fail' true?"

Jonathan: "…No."

Counselor: "Is it honorable? Pure? Christ-centered?"

Jonathan: "Not at all."

Counselor: "So it cannot be from God. Renewing your mind means replacing that lie with truth. What does God say determines your worth?"

Jonathan: "Being His… being in Christ."

Counselor: "Exactly. Truth must override emotion—not the other way around."

Counselor's Strategy Explanation

The counselor guides Jonathan through mind renewal by:

1.Identifying distorted beliefs driving anxiety and perfectionism.

2.Evaluating the belief through Scripture-based criteria (truth, purity, honor).

3.Replacing the lie with biblical truth about identity.

4.Developing a pattern of capturing and evaluating thoughts.

5.Strengthening emotional resilience through truth repetition and discipline.

Mind renewal is a deliberate process requiring consistency, reflection, and biblical grounding.

Action Plan

Jonathan receives a structured renewal plan:

•Thought Capture Journal – Write down anxious thoughts daily and evaluate them using Philippians 4:8.

•Truth Replacement Statements – "My worth is in Christ," "Failure is not final," "God defines my identity."

•Daily Scripture Meditation – Romans 12:2 and 2 Corinthians 10:5 for 14 days.

•Performance Detachment Exercise – Engage in one weekly task with low expectations to reduce perfectionistic pressure.

•Prayer of Reorientation – Daily prayer asking God to renew his mind through truth.

These practices strengthen identity and emotional stability.

Expected Outcome

As Jonathan practices renewing his mind, anxiety will lessen, emotional resilience will increase, and perfectionistic pressure will lose its hold. He will learn to interpret performance through the lens of grace rather than fear, enabling him to live with greater peace, confidence, and spiritual maturity.

INTERVENTION 29: RESTORING HOPE

Restoring hope is one of the most essential biblical interventions for counselees who feel defeated, discouraged, or emotionally exhausted. Scripture consistently presents hope as the anchor of the soul (Hebrews 6:19) and the stabilizing force that allows believers to endure trials with confidence. Hopelessness distorts interpretation, magnifies fear, and shrinks spiritual vision. In contrast, biblical hope reconnects the counselee to God's promises, character, and future. In CCRT, restoring hope involves redirecting the counselee's focus from circumstances to truth, rebuilding expectancy through Scripture, and helping them interpret hardship through God's sovereignty rather than emotional despair.

Case Presentation

Rebecca, a 46-year-old woman, seeks counseling because she feels emotionally numb and spiritually defeated. After two years of financial strain, marital tension, and health issues, she says, "I feel like my life is over. Nothing is ever going to get better." Rebecca avoids friends, struggles with prayer, and has difficulty believing God sees her situation. Her primary distorted belief is: "My circumstances determine my future." This belief produces despair, passivity, and emotional shutdown.

Counseling Objective

The counselor's objective is to help Rebecca identify the beliefs fueling her hopelessness, reconnect her to biblical promises, and shift her expectation from defeat to God-centered hope. The goal is not to promise instant relief but to re-anchor her perspective in God's character, presence, and faithfulness.

CCRT Analysis

PRIMARY NEEDS:

• Security – Desire for stability amid prolonged stress.

• Meaning & Hope – Need for confidence in God's future for her.

Primary Conflicts:

• Belief Conflict – Equating circumstances with destiny.

• Emotional Conflict – Persistent discouragement and despair.

• Insight Conflict – Difficulty recognizing distorted interpretations.

Distorted Beliefs:

• "God has forgotten me."

• "This pain will never end."

• "I have no future."

CCRT Reality Keys Used:

• RK1 – Belief Determines Experience.

• RK3 – Truth Defines Reality.

• RK5 – God Uses Circumstances to Shape Us.

• RK6 – Truth Heals.

• RK12 – God Is Present in Suffering.

Biblical Foundation:

Romans 15:13 – God fills us with hope through the Spirit.

Psalm 42 – The psalmist wrestles with despair but chooses hope.

Jeremiah 29:11 – God's plans include hope and a future.

Counseling Conversation

Counselor: "Rebecca, you've gone through a long and exhausting season. Anyone would feel overwhelmed in your shoes."

Rebecca: (tearful) "But it feels like God doesn't care. Nothing is changing."

Counselor: "Let's explore that belief. What makes you think 'nothing will ever change'?"

Rebecca: "Because everything keeps going wrong."

Counselor: "That's understandable. But does hardship guarantee hopelessness? What does Scripture say about God's involvement in our suffering?"

Rebecca: (quiet) "That He's near the brokenhearted… but it's hard to feel that right now."

Counselor: "Feeling is not the same as fact. Hope isn't based on emotion—it's based on truth. What if the hopelessness you feel is coming from a belief, not from God's reality?"

Rebecca: "…Maybe."

Counselor: "Let's anchor ourselves in truth. Psalm 42 shows us someone in despair speaking hope to themselves. Hope isn't denial—it's choosing to believe God is working even when the evidence is not visible."

Counselor's Strategy Explanation

The counselor uses hope restoration by:

1.Validating Rebecca's pain to reduce shame and emotional resistance.

2.Identifying the hopeless belief shaping her interpretation.

3.Introducing biblical truth that contradicts despair.

4.Reframing her situation through God's promises rather than circumstances.

5.Guiding her toward expectancy rooted in God's character.

Restoring hope does not deny hardship—it reframes it through God's sovereignty.

Action Plan

Rebecca receives a structured hope-building plan:

•Hope Journal – Write one example daily of God's faithfulness from the past.

•Scripture Meditation – Read Romans 15:13 every morning.

•Future Statements – Write three sentences: "God is working," "My story is not over," "I have a future in Christ."

•Connection Step – Attend one weekly church service or small group.

•Prayer of Expectancy – Daily prayer expressing trust in God's future work.

These exercises build emotional stability and forward-looking faith.

Expected Outcome

As Rebecca internalizes hope-based truths, she will regain emotional strength, increase resilience, and reinterpret her situation through God's promises. Over time, despair will diminish as hope reshapes her perspective and restores motivation for growth.

REALITY KEYS AND CCRT PARALLELS (SECTION VI INTERVENTIONS)

This table lists each Reality Key (RK#) used anywhere in Section VI of the Intervention Strategies chapter, alongside a close conceptual parallel found in Dr. Barnett's CCRT text, with page references.

Reality Key (RK# and Title)	Parallel in Barnett (summary + page reference)
RK1 – Belief Determines Experience	Barnett emphasizes that internal reality inevitably expresses itself outwardly: "Abnormal reality takes on mass and form. The individual will always ACT OUT the abnormality physically, mentally, and spiritually" (Chapter 3, p. 43).
RK2 – We Move Toward What We Focus On	Barnett describes how life direction is determined by the forces driving a person: "Abnormal reality always creates out of balanced lives and unnatural forces. The absolute fact is that force always creates motion. Examine closely the long and short-term direction of an individual life and how it is being driven" (Chapter 12, p. 201).
RK3 – Truth Defines Reality	Barnett contrasts normal and abnormal reality and insists that only authentic reality brings cure, summarized in the Reality Key: "Once abnormal is set in motion and left unchanged, it will not self-cure" (Chapter 3, p. 43).
RK4 – Identity Determines Relationship	Barnett grounds identity in God-designed relationship needs: love is defined as a uniquely human and divine need that can only flourish in normalcy, and all abnormality is corrosive to love and relationships (Chapter 2, p. 23).

RK5 – God Uses Circumstances to Shape Us	Barnett shows how God uses consequences and life events to expose abnormal reality and push people toward change—for example, collateral damage from sin that forces individuals and systems to confront their condition (Chapter 5, p. 71).
RK6 – Truth Heals	Barnett repeatedly links cure to truth-based normal reality. Through positive redundancy and resolve, individuals keep doing the right thing until normalized reality replaces abnormality (Chapter 10, pp. 154–155).
RK7 – Identity in Christ	Barnett teaches that real love and real power are rooted in God's design rather than external approval. Love meets emotional, spiritual, and physical needs simultaneously and only grows in normalcy; abnormality always destroys it (Chapter 2, p. 23).
RK8 – Personal Responsibility Leads to Freedom	Barnett stresses personal responsibility for change: using others as an excuse for failure is rejected, and each person must decide to change direction regardless of others' choices (Chapter 3, p. 43).
RK9 – Faithfulness is Success	In his discussion of positive redundancy, Barnett defines success as consistently working the right plan: "Positive redundancy is always planned success. The simple concept is to keep doing the right thing until it works" (Chapter 10, pp. 154–155).
RK10 – Community Strengthens Transformation	Barnett highlights the relational nature of human needs—love, belonging, and shared normal reality—and shows how healthy community, not isolation, supports lasting change (Chapter 2, p. 23; Chapter 5, p. 71).

RK11 – Discipline Produces Emotional and Spiritual Growth	Barnett connects growth to disciplined resolve: "Resolve means each individual works the plan at all costs, no matter the level of resistance... Positive resolve promotes change" (Chapter 10, p. 155; Chapter 12, p. 201).
RK12 – God Is Present in Suffering	Barnett affirms that God is powerful and capable of producing change even where abnormal reality seems entrenched, stressing that God's action within suffering brings transformation (Chapter 3, p. 43).
RK13 – Reflection Exposes Hidden Beliefs	Barnett calls counselees to track recurring patterns, watch for early warning signs, and examine what forces are driving their lives—an intentional reflection that exposes hidden problems (Chapter 12, pp. 200–201).
RK14 – Grace Welcomes Honesty	Barnett's teaching on forgiveness portrays grace as God's gift that reshapes the past and directly affects the future: "Forgiveness is a free gift to man from God... God can change our hearts, reshape our past, and directly affect our futures through forgiveness" (Chapter 12, p. 200).
RK15 – Gratitude Reorients the Heart	Barnett encourages a focus on constructive, normal reality rather than dwelling on abnormality; turning attention toward God's design and blessings shifts the internal posture of the heart (Chapter 2, p. 23).
RK16 – Emotional Awareness Produces Clarity	Barnett urges vigilance and emotional awareness: identify positive and negative signs, recognize recurrence, and notice that all internal problems show themselves outwardly (Chapter 12, pp. 200–201).

The next table shows which Reality Keys are explicitly used under each of the 29 Intervention Strategies.

Intervention	Reality Keys Used (RK#)
Intervention 1: Direct Confrontation of Sin	RK1, RK6, RK8, RK11
Intervention 2: Question-Based Self-Reflection	RK1, RK4, RK6, RK7
Intervention 3: Calling for Repentance	RK1, RK2, RK6, RK8
Intervention 4: Encouragement Toward Faithfulness	RK4, RK6, RK9, RK11
Intervention 5: Teaching and Instruction	RK1, RK3, RK4, RK6
Intervention 6: Reframing Circumstances with God's Sovereignty	RK1, RK3, RK5, RK6
Intervention 7: Accountability	RK1, RK8, RK10, RK11
Intervention 8: Scripture-Based Correction & Training	RK1, RK3, RK4, RK6, RK7
Intervention 9: Validation of Emotion + Truth Alignment	RK1, RK4, RK6, RK7, RK11
Intervention 10: Comfort in Affliction	RK1, RK3, RK5, RK6, RK12
Intervention 11: Narrative Confrontation / Parables	RK1, RK4, RK6, RK8
Intervention 12: Restoration After Failure	RK1, RK4, RK6, RK10, RK12

Intervention 13: Teaching Dependence on God	RK1, RK3, RK5, RK7, RK12
Intervention 14: Challenging Fear and Strengthening Courage	RK1, RK3, RK4, RK5, RK12
Intervention 15: Guiding Lament and Emotional Honesty	RK1, RK6, RK12, RK14, RK16
Intervention 16: Exposure of False Beliefs and Idols	RK1, RK4, RK6, RK7, RK13
Intervention 17: Calling for Responsibility and Action	RK1, RK2, RK3, RK9, RK11
Intervention 18: Mediation and Reconciliation	RK1, RK2, RK4, RK6, RK12
Intervention 19: Use of Consequences to Teach	RK1, RK2, RK3, RK9, RK11
Intervention 20: Cultivating Gratitude	RK1, RK3, RK5, RK6, RK15
Intervention 21: Teaching Wisdom and Discernment	RK1, RK2, RK3, RK8, RK13
Intervention 22: Forgiveness & Release	RK1, RK3, RK6, RK10, RK12
Intervention 23: Intercessory Prayer & Guided Prayer	RK1, RK2, RK3, RK7, RK12
Intervention 24: Confession & Restitution	RK1, RK3, RK6, RK7, RK8
Intervention 25: Redirection Toward God's Purpose	RK1, RK3, RK7, RK9, RK11

Intervention 26: Establishing Boundaries	RK1, RK2, RK7, RK8, RK11
Intervention 27: Clarifying Identity in Christ	RK1, RK4, RK6, RK7, RK14
Intervention 28: Renewing the Mind	RK1, RK3, RK4, RK6, RK11
Intervention 29: Restoring Hope	RK1, RK3, RK5, RK6, RK12

SUMMARY AND CONCLUSION

Section Six provides a comprehensive and practical exploration of twenty-eight biblical intervention strategies forming the backbone of Christ-Centered Reality Therapy (CCRT). These interventions are not abstract theories but concrete, Scripture-anchored methods designed to confront distortion, expose faulty belief systems, and guide counselees toward repentance, responsibility, and transformation. This section demonstrates how deeply CCRT integrates theology, counseling structure, emotional insight, and spiritual formation.

Throughout the interventions, the emphasis is consistent: all lasting change begins by addressing belief, not behavior. Whether confronting sin directly, asking reflective questions, reframing fear, guiding lament, challenging self-reliance, or teaching identity in Christ, each intervention reveals the same pattern—a person's internal belief system determines their emotional state, behavioral choices, relational patterns, and spiritual health. Distorted beliefs lead to abnormal wants, emotional confusion, and destructive patterns; biblical truth, when embraced, produces clarity, repentance, new desires, and renewed obedience.

Each scenario in this section presents a vivid counseling picture. From individuals struggling with anger, insecurity, perfectionism, fear, shame, control, secrecy, anxiety, resentment, and false identity, the interventions demonstrate how a CCRT counselor listens for belief conflicts, identifies internal causes, and strategically guides the counselee from emotional reaction toward spiritual truth. The analysis sections consistently highlight primary needs, primary conflicts, distorted beliefs, and the appropriate Reality Keys, illustrating how CCRT organizes the counseling process with precision and consistency.

A major strength of this section is that it grounds every intervention in Scripture. Verses from Genesis, Psalms, Proverbs, the Gospels, and the Epistles appear not as decoration but as essential tools for correction, evaluation, comfort, accountability, and spiritual reframing. The case presentations also illustrate how CCRT avoids worldly therapeutic assumptions—such as excusing sin, blaming circumstances, or elevating emotion over truth. Instead, the counselor confronts unhealthy patterns with compassion but also clarity, reminding the counselee that healing, freedom, and stability arise only when beliefs and actions submit to God's Word.

Another theme woven throughout Section Six is that God-given needs must be met through God-given means. Many counselees in these examples attempt to meet legitimate needs—love, security, power, belonging, meaning, freedom—through self-exalting strategies that lead only to exhaustion, bondage, and emotional instability. As the interventions show, the counselor's role is to redirect these desires back to Christ, where the counselee learns dependence, humility, trust, and a renewed identity that reshapes their emotional reality.

CONCLUSION

Section Six stands as the practical engine room of Christ-Centered Reality Therapy. It brings the core principles of CCRT to life by showing how intervention strategies flow out of Scripture, address real human struggles, and lead people toward renewed faith, responsibility, obedience, and emotional stability. Each intervention reinforces the truth that counseling is not merely about solving problems—it is about restoring the counselee to a Christ-centered way of living and thinking.

Through biblical confrontation, reflective questioning, accountability, identity clarification, emotional validation, encouragement, correction, and guided repentance, CCRT equips counselors to shepherd people into spiritual transformation. This section demonstrates that change is not accidental but intentional, structured, and anchored in God's truth. Ultimately, the goal of every intervention is the same: to help people abandon self-centered living and embrace a Christ-centered reality where truth heals, identity stabilizes, and obedience produces lasting wholeness.

SUMMARY AND CONCLUSION FOR THE ENTIRE BOOK

Using Christ-Centered Reality Therapy (Volume II)

This volume, Using Christ-Centered Reality Therapy, brings together the full methodology of CCRT and demonstrates how biblical truth becomes a structured, actionable counseling process. Building upon the theological and philosophical model established in Volume I, this book moves from understanding to implementation, from concept to practice, and from explanation to transformation. The central conviction of CCRT—that belief determines behavior and that all meaningful change requires realignment with God's truth—shapes every chapter, tool, and intervention presented in this volume.

Throughout the book, the reader is taught how to identify distorted beliefs, abnormal wants, unmet needs, and the internal conflicts that drive emotional instability and relational dysfunction. Rather than treating emotions, circumstances, or external behaviors as the problem, CCRT leads the counselor to examine the counselee's underlying belief systems, uncovering the theological and psychological assumptions that shape their choices. This volume emphasizes repeatedly that problems are not fundamentally circumstantial or emotional—they are spiritual, arising from a departure from God's design for normality. True transformation occurs when the counselee brings their beliefs, behavior, and desires under the authority of Scripture.

The book also provides a full suite of structured tools that make CCRT both measurable and reproducible: The Therapeutic Plan (Mind–Body–Spirit), the Five Needs/Five Conflicts diagnostic system, the Action Plan worksheet, the Rule of 52, the Reality Keys, Here-and-Now questioning, Session Mapping, and numerous other aids designed to bring clarity and structure to the counseling process. Each tool helps the counselor move the counselee from emotional reaction to responsible action, guiding them step-by-step toward obedience, renewal, and Christ-centered living.

Sections IV, V, and VI bring the methodology to life through detailed teaching, biblical case studies, and 29 intervention strategies. These interventions demonstrate how Scripture addresses fear, anger, guilt, shame, rebellion, insecurity, perfectionism, dependency, pride, despair, and misplaced desires. Each example shows that human struggles today mirror the struggles of biblical figures—and that God's methods for confronting, correcting, and restoring people have never changed. The counseling conversations and case analyses reveal how the counselor discerns belief conflicts, asks precise questions, assigns responsibility, confronts self-deception, and consistently points the counselee toward repentance and renewed obedience.

This volume stresses repeatedly that counseling cannot ignore Scripture or spiritual absolutes. Secular therapy may offer coping strategies, emotional processing, or surface-level encouragement, but CCRT insists that nothing short of alignment with biblical truth produces lasting change. This book equips counselors, pastors, and ministry leaders to diagnose problems biblically, confront sinful patterns with clarity and compassion, redirect unhealthy wants, identify unmet needs, and guide individuals into responsible, God-centered choices. The consistent message is that emotions are messengers, but truth is the cure; Scripture is the absolute standard for normality; and Christ is the source of all transformation.

In conclusion, Using Christ-Centered Reality Therapy stands as a complete guide for implementing a fully biblical counseling methodology. It provides the counselor with the theological insight, diagnostic framework, practical tools, session structure, and intervention strategies necessary to help people experience real change. When paired with Volume I, the two books form a unified system—one that defines the truth about human nature and one that applies that truth in counseling practice.

Ultimately, this book affirms that genuine healing does not come from technique alone but from the redemptive work of Jesus Christ. Transformation begins when the counselee confronts the truth, repents of distorted beliefs, embraces biblical responsibility, and chooses obedience. As this volume demonstrates, Christ-centered reality is not merely a therapeutic model—it is the only pathway to restoration, wholeness, and spiritual maturity. May every counselor who uses this methodology do so with humility, clarity, and confidence, trusting that God's Word is sufficient and that His Spirit is faithful to complete the work He begins in every counselee who submits to His truth.

In HIS Service,
Dr. Alan Kitay
Dr. Carrie Kitay

ABOUT THE AUTHOR
DR. ALAN KITAY

Dr. Alan Kitay holds a Master's degree (MS) and Doctorate degree (PhD) in Psychology from International Christian University, A Doctorate degree in Theology from the Institute of Theology and Christian Therapy (ITCT), and a Master's degree in Counseling from Prairie View A&M. He is a Licensed Professional Christian Therapist and a Board-Certified Christian Counselor through the American Association of Christian Therapists. His experience includes over 25 years as an educator and over 40 years as a minister. Dr. Kitay entered the ministry in 1984.

Since 1999 when he founded Grace Christian Counseling Ministries, he has provided Christian counseling to men, women. children, and families and has taught Christian Psychology and Counseling classes through the various Churches he has attended and various institutions such as Grace Bible Institute, Houston Bible College, and now Destiny Bible College.

He has served as an Evangelist, Assistant Pastor, Director of Education, and Dean of two Bible Schools. Upon retirement from teaching in the Public School System, Dr Kitay is now servings as an Assistant Pastor at Destiny Church in Clute, Texas, under Pastor Dr. Cedric Johnson, and is now the Director of Destiny Cares Christian Counseling and the Dean and Senior Instructor for Destiny Bible College.

Dr Kitay is a permanent member, and former vice-president, of the American Association of Christian Therapists, and is certified through AACT as an Approved Academic Professor. and an Approved Conference Instructor. He is also a member of the American Association of Christian Counselors.

In addition to his work in the ministry, from 1988 to 2022, Dr. Kitay worked in the public-school system as a middle school Language Arts teacher, middle school Counselor, and as an Irlen and Dyslexia Specialist. He retired from Aldine Independent School District in February of 2022.

Education

- BS Liberal Arts – Univ. of the State of New York (1985) Majors - Psychology and Sociology
- Secondary Texas Teaching Certificate - Lamar University (1988) Reading and Sociology
- MS Psychology – Int'l Christian Institute, Houston, Texas (2000) Psychology
- Ph.D., Psychology – Int'l Christian Institute, Houston, Texas (2002) Psychology
- Ph.D. Theology – Institute of Theology and Christian Therapy (2004) Theology
- MS Educational Counseling - Prairie View A&M University (2008) Counseling

Certifications

- Certified Christ Centered Reality Therapist
- Certified Basic Mediator
- Certified Marriage and Family Mediator
- Board Certified Chaplain
- Ordained Minister – Grace International

ABOUT THE AUTHOR
DR. CARRIE KITAY

Dr. Carrie Kitay holds a Bachelor's, Master's, and Doctorate degree in Psychology from The Institute of Theology and Christian Therapy. She is also a Certified Christian Counselor and a Board-Certified Christian Therapist. She is the Director of Grace Christian Counseling Ministries.

Dr. Carrie Kitay specializes in the assessment, counseling, and consultation in the area of Domestic Violence, Spousal Abuse, and Child Abuse. She has extensive experience working with individuals and families who have been victims of violence. As a manager and case worker of a battered women's shelter, and as a counselor in private practice, she has seen both perpetrators and victims of domestic violence and abuse and has worked closely with law enforcement agencies, care providers, and service organizations.

In addition to her Administration and Counseling ministry, Carrie is also one of the Senior instructors at Destiny Bible College. She has co-authored the Certified Christian Counseling Program course materials and teaches all of the C*ertified Christian Counselor* courses and the Anxiety, Anger, and Depression workshops offered through Destiny Bible College and individual workshops. She co-authored Understanding Christ Centered Reality Therapy and Using Christ Centered Reality Therapy with her husband, Dr. Alan Kitay. She has a new book, Counseling Survivors of Domestic Abuse coming out in early 2026.

She has conducted training and workshops explaining the dynamics and consequences of grooming (finding and ensnaring) child and adult victims, battered women syndrome, bullying, anger, and myths and misconceptions of family and personal violence. Over the last 20 years Carrie has served in a variety of positions in her local Church. She has taught Sunday school, been active in women's ministry, and as intercessor / prayer partner. In addition to her counseling and ministry, she has worked as an adult counselor at a local battered women's shelter. Her passion reaches outside the walls of the church. She has been in lay ministry for over 20 years ministering, counseling, and educating women and teens who are struggling in with the issues of life and works to help them find their position and function in the body of Christ.

Education

2008–2013 Institute of Theology and Christian Therapy, Houston, TX
• Doctorate in Psychology, 2013
• Masters in Psychology, 2009
• Bachelors in Psychology, 2007

2007–2008 Grace Bible Institute, Humble, TX
• Board Certified Christian Therapist
• Certified Christian Counselor

2003–2006 Montgomery Community College, Conroe, TX
• Associates Degree in Human Services
• Advanced Certificate in Chemical Dependency Counseling
• Graduated Phi Theta Kappa, Beta Delta Iota Chapter, Summa Cum Laude

1980–1982 Houston Community College, Houston, TX
• Associates Degree in Applied Sciences

Certifications

- Certified Christ Centered Reality Therapist
- Certified Basic Mediator
- Certified Marriage and Family Mediator
- Board Certified Chaplain

www.ingramcontent.com/pod-product-compliance
Lightning Source LLC
LaVergne TN
LVHW070908210926
848482LV00017B/1024